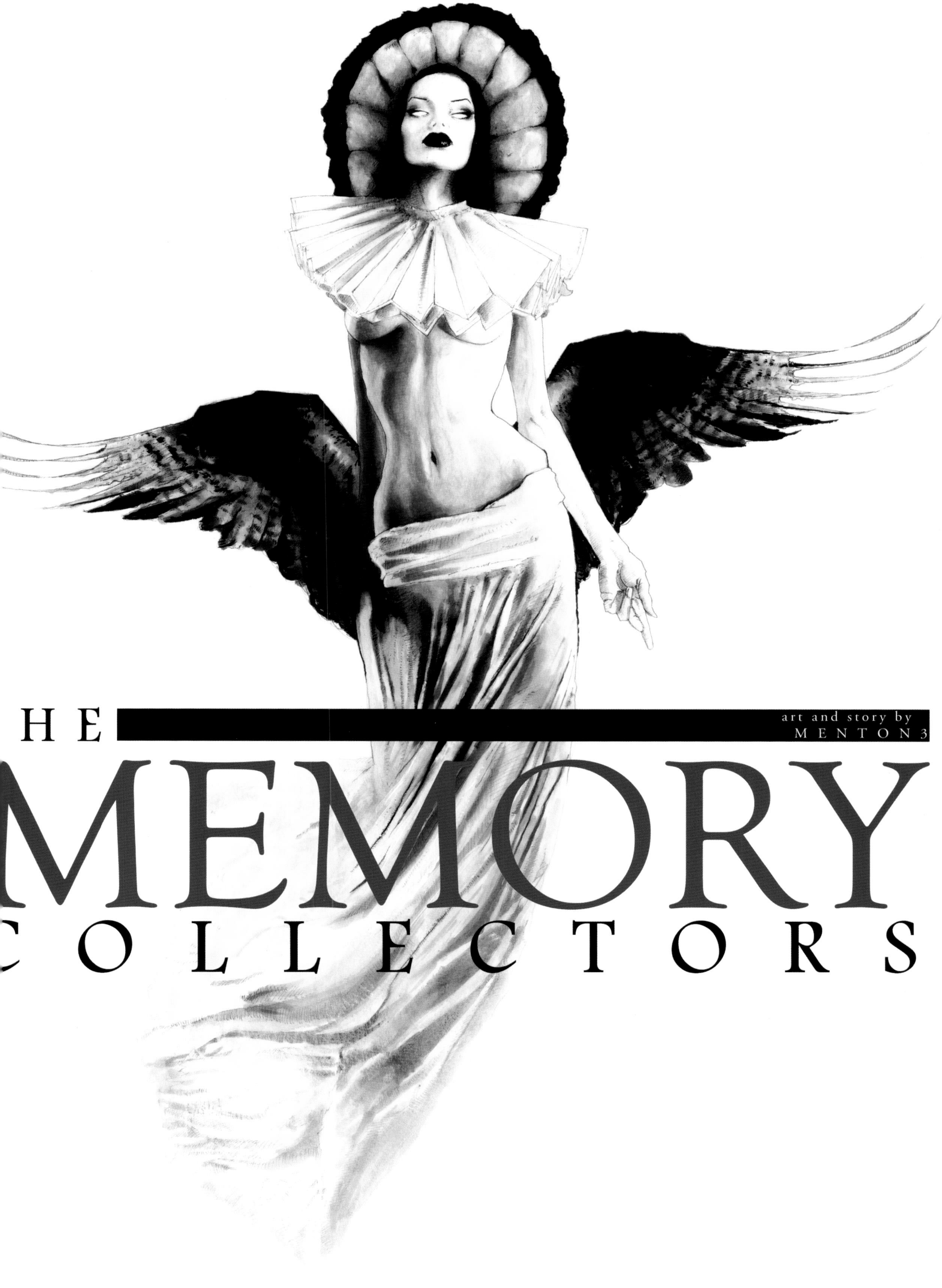

HE MEMORY COLLECTORS

art and story by
MENTON3

THE MEM COLLE

ISBN: 978-1-61377-892-0

17 16 15 14   1 2 3 4

IDW®
www.IDWPUBLISHING.com
IDW founded by Ted Adams, Alex Garner, Kris Oprisko, and Robbie Robbins

Ted Adams, CEO & Publisher
Greg Goldstein, President & COO
Robbie Robbins, EVP/Sr. Graphic Artist
Chris Ryall, Chief Creative Officer/Editor-in-Chief
Matthew Ruzicka, CPA, Chief Financial Officer
Alan Payne, VP of Sales
Dirk Wood, VP of Marketing
Lorelei Bunjes, VP of Digital Services
Jeff Webber, VP of Digital Publishing & Business Development

Facebook: **facebook.com/idwpublishing**
Twitter: **@idwpublishing**
YouTube: **youtube.com/idwpublishing**
Instagram: **instagram.com/idwpublishing**
deviantART: **idwpublishing.deviantart.com**
Pinterest: **pinterest.com/idwpublishing/idw-staff-faves**

Originally published as THE MEMORY COLLECTORS issues #1–3.

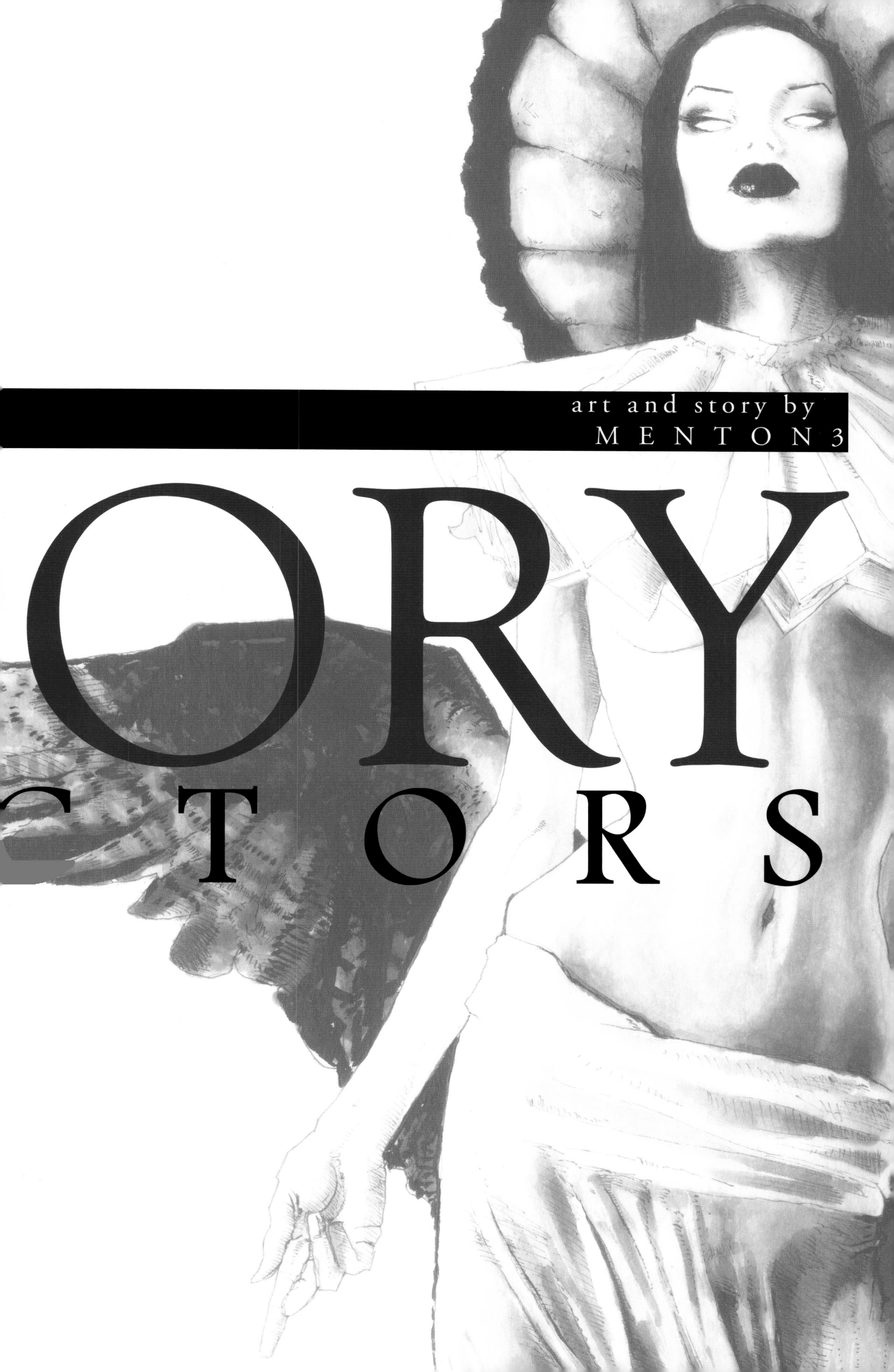
art and story by
MENTON 3
ORY
TORS

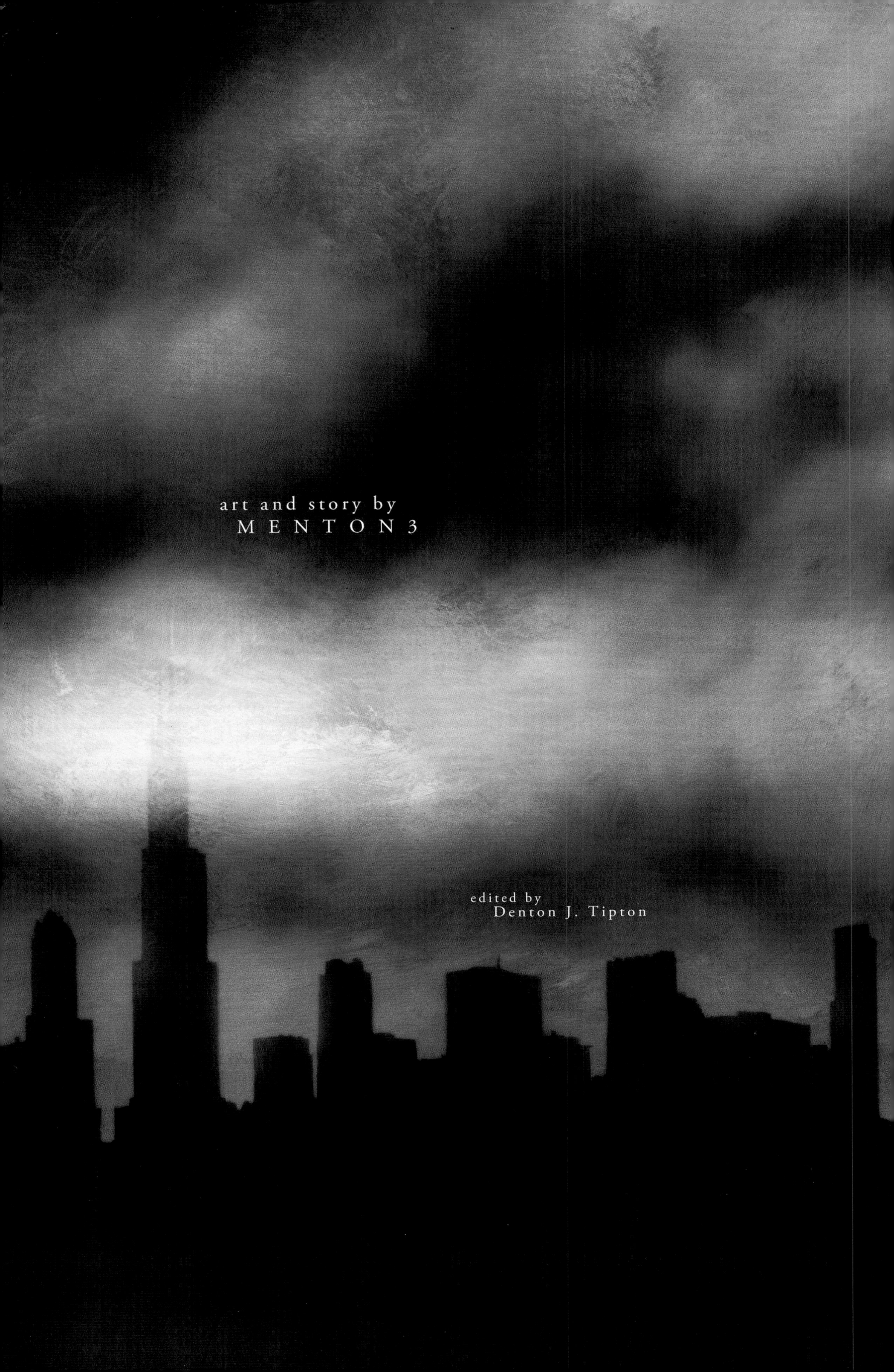
art and story by
MENTON3
edited by
Denton J. Tipton

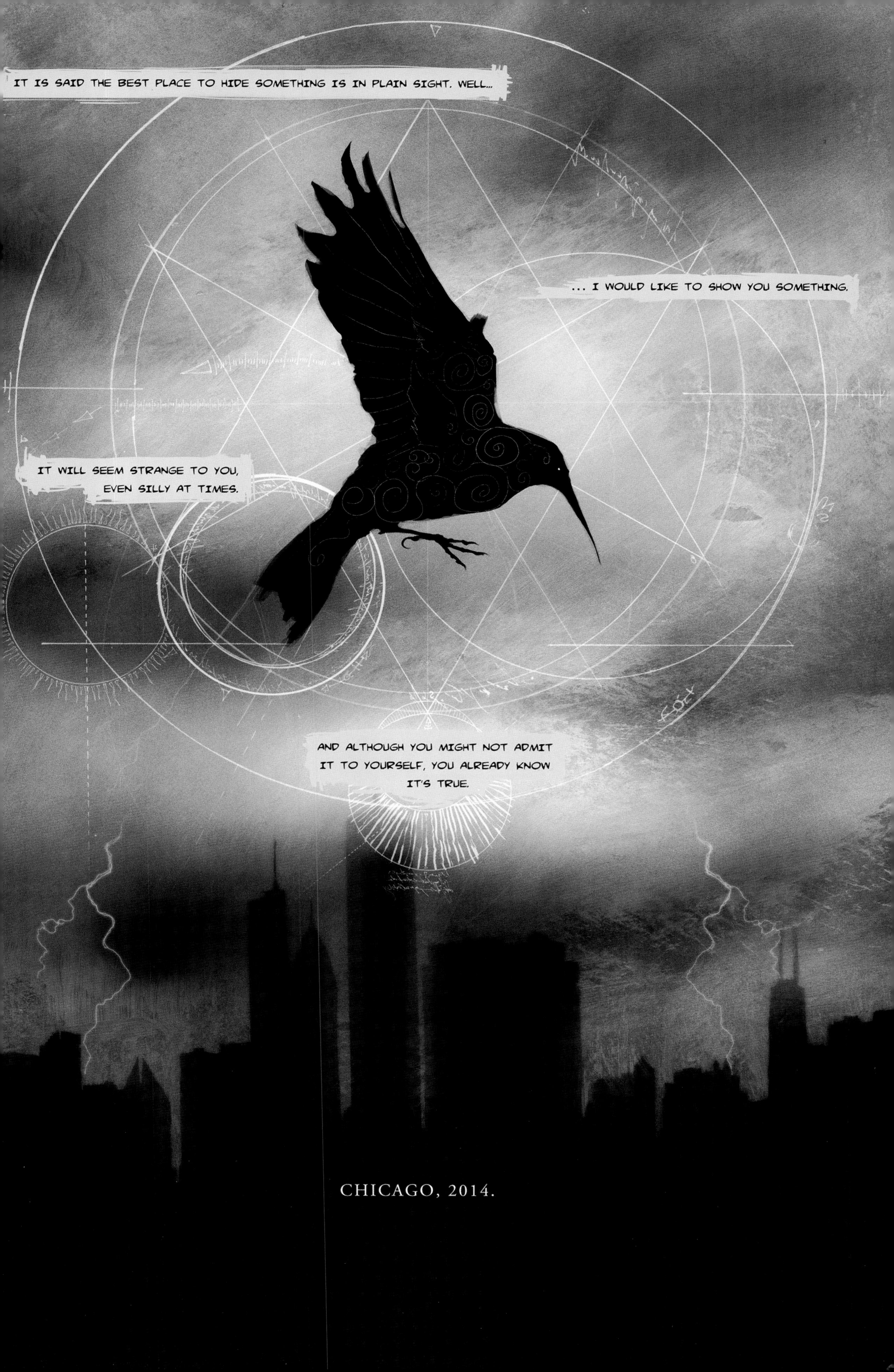
IT IS SAID THE BEST PLACE TO HIDE SOMETHING IS IN PLAIN SIGHT. WELL...
... I WOULD LIKE TO SHOW YOU SOMETHING.
IT WILL SEEM STRANGE TO YOU, EVEN SILLY AT TIMES.
AND ALTHOUGH YOU MIGHT NOT ADMIT IT TO YOURSELF, YOU ALREADY KNOW IT'S TRUE.
CHICAGO, 2014.

11:52 P.M. DOWNTOWN, OUTSIDE OF A COMIC-BOOK CONVENTION.

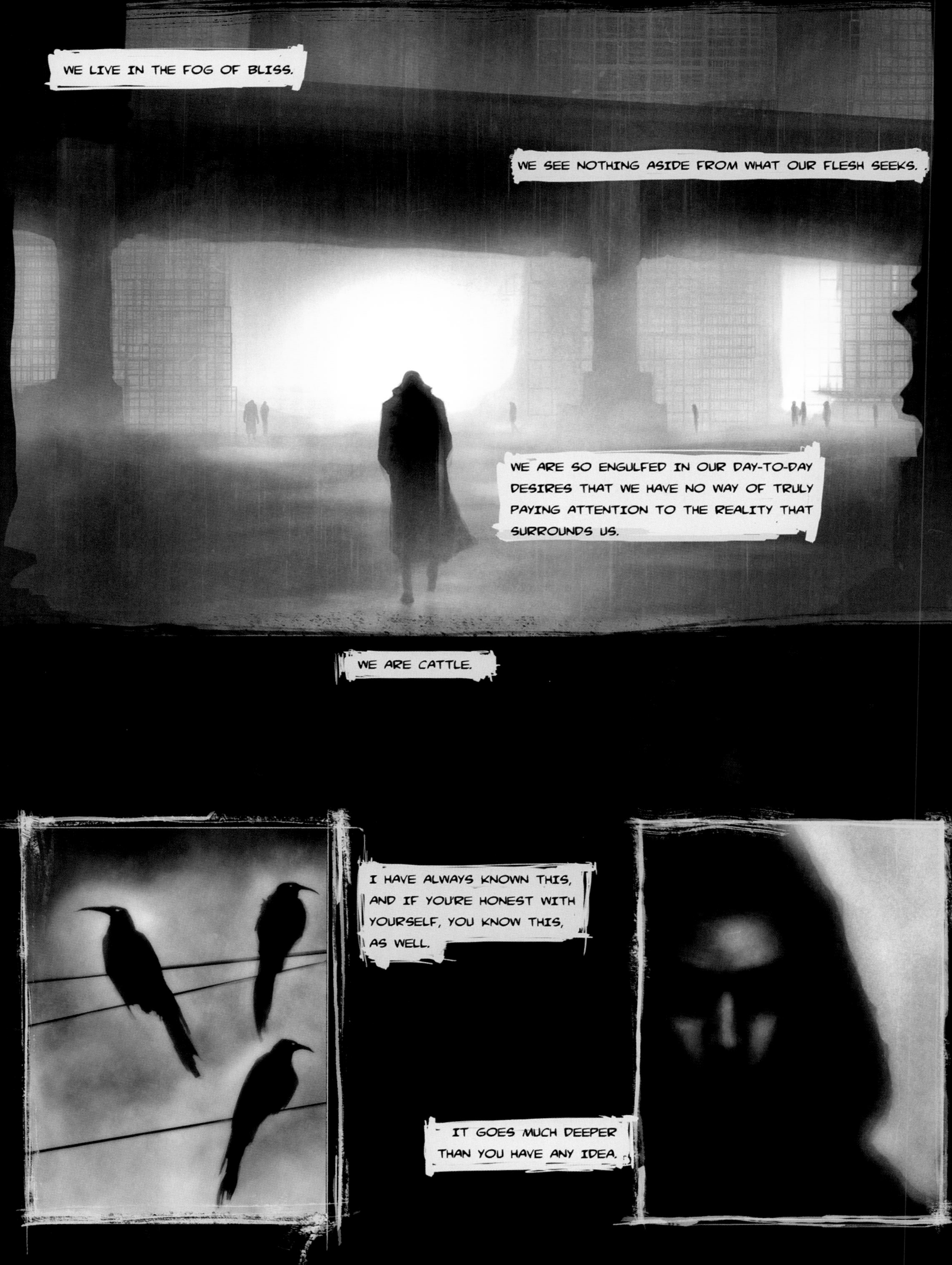
WE LIVE IN THE FOG OF BLISS.
WE SEE NOTHING ASIDE FROM WHAT OUR FLESH SEEKS.
WE ARE SO ENGULFED IN OUR DAY-TO-DAY DESIRES THAT WE HAVE NO WAY OF TRULY PAYING ATTENTION TO THE REALITY THAT SURROUNDS US.
WE ARE CATTLE.
I HAVE ALWAYS KNOWN THIS, AND IF YOU'RE HONEST WITH YOURSELF, YOU KNOW THIS, AS WELL.
IT GOES MUCH DEEPER THAN YOU HAVE ANY IDEA.

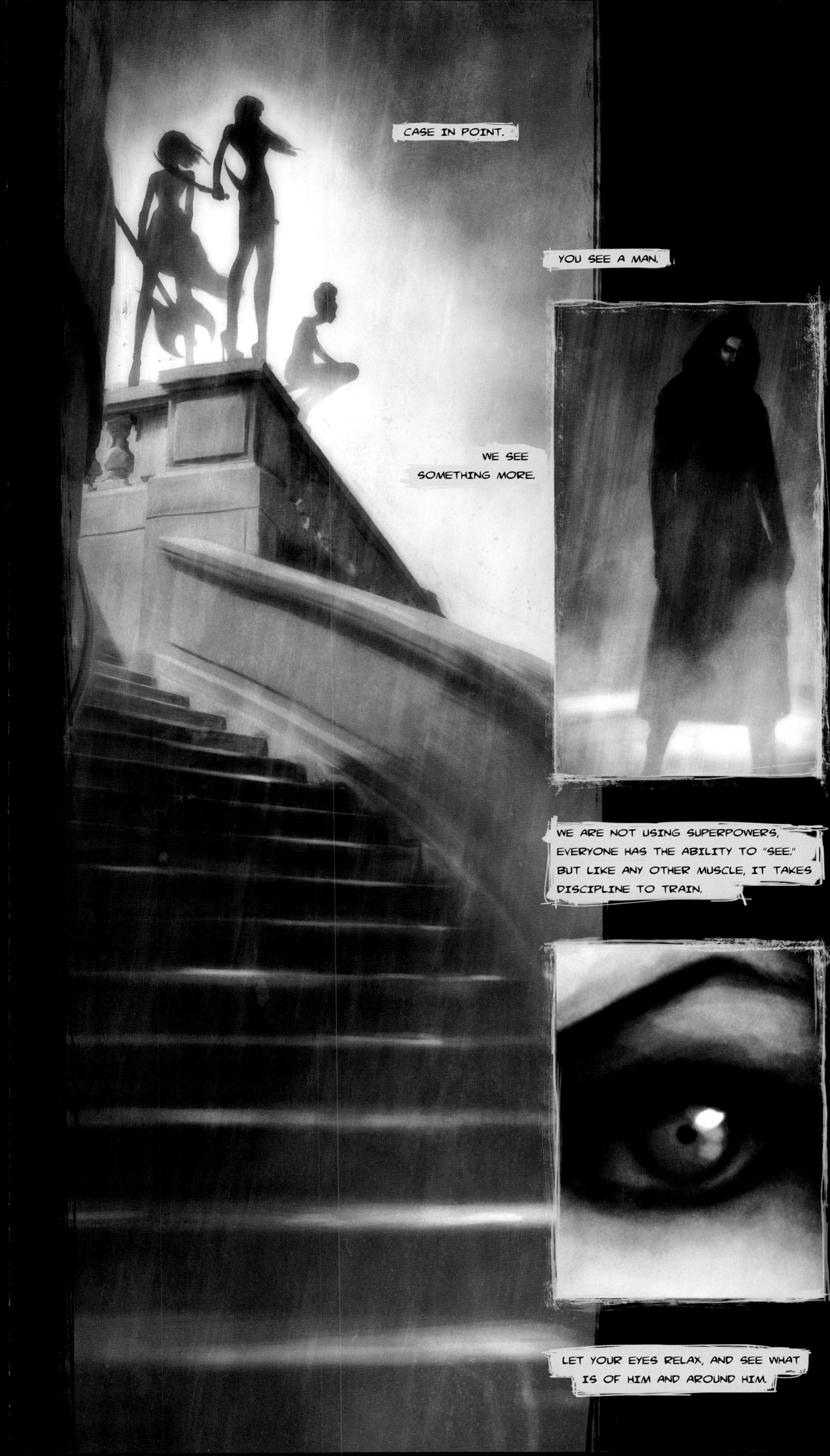
CASE IN POINT.
YOU SEE A MAN.
WE SEE SOMETHING MORE.
WE ARE NOT USING SUPERPOWERS, EVERYONE HAS THE ABILITY TO "SEE." BUT LIKE ANY OTHER MUSCLE, IT TAKES DISCIPLINE TO TRAIN.
LET YOUR EYES RELAX, AND SEE WHAT IS OF HIM AND AROUND HIM.

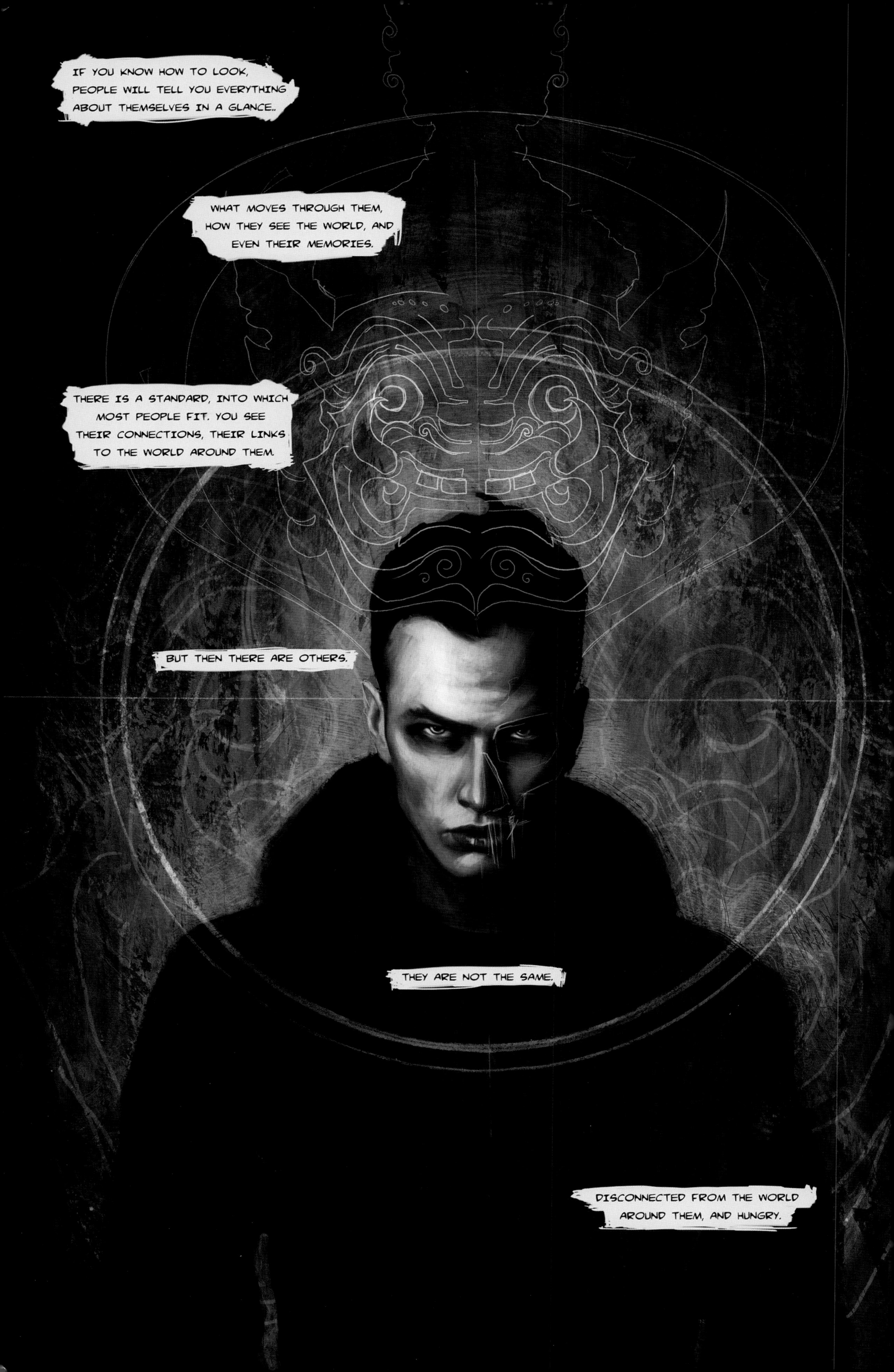
IF YOU KNOW HOW TO LOOK, PEOPLE WILL TELL YOU EVERYTHING ABOUT THEMSELVES IN A GLANCE..
WHAT MOVES THROUGH THEM, HOW THEY SEE THE WORLD, AND EVEN THEIR MEMORIES.
THERE IS A STANDARD, INTO WHICH MOST PEOPLE FIT. YOU SEE THEIR CONNECTIONS, THEIR LINKS TO THE WORLD AROUND THEM.
BUT THEN THERE ARE OTHERS.
THEY ARE NOT THE SAME.
DISCONNECTED FROM THE WORLD AROUND THEM, AND HUNGRY.

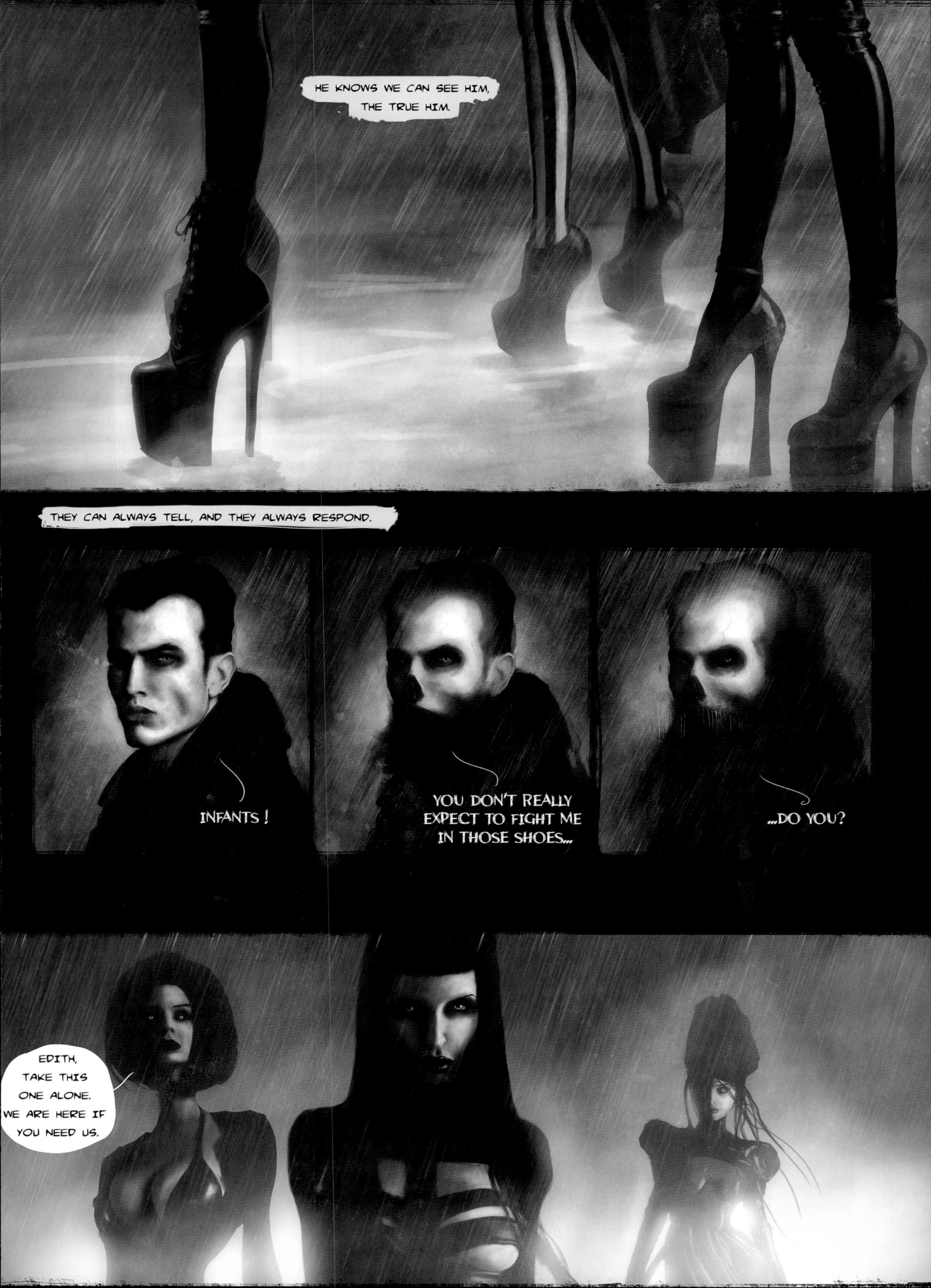

HE KNOWS WE CAN SEE HIM, THE TRUE HIM.
THEY CAN ALWAYS TELL, AND THEY ALWAYS RESPOND.
INFANTS !
YOU DON'T REALLY EXPECT TO FIGHT ME IN THOSE SHOES...
...DO YOU?
EDITH, TAKE THIS ONE ALONE. WE ARE HERE IF YOU NEED US.

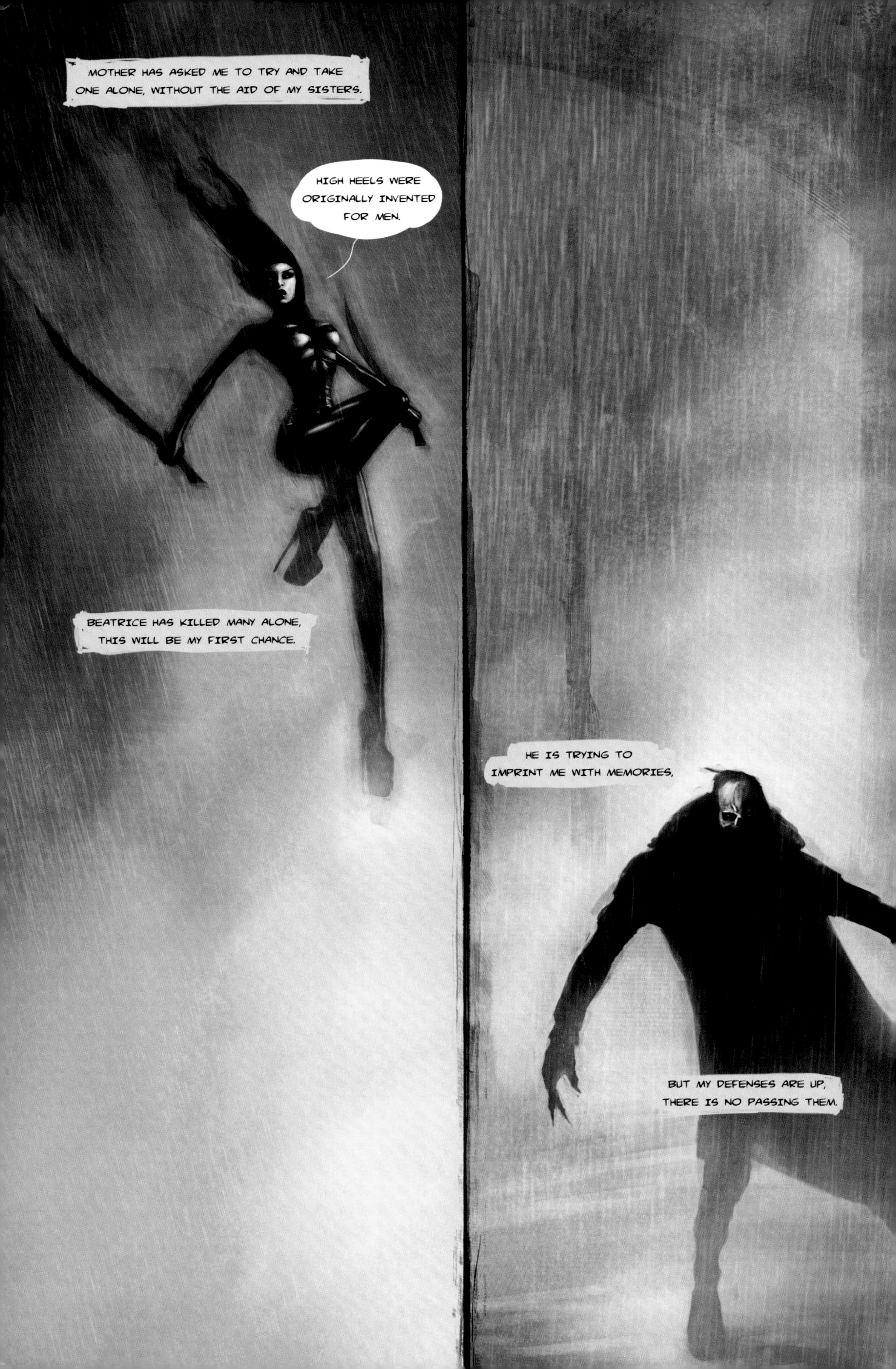
MOTHER HAS ASKED ME TO TRY AND TAKE ONE ALONE, WITHOUT THE AID OF MY SISTERS.
HIGH HEELS WERE ORIGINALLY INVENTED FOR MEN.
BEATRICE HAS KILLED MANY ALONE, THIS WILL BE MY FIRST CHANCE.
HE IS TRYING TO IMPRINT ME WITH MEMORIES,
BUT MY DEFENSES ARE UP, THERE IS NO PASSING THEM.

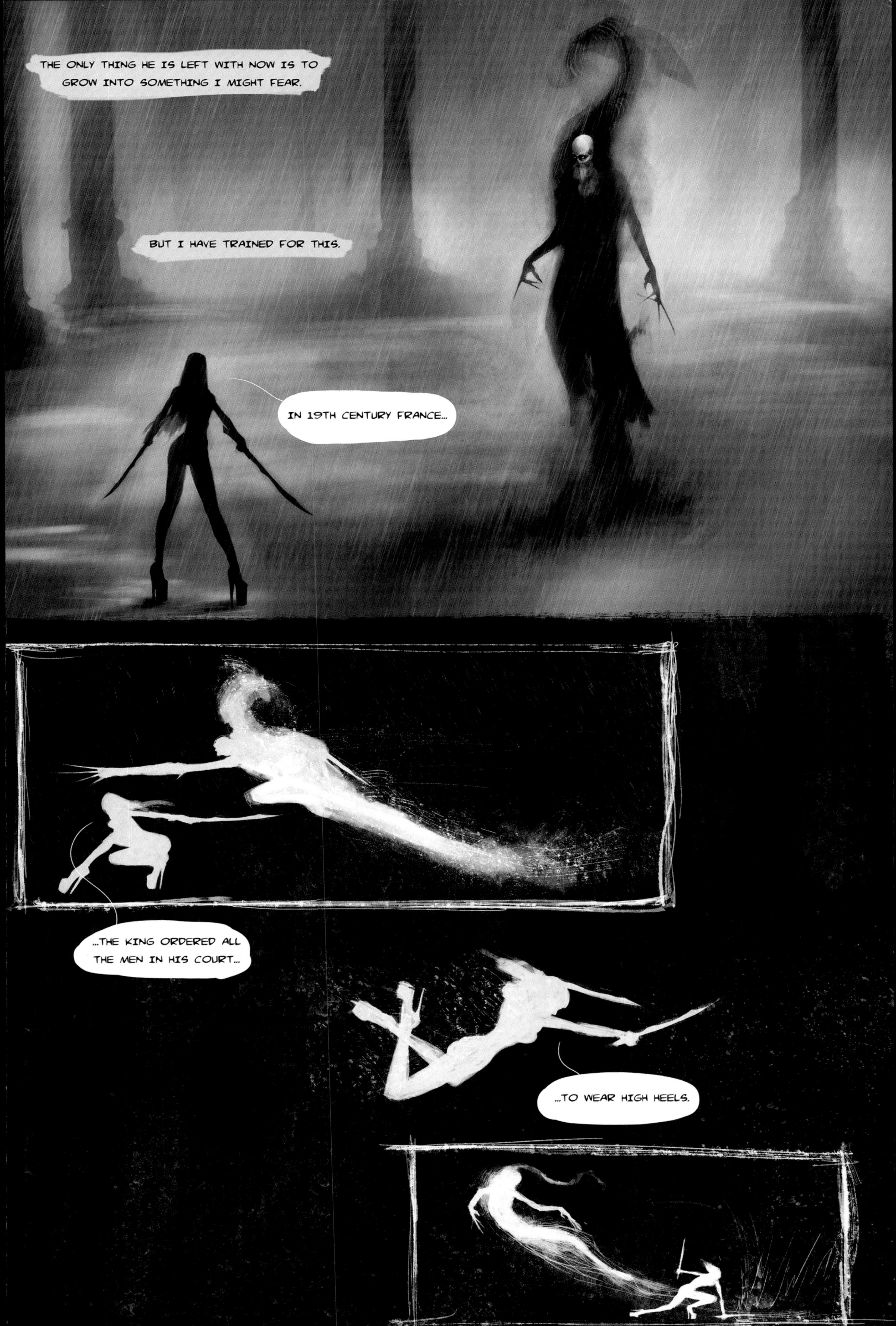
THE ONLY THING HE IS LEFT WITH NOW IS TO GROW INTO SOMETHING I MIGHT FEAR.
BUT I HAVE TRAINED FOR THIS.
IN 19TH CENTURY FRANCE...
...THE KING ORDERED ALL THE MEN IN HIS COURT...
...TO WEAR HIGH HEELS.

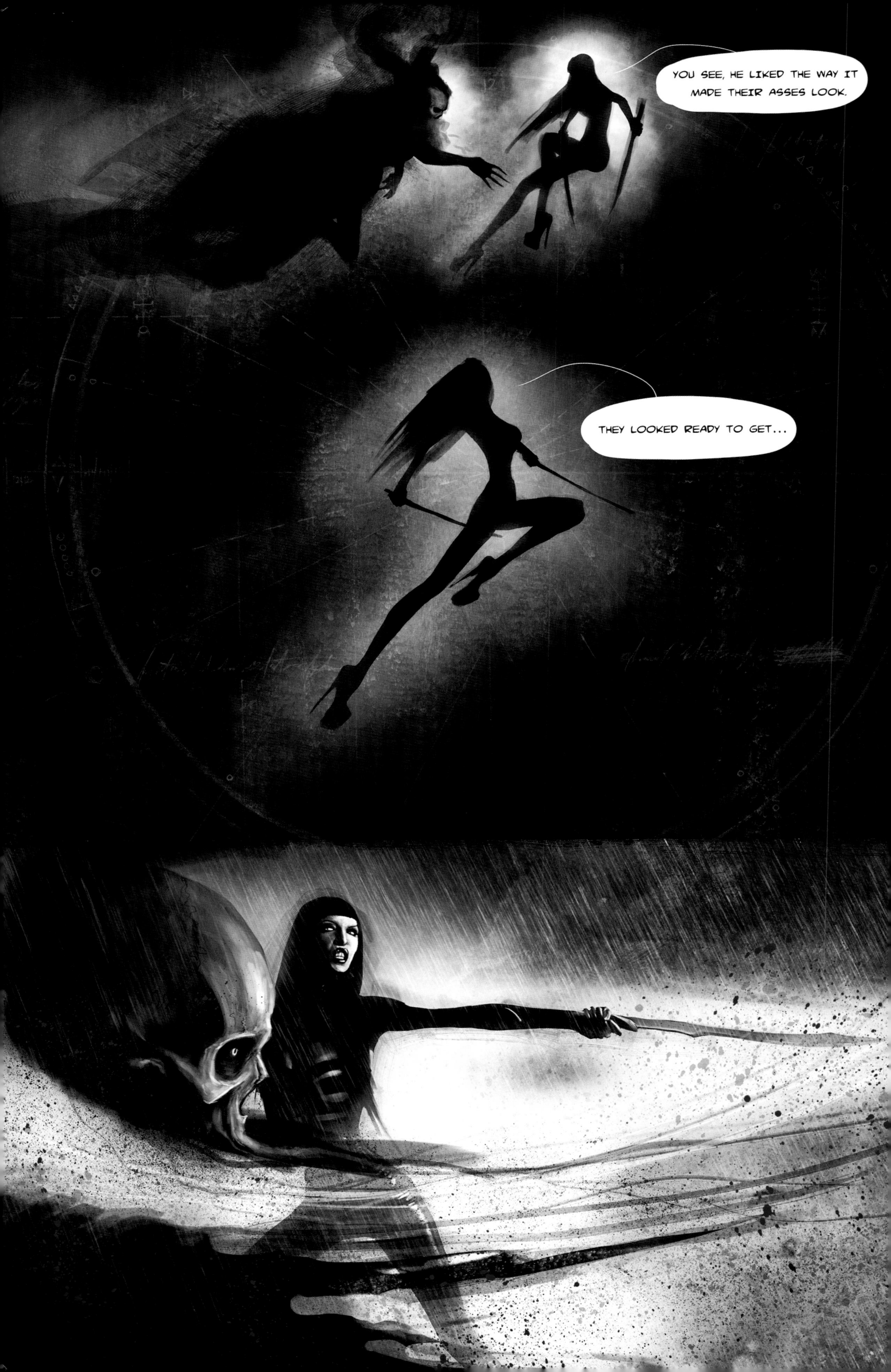
YOU SEE, HE LIKED THE WAY IT MADE THEIR ASSES LOOK.
THEY LOOKED READY TO GET...

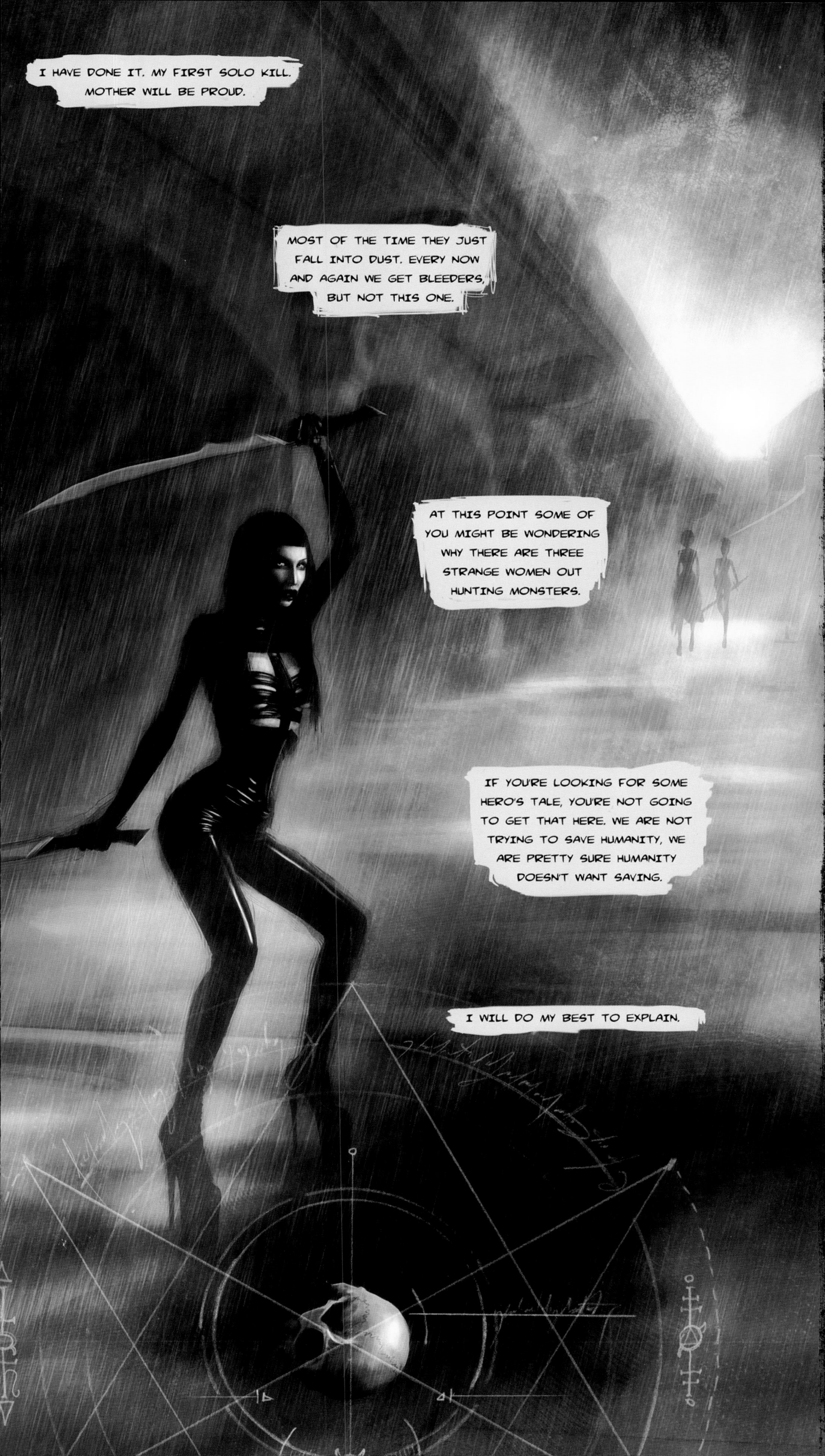
I HAVE DONE IT. MY FIRST SOLO KILL. MOTHER WILL BE PROUD.
MOST OF THE TIME THEY JUST FALL INTO DUST. EVERY NOW AND AGAIN WE GET BLEEDERS, BUT NOT THIS ONE.
AT THIS POINT SOME OF YOU MIGHT BE WONDERING WHY THERE ARE THREE STRANGE WOMEN OUT HUNTING MONSTERS.
IF YOU'RE LOOKING FOR SOME HERO'S TALE, YOU'RE NOT GOING TO GET THAT HERE. WE ARE NOT TRYING TO SAVE HUMANITY, WE ARE PRETTY SURE HUMANITY DOESN'T WANT SAVING.
I WILL DO MY BEST TO EXPLAIN.

New York City 2012

I had been hired to be one of the models in a latex fashion show at a premier fetish club in New York. This was their big annual event, no expense spared. Not being invited to be one of the models in this event was death to any modeling career in the industry, so of course the models were never paid. We had to be there.

I had seen it all. There was nothing new to see. I once enjoyed this scene and the people in it, but that was before I really understood it.

You see, like all scenes there are cliques, and I had never fit into any of them. Most of the girls hated me, and most of the photographers hate you when they find out you're not trying to sleep with them. I wanted to make art, however silly that sounds. I thought that modeling could lead to something moving beyond sexual tension and repression.

I had a few friends here and there, and they normally would help make nights like this bearable. But in the last few years, two of my best friends in this industry died, one from an overdose, and the other got married. Sure, I had girls talk to me, but they would just turn around and talk shit behind my back. I was truly alone this night, but I would do my job anyway. The modeling had become my main source of income, and there was no way I was willing to let that go.

Sitting there at the bar waiting for my chance to go backstage feeling alone and trying to pep talk myself into doing this show, I was reminded of my youth, when I never fit in anywhere. Every school, every church, and even my own home, I did not belong anywhere. I always wondered if this was a result of that horrible family member who made sure I would have issues with intimacy the rest of my life. What he did to me... how can anyone really look at a child like that? Images of those times rushed into my mind's eye, sometimes you can't help seeing the painful images as they push in. I had not thought of this for years, and something in me woke up. Something was wrong.

I looked up, and this very normal-looking but very strange feeling man was standing about 15 feet away. And I don't know how to explain it, but I knew he was feeling what I was remembering.

I stood up and forced my way to the backstage dressing room. I felt like I had been in a fight, shaking and upset, but for what? Nothing had happened, just looked up at a strange man, and what? I felt crazy again. It was probably just my nerves about tonight. Brush it off and move on, girl.

I was sitting back in the dressing room, trying to get my heart rate down when one of the other models stormed in looking a bit like a wreck. Her name and what we used to call ourselves is not important. This girl is now known to me as Magdalena, and that is how I will refer to her. She was one of the models I always hated working with, from some foreign country somewhere, terrible accent, loaded, and always getting too drunk to work. Modeling gigs with her always ended up with her on the floor passed out from some drug. She was a mess, but I had never seen her like this before, her eyes wide and quiet. Trying to be the better person, I asked if she was okay. She began telling me a story very similar to the one I just had Experienced. The strange man had upset her, as well. One thing the clubs did give the models was the power to get anyone thrown out of the club for any reason. We were all used to strange, pervy people. I grabbed Magdalena's hand, and we stormed off to find a bouncer. We pointed the man out, and the bouncer went over to him. I was expecting some kind of fight, but the strange man almost seemed fine with being kicked out. The only thing he did was make a small circle motion with his right index finger, and then pointed to me. But this is New York, I am used to the crazy.

The strange man was gone. I felt a great deal better, and it was off to the bar to do shots with Magdalena to calm our nerves. It was then that I first saw her. I had never seen her before, and my first thought was she was a new model.

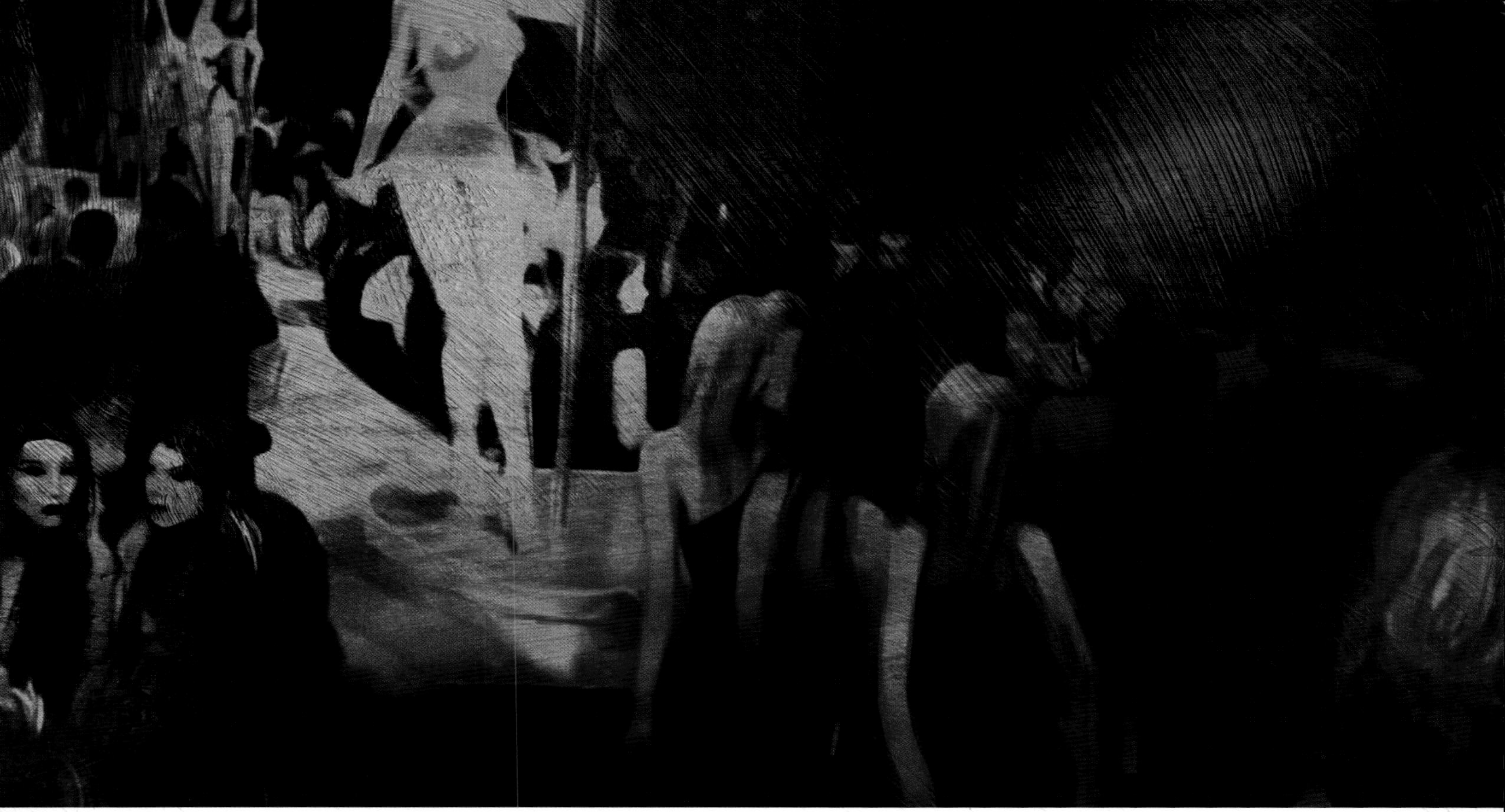

he looked amazing, and dressed to the nines. And that is ne thing I love about this scene, the clothes. I loved hem, they made me feel so powerful. They are my drug, hey take me so far away from where I grew up and made me el new, like I had control over myself. But this woman emed strangely comforting and calm. She looked like I anted to be. One of the things I noticed were her white es. I almost could not tell if they were contacts or not. felt like she was almost watching over me in some strange ay. But just as I put my head down to drink my first shot, he was gone.

) six shots of tequila and hours later, it was time for the shion show. I had a great outfit, the latex designer and loved each other, and she saved me the best outfit, an mazing new dress. I would be last in the show, the finale, nd this would help my next year of trying to get paid hoots. I sat backstage waiting for my time to go out, xtremely excited. Magdalena was going out on stage right efore me. When she came back and I got my cue to go, I ould see in her face something was wrong, but I had no me to ask. I had to get out on stage. I turned the corner, nd boom... insecurity hit me. I was not pretty enough to be he finale. I did not have the best body of the models orking tonight. I was single and a lot of the other odels had boyfriends, but I could not get a good date to ve my life. As I walked out into the catwalk, I knew I was ooling no one, just like in high school how they all new was shit, white trash, good-for-nothing. The images of my me in high school started rushing back, then it clicked. omething was wrong. I saw him. A man at the very end of he catwalk. He looked nothing like the man I saw before, completely different person. But then he made a small rcle motion with his right index finger and pointed to e. It was him. Everything in me told me to run. Then as if ut of nowhere, the woman with the white eyes jumped rom the floor onto the the stage right in front of me. he man saw her and ran out of the club. No one really new what was going on, but security grabbed the woman ith the white eyes and escorted her out of the club.

I was completely shaken. Getting backstage, I saw Magdalena. We did not even talk about it, it scared us too much. Quickly, we made plans with all the other models that night to walk together back to a hotel party. There is power in numbers. So at three in the morning, me, Magdalena, and twelve other models started to walk the streets of New York back to the hotel. It was a blur now, I do not know how we got into that alleyway. What I do remember is waking up coverd in blood, many of the other models laying in parts all around me, all of them dead. It seemed the only ones alive were me and Magdalena. Then from the shadows came the woman with the white eyes holding a huge battle axe.

"My name is Beatrice. I am not the one who has killed your friends. I killed your attacker, and you know who I am referring to. You have been marked. You may trust me and come with me, or stay in your lives and be worse than cattle. You must choose now."

Although I felt more fear in that moment than any time before or since, I did trust Beatrice, I would go. I looked over at Magdalena whose face was covered in blood and tears. All she could bring herself to do was nod yes, and from that night forward I have never heard Magdalena speak a word.

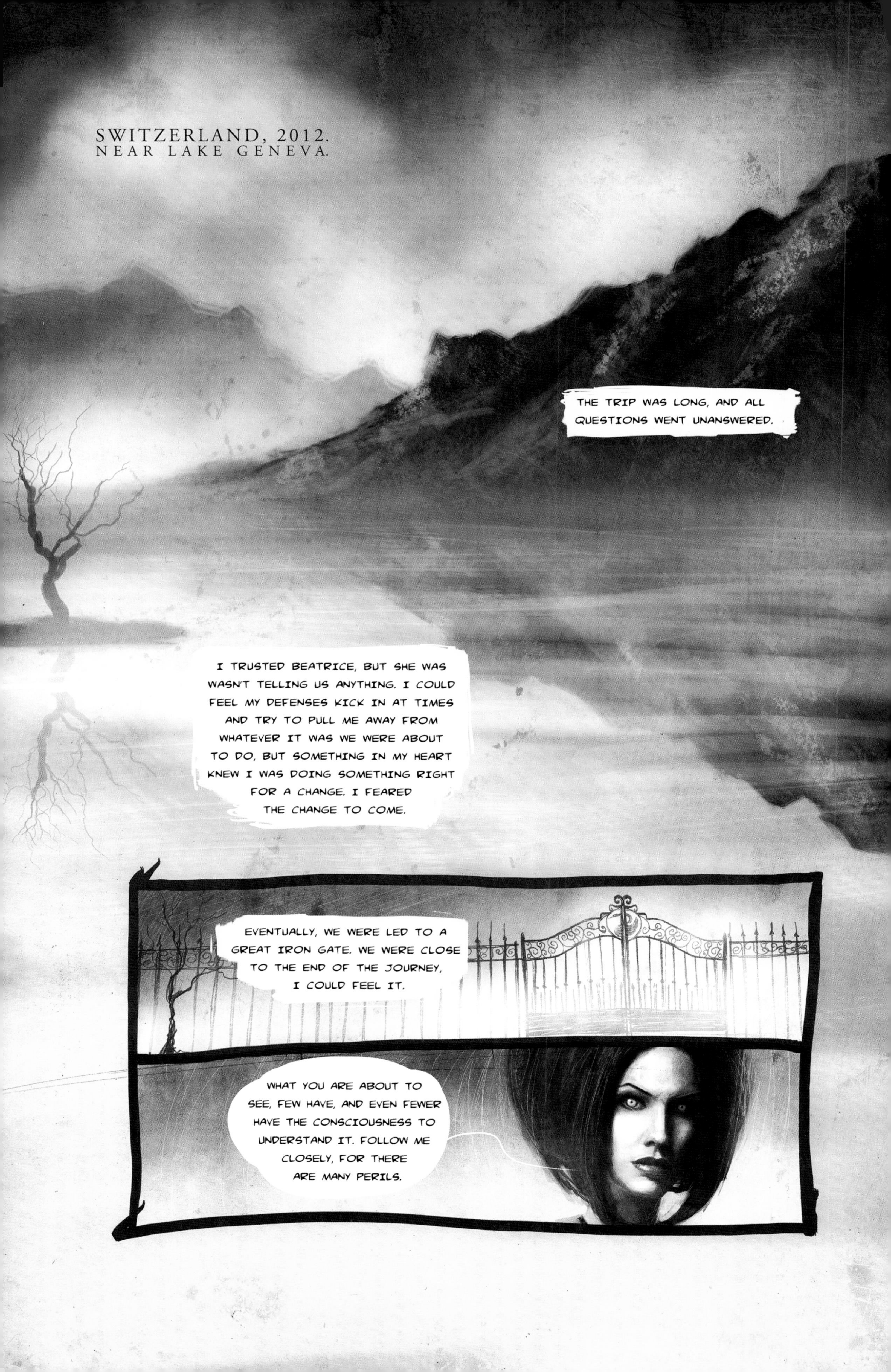
SWITZERLAND, 2012.
NEAR LAKE GENEVA.
THE TRIP WAS LONG, AND ALL QUESTIONS WENT UNANSWERED.
I TRUSTED BEATRICE, BUT SHE WAS WASN'T TELLING US ANYTHING. I COULD FEEL MY DEFENSES KICK IN AT TIMES AND TRY TO PULL ME AWAY FROM WHATEVER IT WAS WE WERE ABOUT TO DO, BUT SOMETHING IN MY HEART KNEW I WAS DOING SOMETHING RIGHT FOR A CHANGE. I FEARED THE CHANGE TO COME.
EVENTUALLY, WE WERE LED TO A GREAT IRON GATE. WE WERE CLOSE TO THE END OF THE JOURNEY, I COULD FEEL IT.
WHAT YOU ARE ABOUT TO SEE, FEW HAVE, AND EVEN FEWER HAVE THE CONSCIOUSNESS TO UNDERSTAND IT. FOLLOW ME CLOSELY, FOR THERE ARE MANY PERILS.

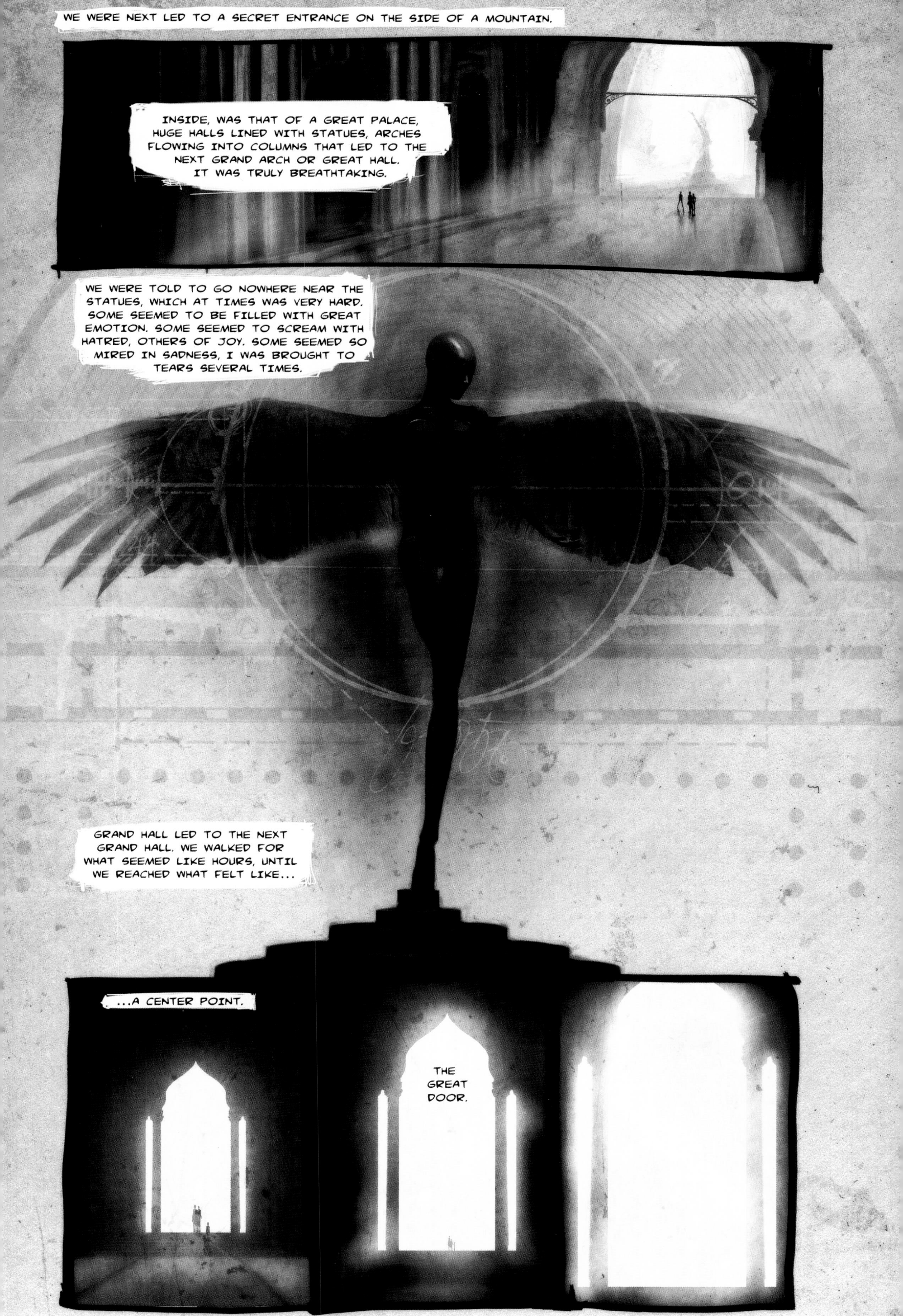
WE WERE NEXT LED TO A SECRET ENTRANCE ON THE SIDE OF A MOUNTAIN.
INSIDE, WAS THAT OF A GREAT PALACE, HUGE HALLS LINED WITH STATUES, ARCHES FLOWING INTO COLUMNS THAT LED TO THE NEXT GRAND ARCH OR GREAT HALL. IT WAS TRULY BREATHTAKING.
WE WERE TOLD TO GO NOWHERE NEAR THE STATUES, WHICH AT TIMES WAS VERY HARD. SOME SEEMED TO BE FILLED WITH GREAT EMOTION. SOME SEEMED TO SCREAM WITH HATRED, OTHERS OF JOY. SOME SEEMED SO MIRED IN SADNESS, I WAS BROUGHT TO TEARS SEVERAL TIMES.
GRAND HALL LED TO THE NEXT GRAND HALL. WE WALKED FOR WHAT SEEMED LIKE HOURS, UNTIL WE REACHED WHAT FELT LIKE...
...A CENTER POINT.
THE GREAT DOOR.

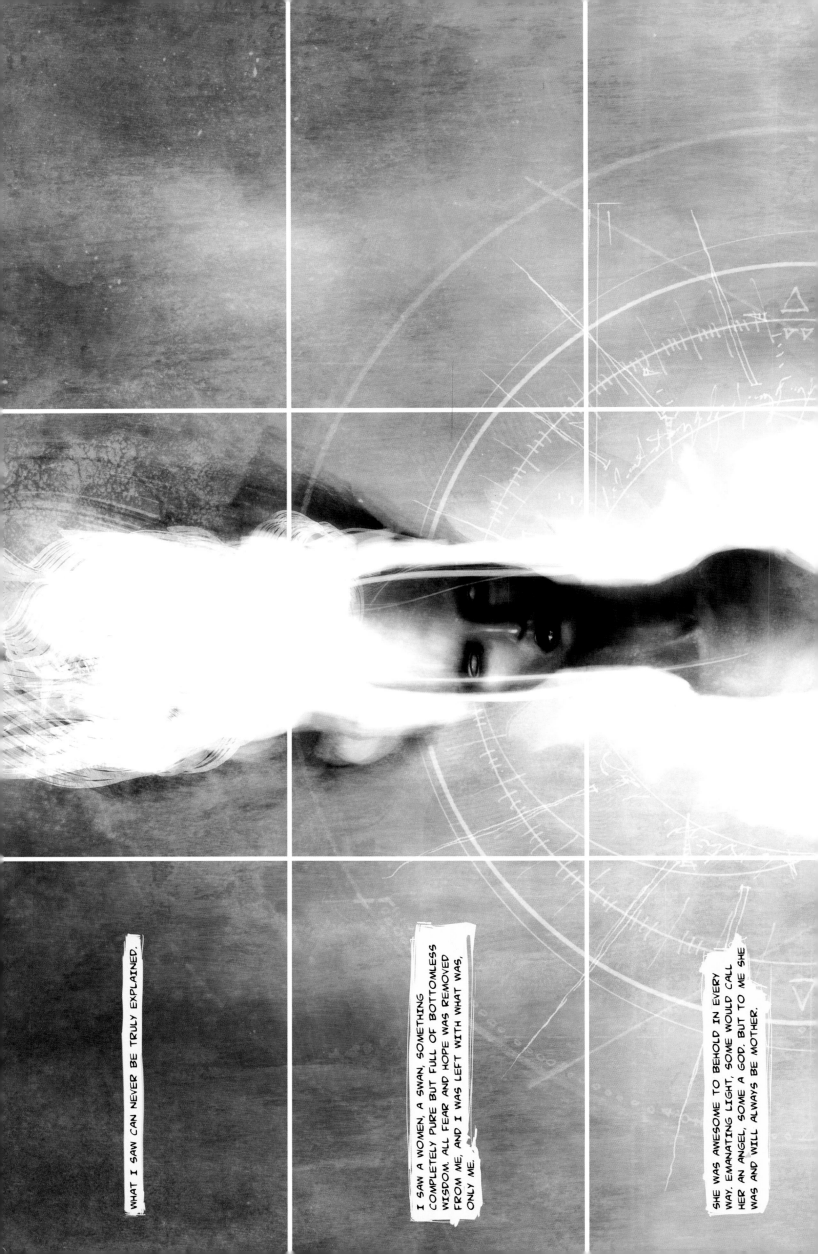

WHAT I SAW CAN NEVER BE TRULY EXPLAINED.

I SAW A WOMEN, A SWAN, SOMETHING COMPLETELY PURE BUT FULL OF BOTTOMLESS WISDOM. ALL FEAR AND HOPE WAS REMOVED FROM ME, AND I WAS LEFT WITH WHAT WAS, ONLY ME.

SHE WAS AWESOME TO BEHOLD IN EVERY WAY, EMANATING LIGHT, SOME WOULD CALL HER AN ANGEL, SOME A GOD, BUT TO ME SHE WAS AND WILL ALWAYS BE MOTHER.

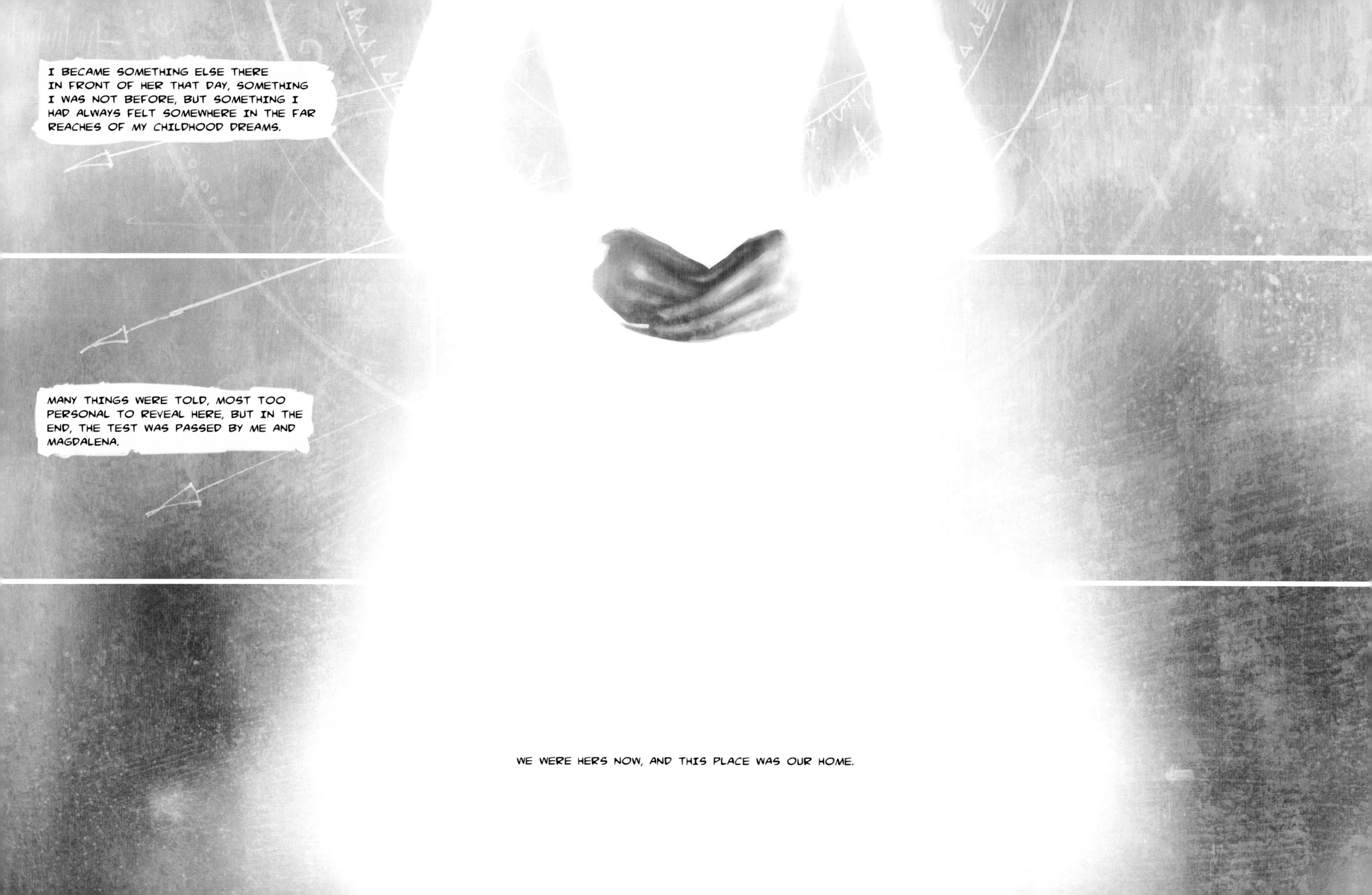
I BECAME SOMETHING ELSE THERE IN FRONT OF HER THAT DAY, SOMETHING I WAS NOT BEFORE, BUT SOMETHING I HAD ALWAYS FELT SOMEWHERE IN THE FAR REACHES OF MY CHILDHOOD DREAMS.
MANY THINGS WERE TOLD, MOST TOO PERSONAL TO REVEAL HERE, BUT IN THE END, THE TEST WAS PASSED BY ME AND MAGDALENA.
WE WERE HERS NOW, AND THIS PLACE WAS OUR HOME.

TRAINING BEGAN IMMEDIATELY. BEATRICE STARTED BY TEACHING US ABOUT THE THING THAT ATTACKED US. IT TURNS OUT THEY ARE EVERYWHERE, AND THIS KIND OF ATTACK IS VERY COMMON. IT WAS MY ABILITY TO SEE WHAT WAS HAPPENING THAT MADE BEATRICE NOTICE ME.

SOME WOULD CALL THEM VAMPIRES, AND OTHERS MIGHT CALL THEM DEMONS OR EVEN WEREWOLVES, BUT THEY WOULD ALL BE WRONG. THEY ARE SOMETHING MUCH MORE. DO YOU KNOW THAT FEELING YOU GET WITH A FIRST KISS? A BABY SMILING AT YOU? WHEN YOU SEE A PAINTING THAT TRULY MOVES YOU? THE SICK FEELING YOU GET WHEN YOU WATCH VIDEOS OF PEOPLE DYING? THAT EMOTIONAL BURST YOU GET WHEN YOU BREAK A BONE? YOU ARE ABLE TO FEEL THOSE THINGS BECAUSE YOU ARE CONNECTED TO WHAT SOME PEOPLE WOULD CALL A SOUL. IT TURNS OUT IF YOU CUT YOURSELF OFF FROM YOUR SOUL, YOUR PHYSICAL MANIFESTATION CAN LIVE ON. BUT YOU NEED TO STEAL THE CHARGED EMOTIONAL MEMORIES FROM OTHERS TO REMAIN CORPO-REAL. THESE CREATURES, THESE THINGS, ARE NO LONGER ABLE TO GENERATE ANYTHING LIKE THAT. IF THEY LOOK AT AN AMAZING PAINTING, ALL THEY ARE ABLE TO SEE ARE THE BRUSH STOKES, THE WAY IN WHICH THE COLORS INTERACT. BUT THEY CAN NOT BE MOVED BY IT, FOR A FIRST KISS THEY WOULD FEEL NOTHING BUT LIPS PUSHING AGAINST LIPS. EVERYTHING IS HOLLOW. THEY NEED THE FEELINGS AND MEMORIES OF OTHERS STILL CONNECTED IN THE NATURAL WAY.

THIS BRINGS ALL-NEW MEANING TO ANCIENT WORLD HUMAN SACRIFICE, AS THE EMOTIONS THAT WOULD BE GENERATED WOULD BE INCREDIBLE TO ONE OF THESE THINGS. THE MORE YOU FEEL INSIDE OF A MEMORY, THE MORE THEY GET OUT OF IT. THEY CAN EVEN STEAL YOUR MEMORIES. YOU WOULD NEVER KNOW, OR THEY CAN PLACE ALL NEW MEMORIES THERE. IT IS ALL ABOUT GETTING YOU TO FEEL AS MUCH AS THEY CAN. WE BECOME LIKE BOTTLES OF WINE TO THEM. THEY WILL EVEN CULTIVATE A PERSON OVER YEARS, TORMENTING THEM UNTIL THEY REACH JUST THE RIGHT FLAVOR THEY WANT.

THIS IS WHY WE CALL THEM THE MEMORY COLLECTORS.

DON'T WORRY, IT IS NOT A SIMPLE THING THEY HAVE DONE. CUTTING YOURSELF OFF FROM YOUR SOUL OR YOUR HIGHER SELF IS NOT AN EASY TASK. IT INVOLVES KILLING YOURSELF AND BEING ABLE TO REFORM YOUR MANIFESTATION AGAIN AT THE MOMENT OF DEATH. MANY SECRET KNOWLEDGES HAVE TO BE MASTERED TO BE ABLE TO DO IT. NO ONE IS IN ANY DANGER OF BECOMING SOMETHING LIKE THAT ON ACCIDENT, YOU REALLY HAVE TO KNOW WHAT YOU'RE DOING.

THEY ALL HIDE AMONG US, AIRPORTS AN MALLS ARE GREAT PLACES FOR THEM NOT TO B NOTICED. THEY ARE ALWAYS THE PERSON I THE CROWD YOU WOULD NEVER THINK WOUL BE DOING SOMETHING LIKE THAT, NORMALI VERY SHORT OR UGLY, BUT NOT TOO UGL SOMETIMES THEY PLAY AS THE HOMELESS O CAB DRIVERS, ANYTHING THAT DOES NOT DRA ATTENTION TO THEMSELVES.

TO HUNT THEM, WE WOULD NEED TO BE ABI TO SEE THEM, SO SIGHT IS FIRST AN FOREMOST. THIS IS WHERE BEATRICE STARTE WITH US. WE SPENT FULL DAYS AND WEEK MEDITATING, AND THEN SEEING THEM WAS REI ATIVELY EASY. IT SEEMS WE ARE ALL BORN WIT THIS KIND OF SIGHT, BUT LIKE ANY MUSCL YOU HAVE TO BUILD STRENGTH WITH IT.

NEXT CAME THE WEAPONS TRAINING. NO JUST ANY WEAPON CAN HURT THEM, THEY HAV TO BE WEAPONS MADE WITH PURE, MANIFESTE CONSCIOUSNESS. THIS WAS MUCH HARDE TOOK A GREAT AMOUNT TIME, AND WA EXTREMELY PAINFUL. MAGDALENA WAS ABLE T ACHIEVE THIS WEEKS BEFORE ME. WE LEARNE A GREAT DEAL OVER THOSE YEARS, AN NOWADAYS IT IS HARD FOR ME TO REMEMBE WHAT IT'S LIKE TO LIVE LIFE WITHOUT THOS ABILITIES. THE MOST SHOCKING THING ABOU ALL OF THE TRAINING WAS THAT EVERYTHING LEARNED, THE MOMENT I TRULY UNDERSTOO IT, WAS MORE LIKE A MEMORY THEN SOM THING NEW. EVERYONE HAS THESE ABILITIE THEY ARE ALL INSIDE OF ALL OF US, IT IS JUST MATTER OF REMEMBERING THEM.

WHAT I BECAME, WHAT I AM NOW, LONG AG WAS CALLED A SWAN MAIDEN OR A RAVE MAIDEN. WE JUST HIDE THE SKINS, OR ROBE WELL.

WHEN ALL THE TRAINING WAS DONE AN MOTHER FINALLY SAID IT WAS OKAY TO HUN THERE WAS A GREAT DEAL OF FEAR ON MY PAR I KNOW IT SOUNDS SILLY, BUT I WANTED T WEAR MY OLD FEITSH OUTFITS. I KNEW WOULD MAKE ME FEEL MORE POWERFUL, MOR IN CONTROL, AND I WOULD NOT BE TRYING T HIDE LIKE THE ONES WE ARE HUNTING. WHE I BROUGHT THIS UP TO THE GROUP, THEY A LOVED IT. WE EVEN CAME UP WITH THE IDE TO START HUNTING AT COMIC-BOOK CONVEN TIONS, AS THE OUTFITS WOULD JUST LOOK LIK COSPLAY. IT WAS ALL KIND OF PERFECT, AND W COULD GET OUT OUR DESIRES TO BE SUPE HEROES, AS WELL. IT ALL WORKED BETTE THAN WE HAD HOPED. WE EVEN HAD A CHANC TO CONVINCE A STRANGE LITTLE MAN WITH CRAZY BEARD TO MAKE A COMIC ABOUT US, S THAT WHEN WE WENT TO CONVENTION PEOPLE EVEN KNEW THE CHARACTERS WE WER "PRETENDING" TO BE.

WE DO NOT HUNT THEM BECAUSE WE WANT TO SAVE HUMANITY. WE HUNT THEM BECAUSE WE LIKE KILLING THEM. MORE THAN A CALLING, THIS IS EVERYTHING TO US, OUR ONLY TRUE REASON FOR LIVING. THE HOLLOW PLACE IN OUR HEARTS ARE FILLED WITH EACH OF THEIR DEATHS.

WE WILL NEVER STOP.

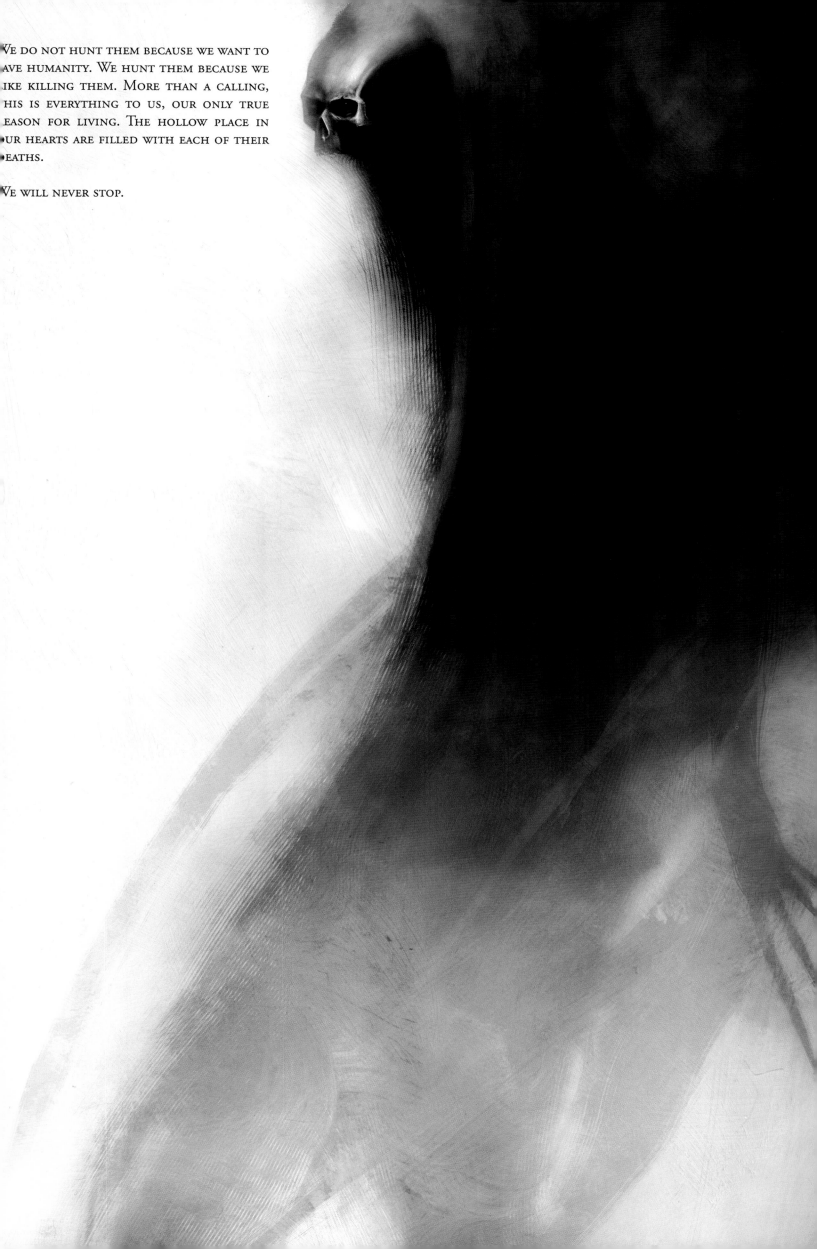

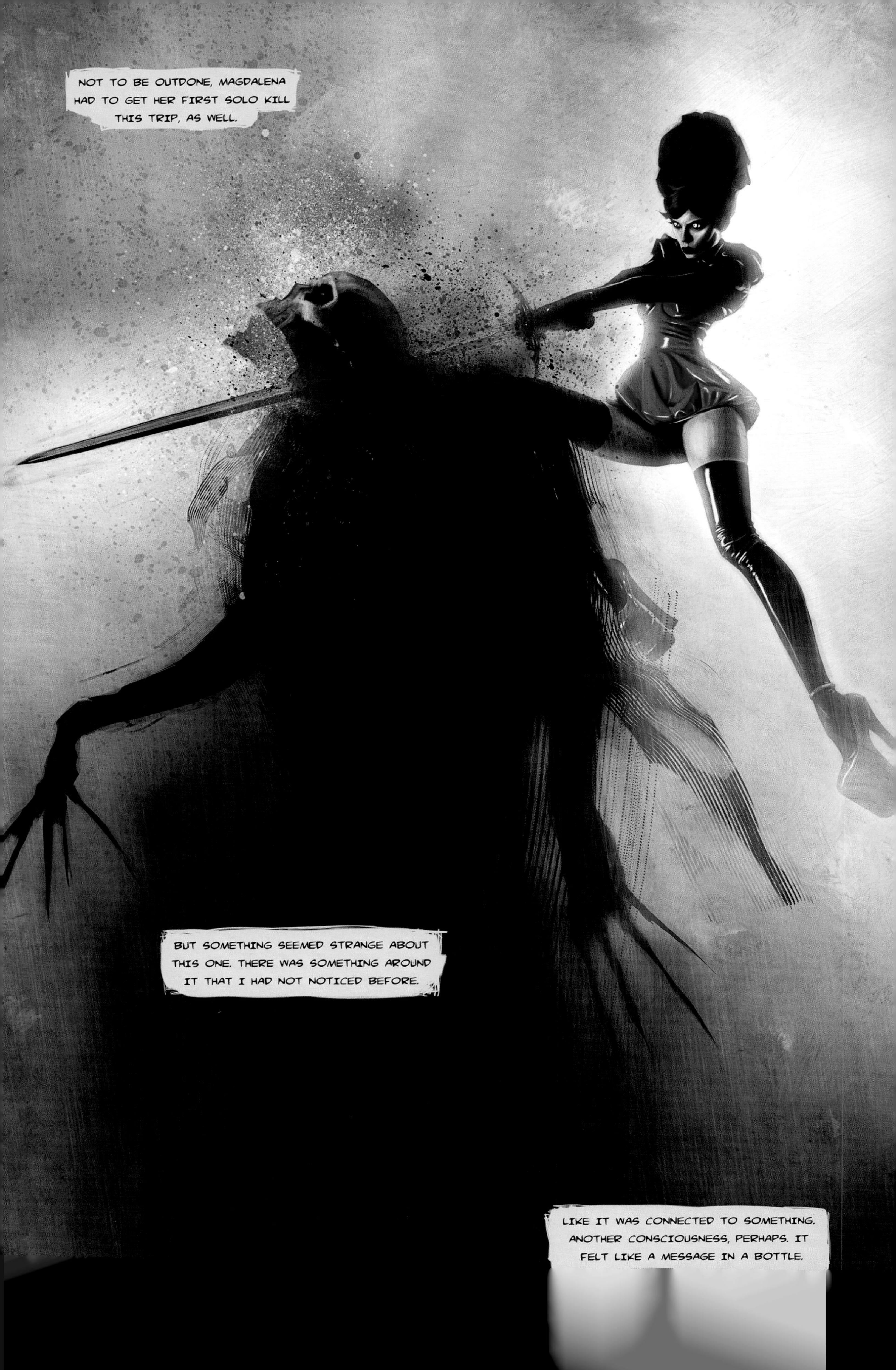
NOT TO BE OUTDONE, MAGDALENA HAD TO GET HER FIRST SOLO KILL THIS TRIP, AS WELL.
BUT SOMETHING SEEMED STRANGE ABOUT THIS ONE. THERE WAS SOMETHING AROUND IT THAT I HAD NOT NOTICED BEFORE.
LIKE IT WAS CONNECTED TO SOMETHING. ANOTHER CONSCIOUSNESS, PERHAPS. IT FELT LIKE A MESSAGE IN A BOTTLE.

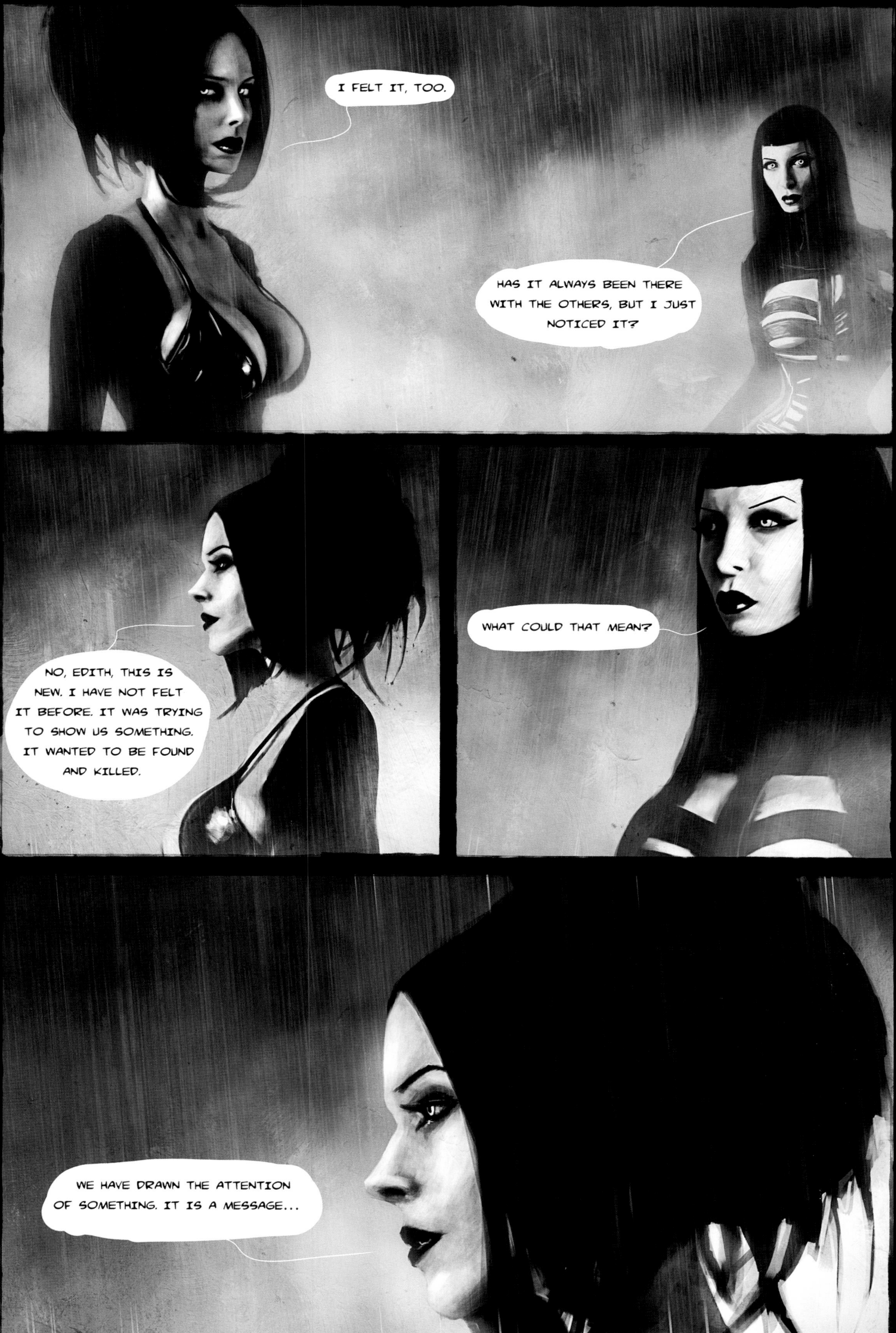
I FELT IT, TOO.
HAS IT ALWAYS BEEN THERE WITH THE OTHERS, BUT I JUST NOTICED IT?
NO, EDITH, THIS IS NEW. I HAVE NOT FELT IT BEFORE. IT WAS TRYING TO SHOW US SOMETHING. IT WANTED TO BE FOUND AND KILLED.
WHAT COULD THAT MEAN?
WE HAVE DRAWN THE ATTENTION OF SOMETHING. IT IS A MESSAGE...

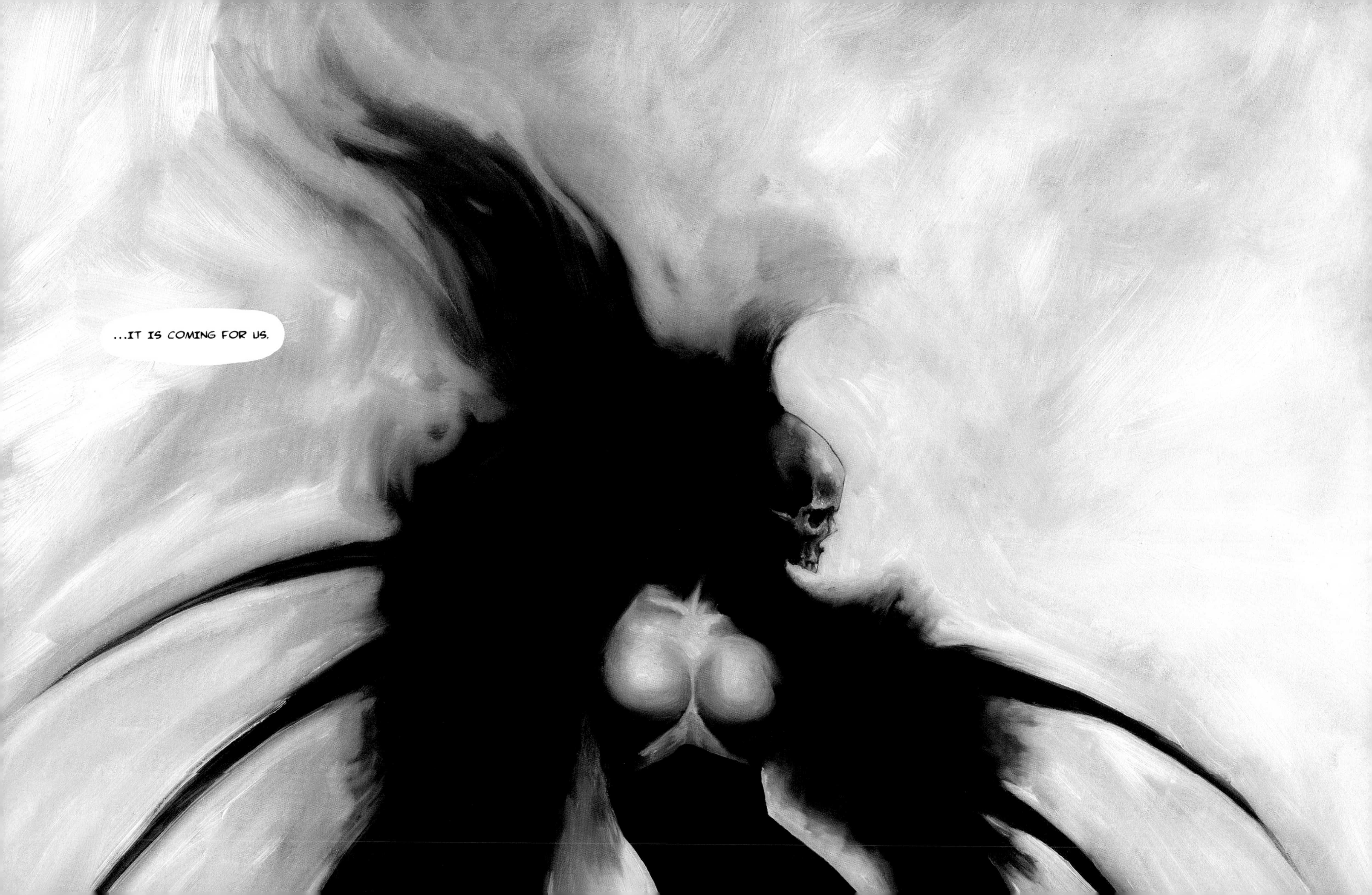
...IT IS COMING FOR US.

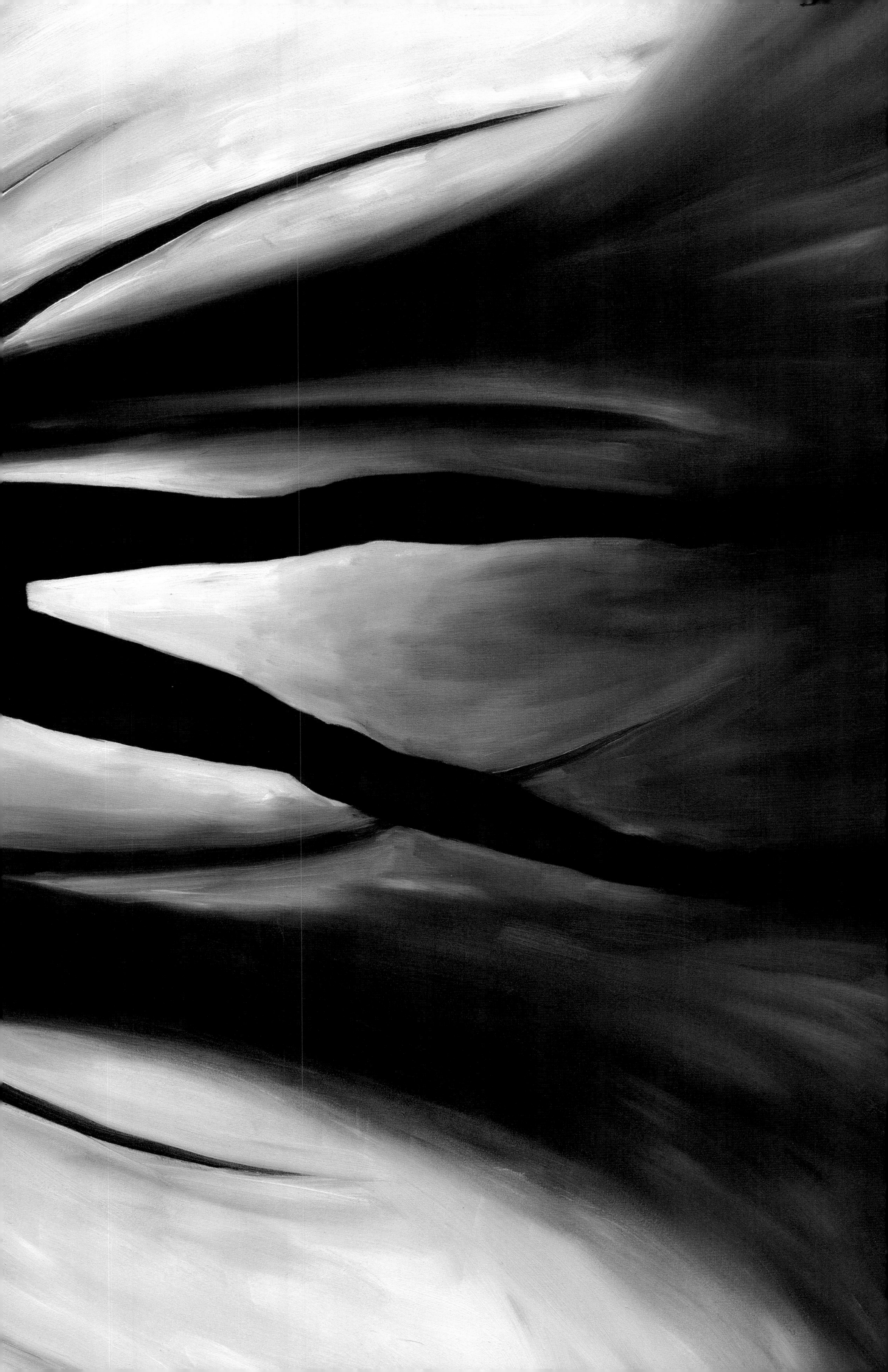

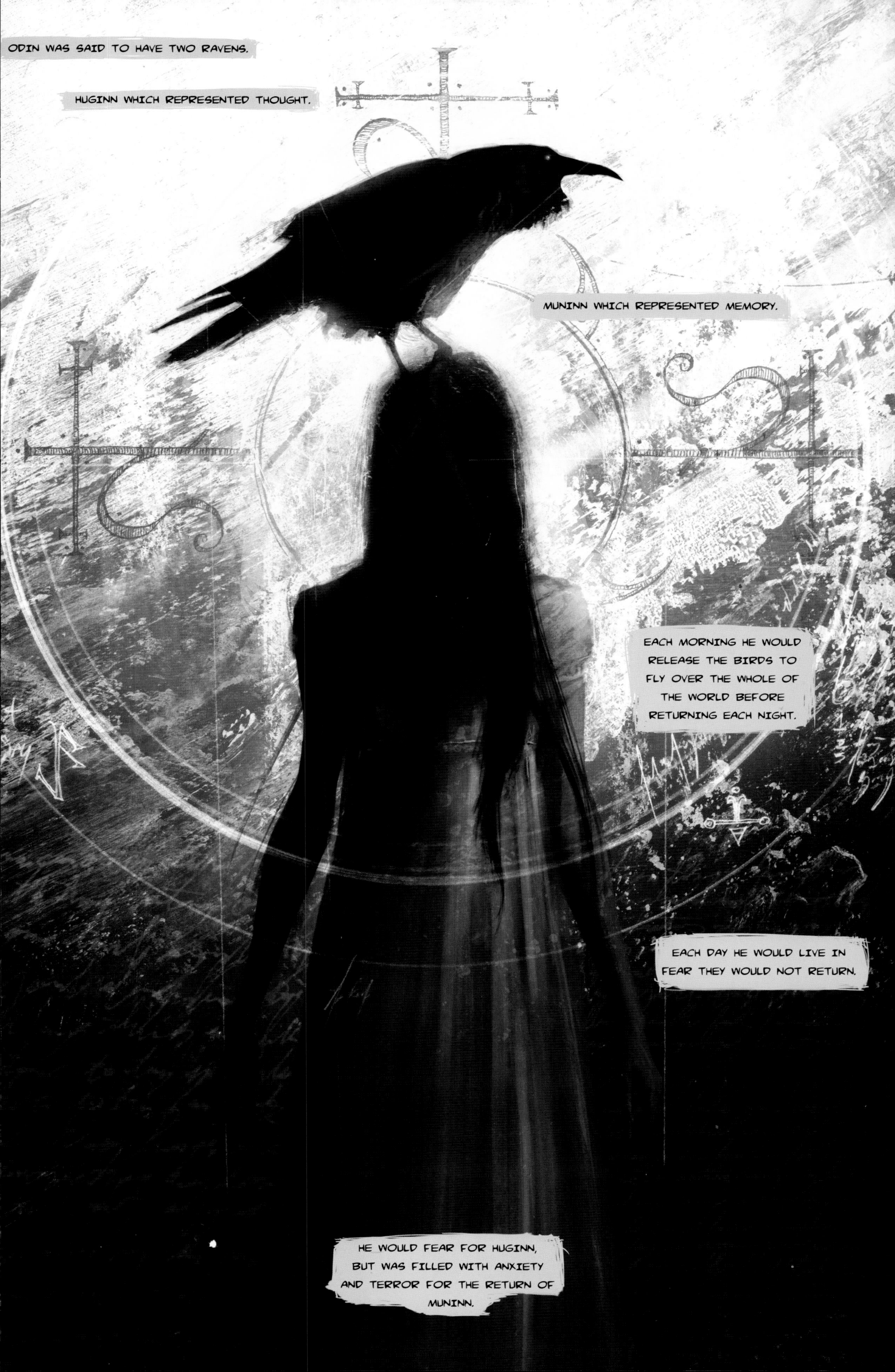
ODIN WAS SAID TO HAVE TWO RAVENS.
HUGINN WHICH REPRESENTED THOUGHT.
MUNINN WHICH REPRESENTED MEMORY.
EACH MORNING HE WOULD RELEASE THE BIRDS TO FLY OVER THE WHOLE OF THE WORLD BEFORE RETURNING EACH NIGHT.
EACH DAY HE WOULD LIVE IN FEAR THEY WOULD NOT RETURN.
HE WOULD FEAR FOR HUGINN, BUT WAS FILLED WITH ANXIETY AND TERROR FOR THE RETURN OF MUNINN.

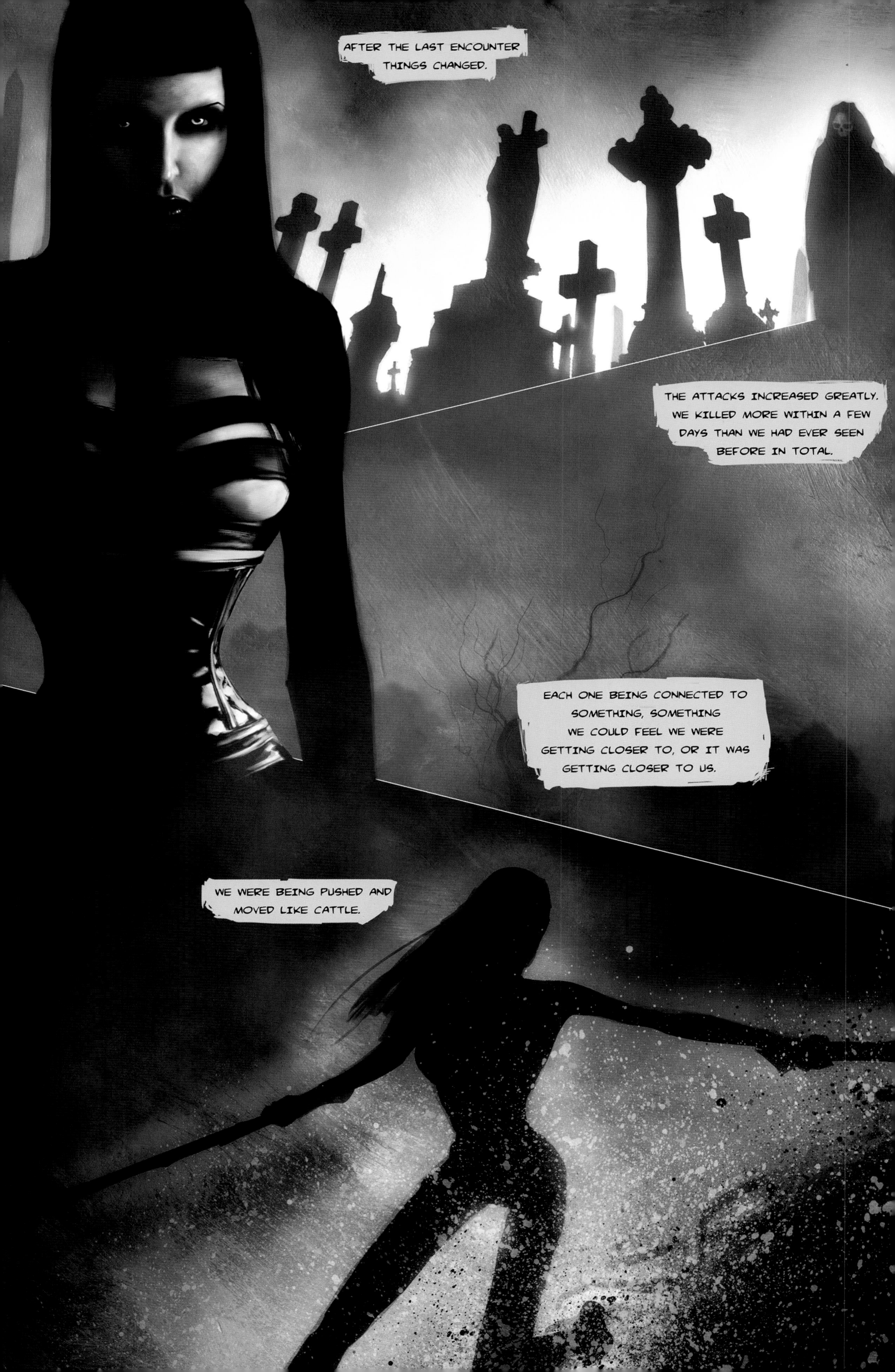
AFTER THE LAST ENCOUNTER THINGS CHANGED.
THE ATTACKS INCREASED GREATLY. WE KILLED MORE WITHIN A FEW DAYS THAN WE HAD EVER SEEN BEFORE IN TOTAL.
EACH ONE BEING CONNECTED TO SOMETHING, SOMETHING WE COULD FEEL WE WERE GETTING CLOSER TO, OR IT WAS GETTING CLOSER TO US.
WE WERE BEING PUSHED AND MOVED LIKE CATTLE.

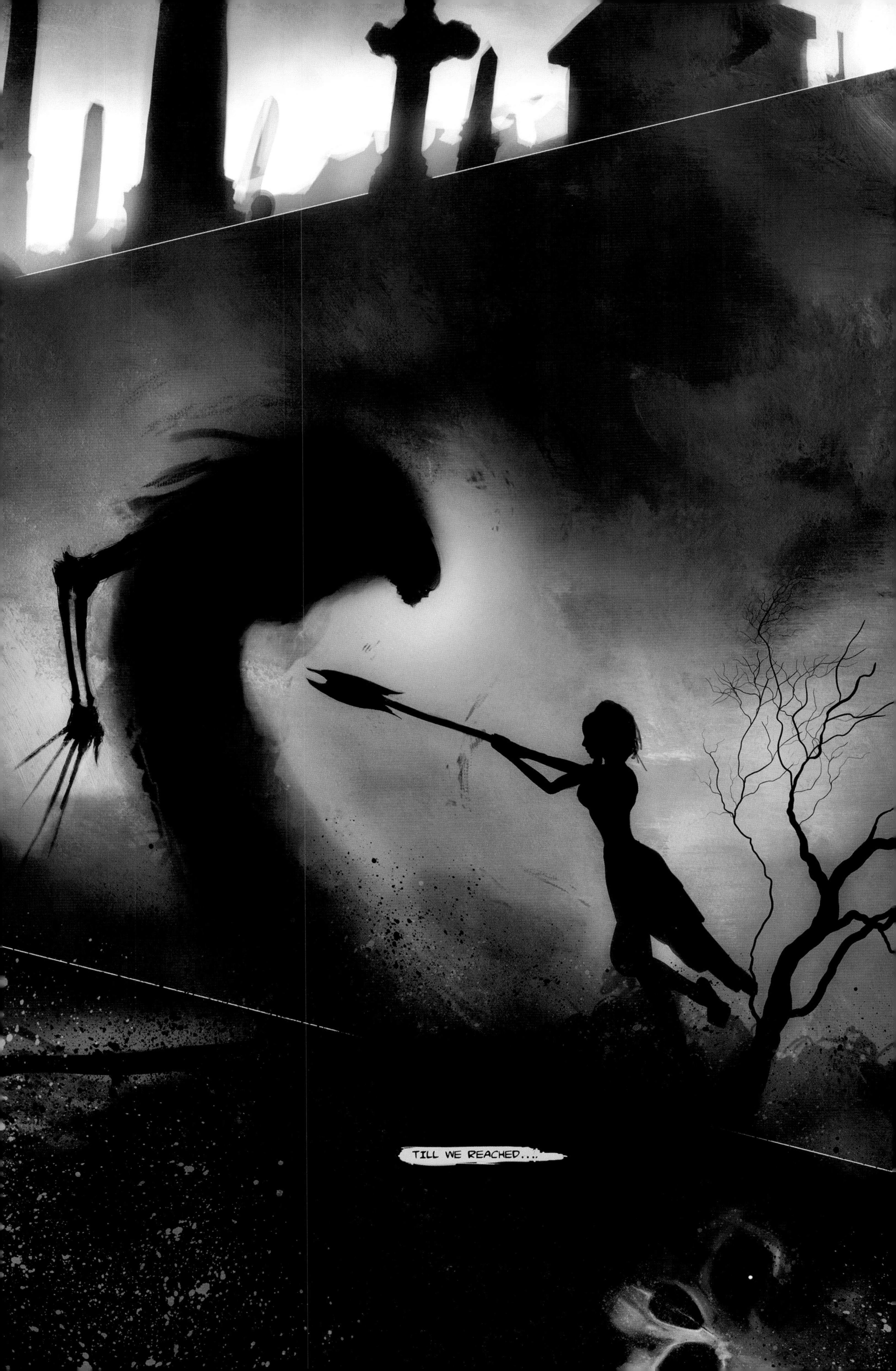
TILL WE REACHED....

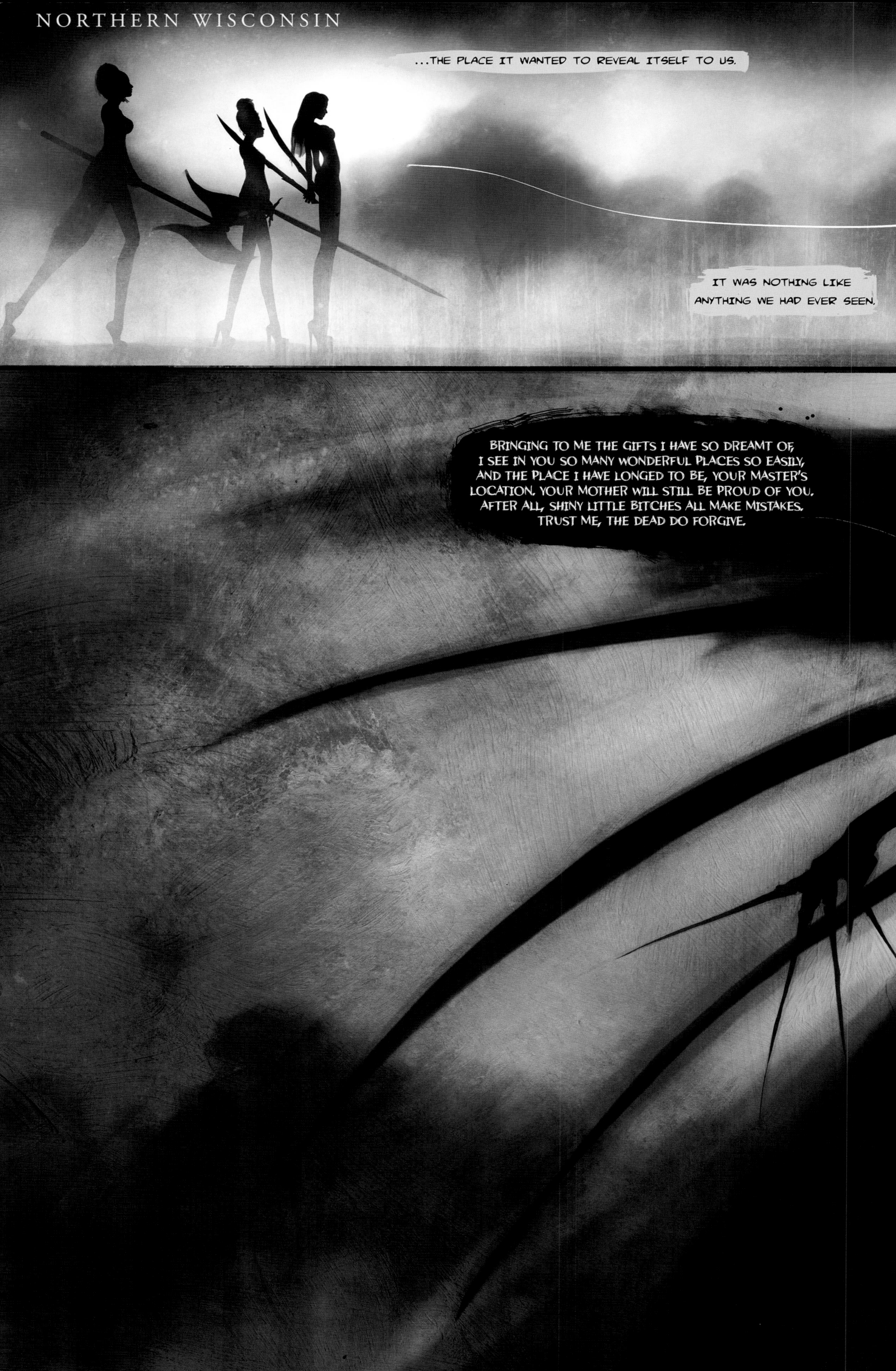
NORTHERN WISCONSIN
...THE PLACE IT WANTED TO REVEAL ITSELF TO US.
IT WAS NOTHING LIKE ANYTHING WE HAD EVER SEEN.
BRINGING TO ME THE GIFTS I HAVE SO DREAMT OF, I SEE IN YOU SO MANY WONDERFUL PLACES SO EASILY, AND THE PLACE I HAVE LONGED TO BE, YOUR MASTER'S LOCATION. YOUR MOTHER WILL STILL BE PROUD OF YOU. AFTER ALL, SHINY LITTLE BITCHES ALL MAKE MISTAKES. TRUST ME, THE DEAD DO FORGIVE.

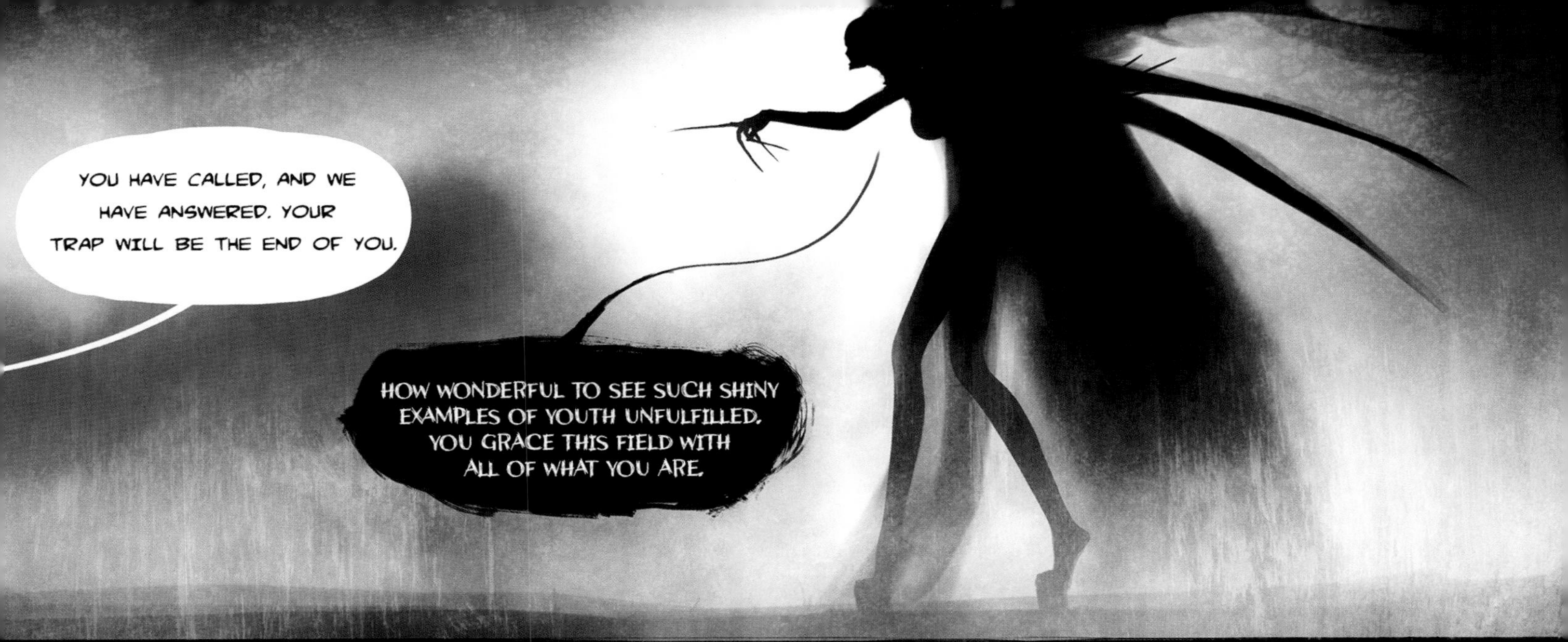
YOU HAVE CALLED, AND WE HAVE ANSWERED. YOUR TRAP WILL BE THE END OF YOU.
HOW WONDERFUL TO SEE SUCH SHINY EXAMPLES OF YOUTH UNFULFILLED. YOU GRACE THIS FIELD WITH ALL OF WHAT YOU ARE.

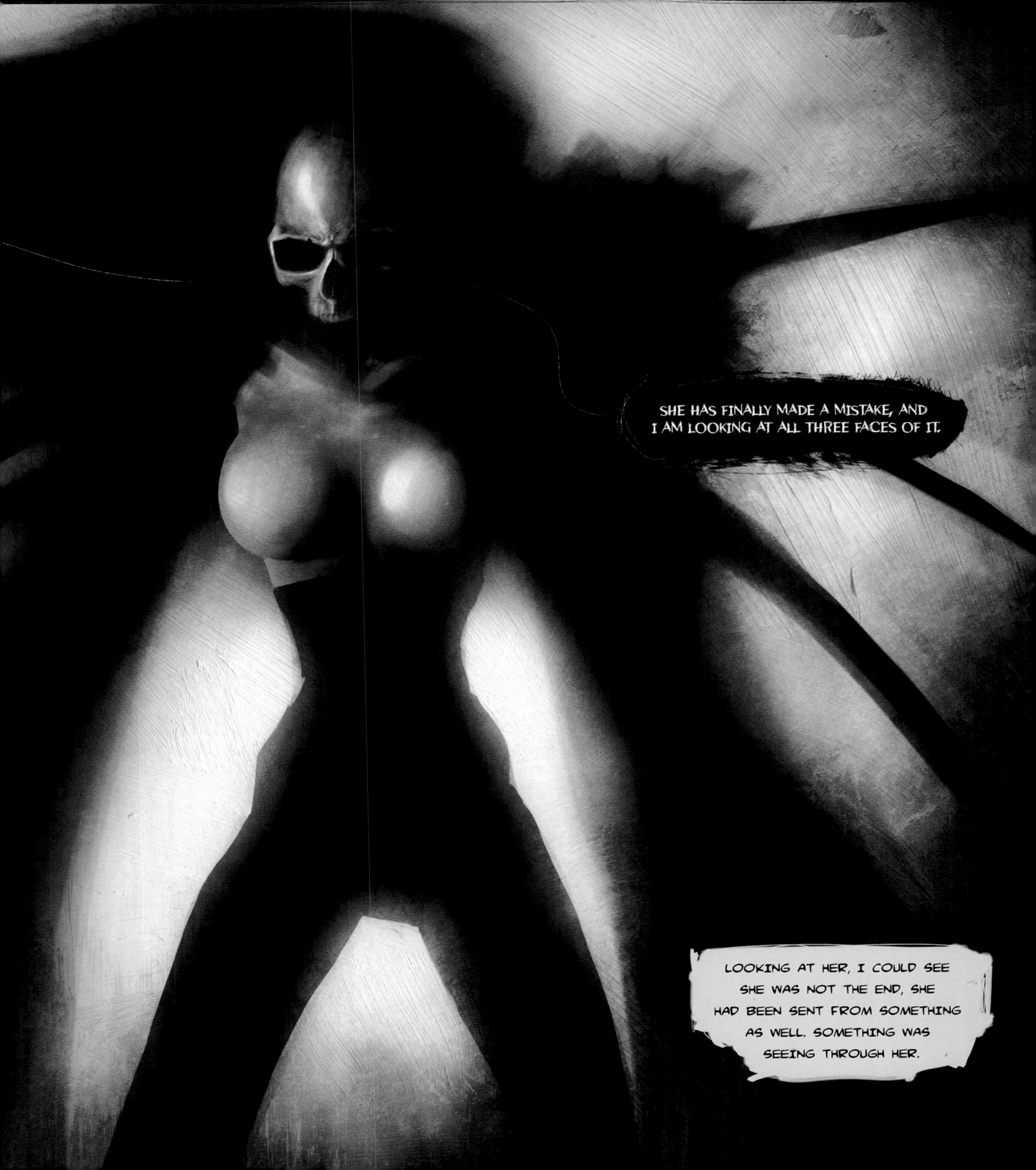
SHE HAS FINALLY MADE A MISTAKE, AND I AM LOOKING AT ALL THREE FACES OF IT.
LOOKING AT HER, I COULD SEE SHE WAS NOT THE END, SHE HAD BEEN SENT FROM SOMETHING AS WELL. SOMETHING WAS SEEING THROUGH HER.

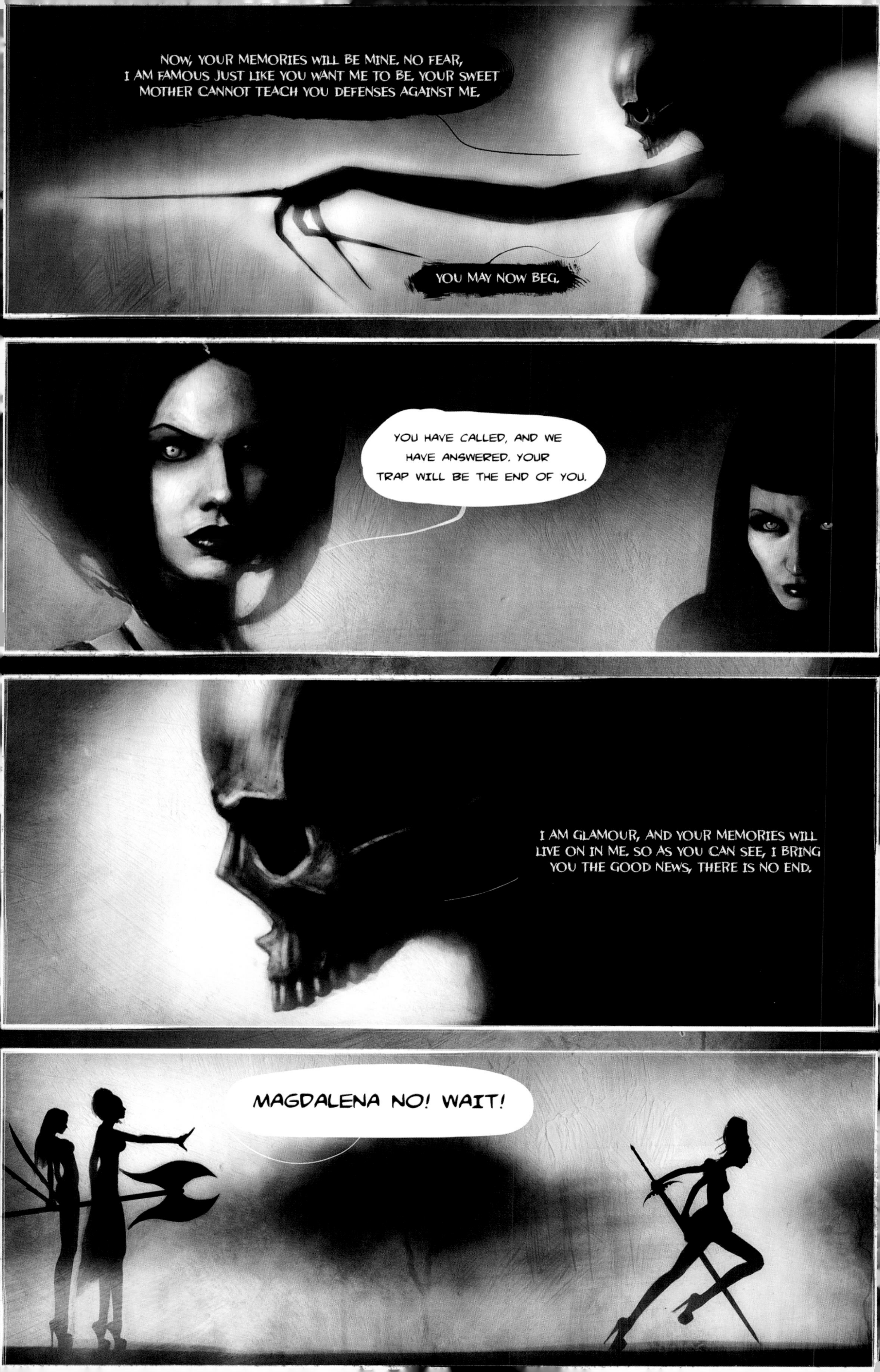
NOW, YOUR MEMORIES WILL BE MINE. NO FEAR, I AM FAMOUS JUST LIKE YOU WANT ME TO BE. YOUR SWEET MOTHER CANNOT TEACH YOU DEFENSES AGAINST ME.
YOU MAY NOW BEG.
YOU HAVE CALLED, AND WE HAVE ANSWERED. YOUR TRAP WILL BE THE END OF YOU.
I AM GLAMOUR, AND YOUR MEMORIES WILL LIVE ON IN ME. SO AS YOU CAN SEE, I BRING YOU THE GOOD NEWS, THERE IS NO END.
MAGDALENA NO! WAIT!

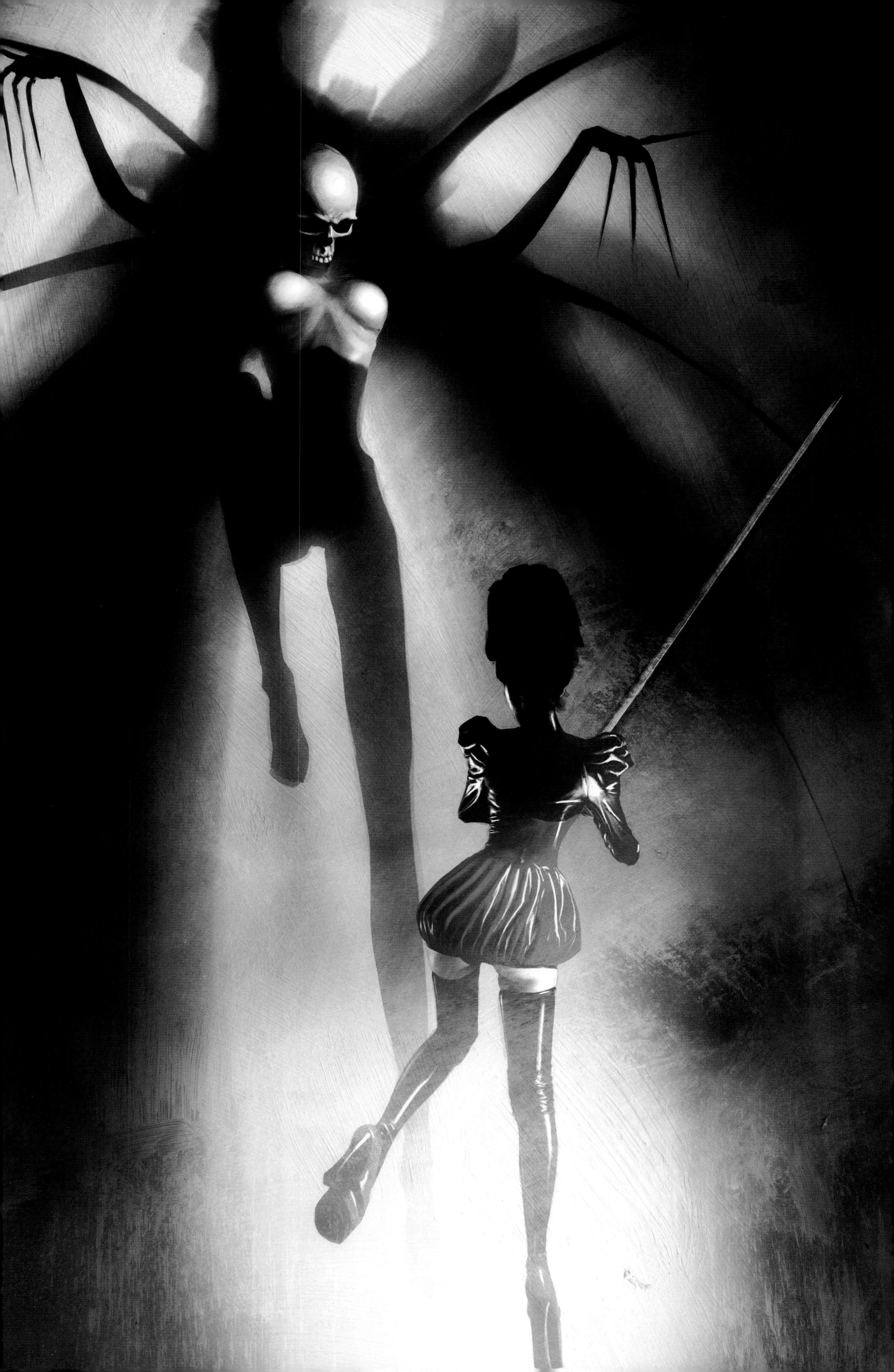

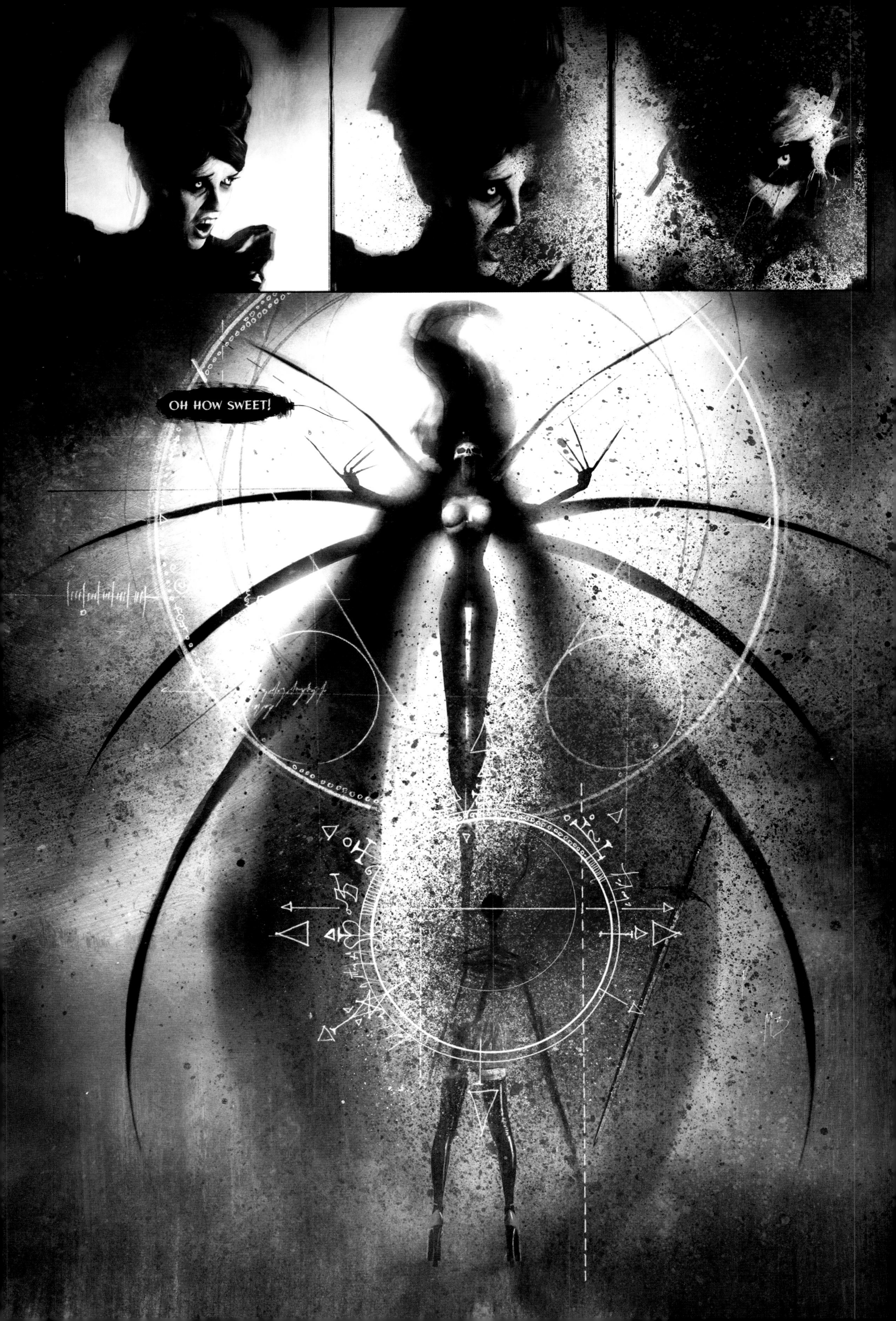
OH HOW SWEET!

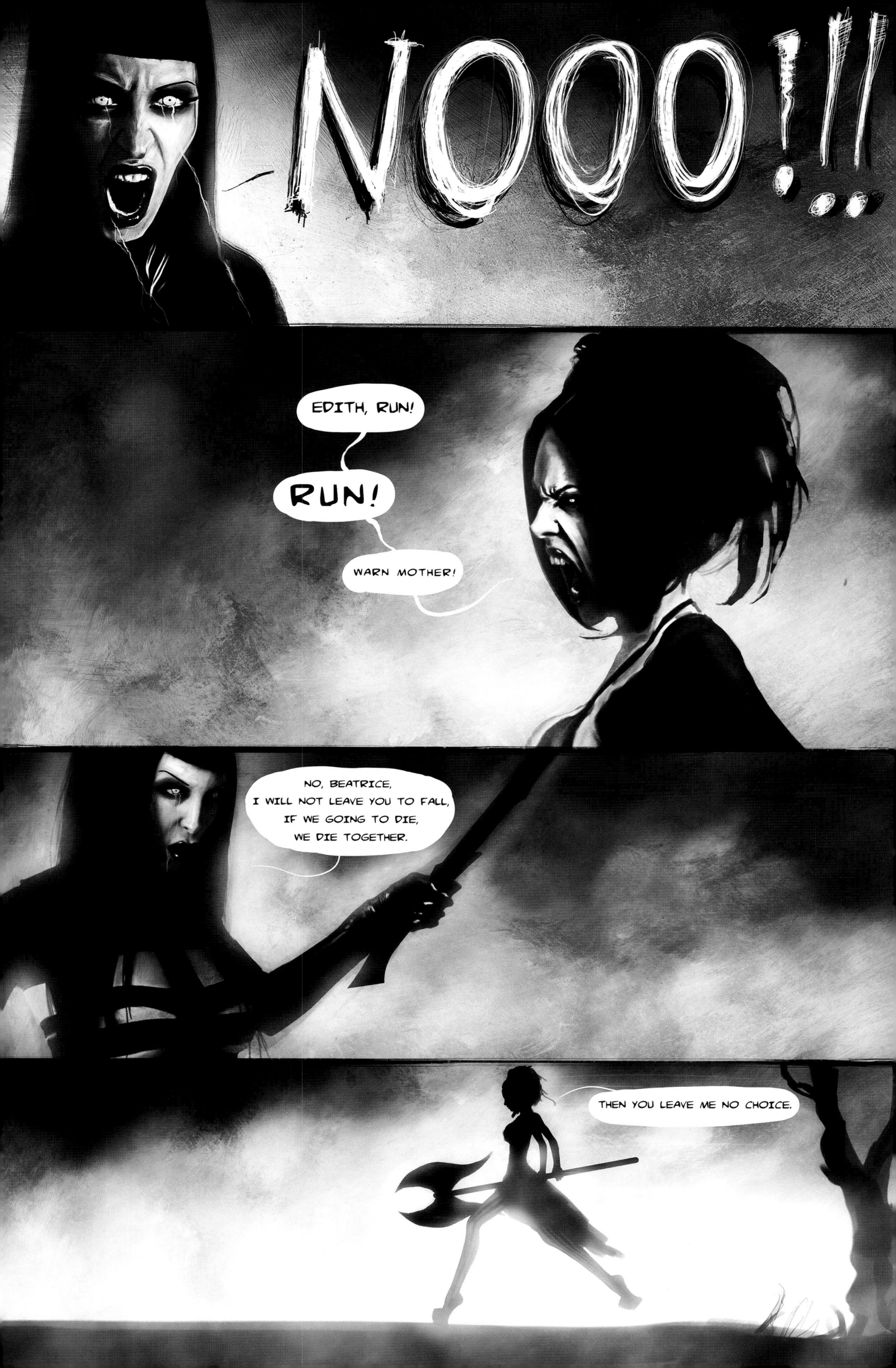
NOOO!!!...
EDITH, RUN!
RUN!
WARN MOTHER!
NO, BEATRICE,
I WILL NOT LEAVE YOU TO FALL,
IF WE GOING TO DIE,
WE DIE TOGETHER.
THEN YOU LEAVE ME NO CHOICE.

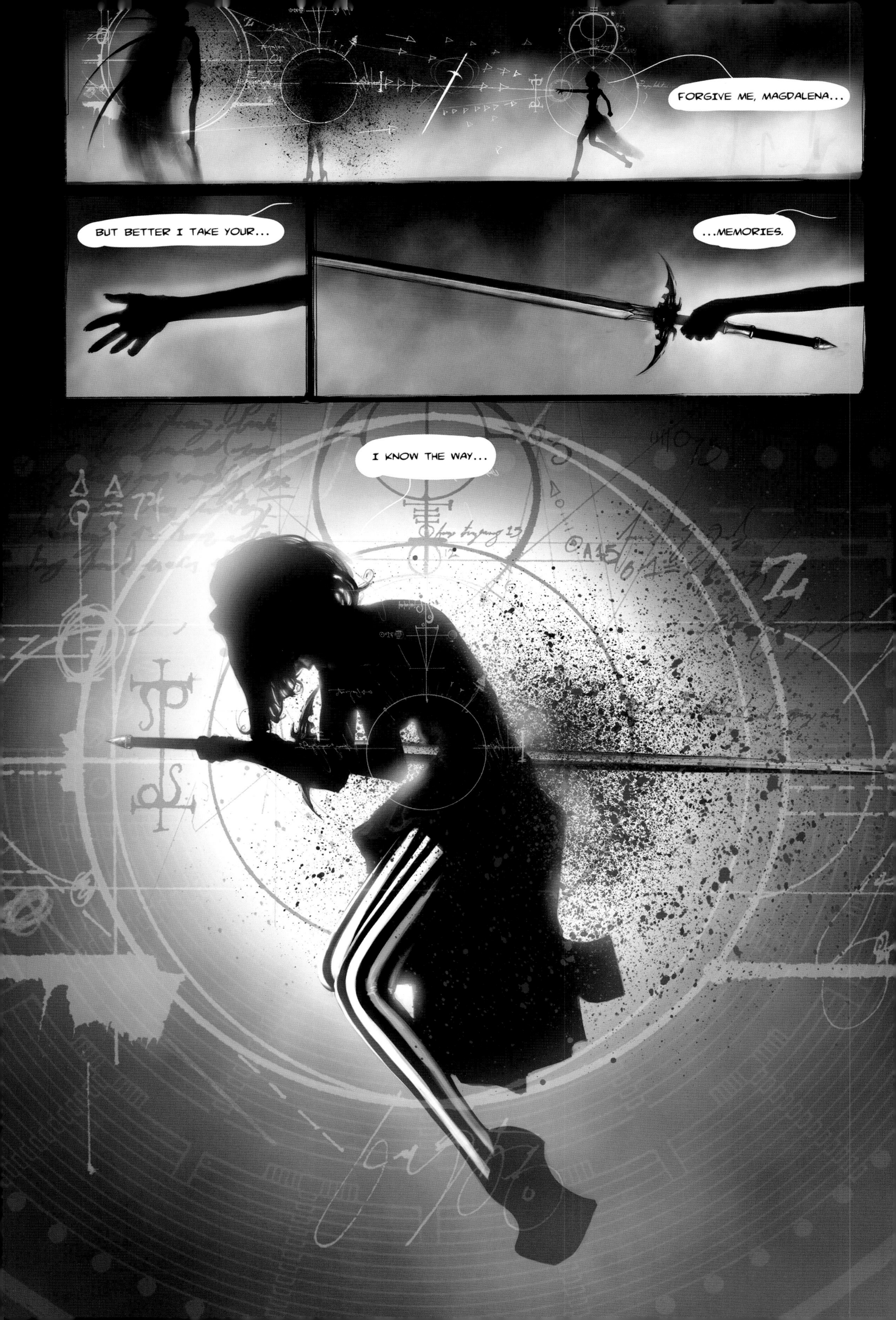
FORGIVE ME, MAGDALENA...
BUT BETTER I TAKE YOUR...
...MEMORIES.
I KNOW THE WAY...

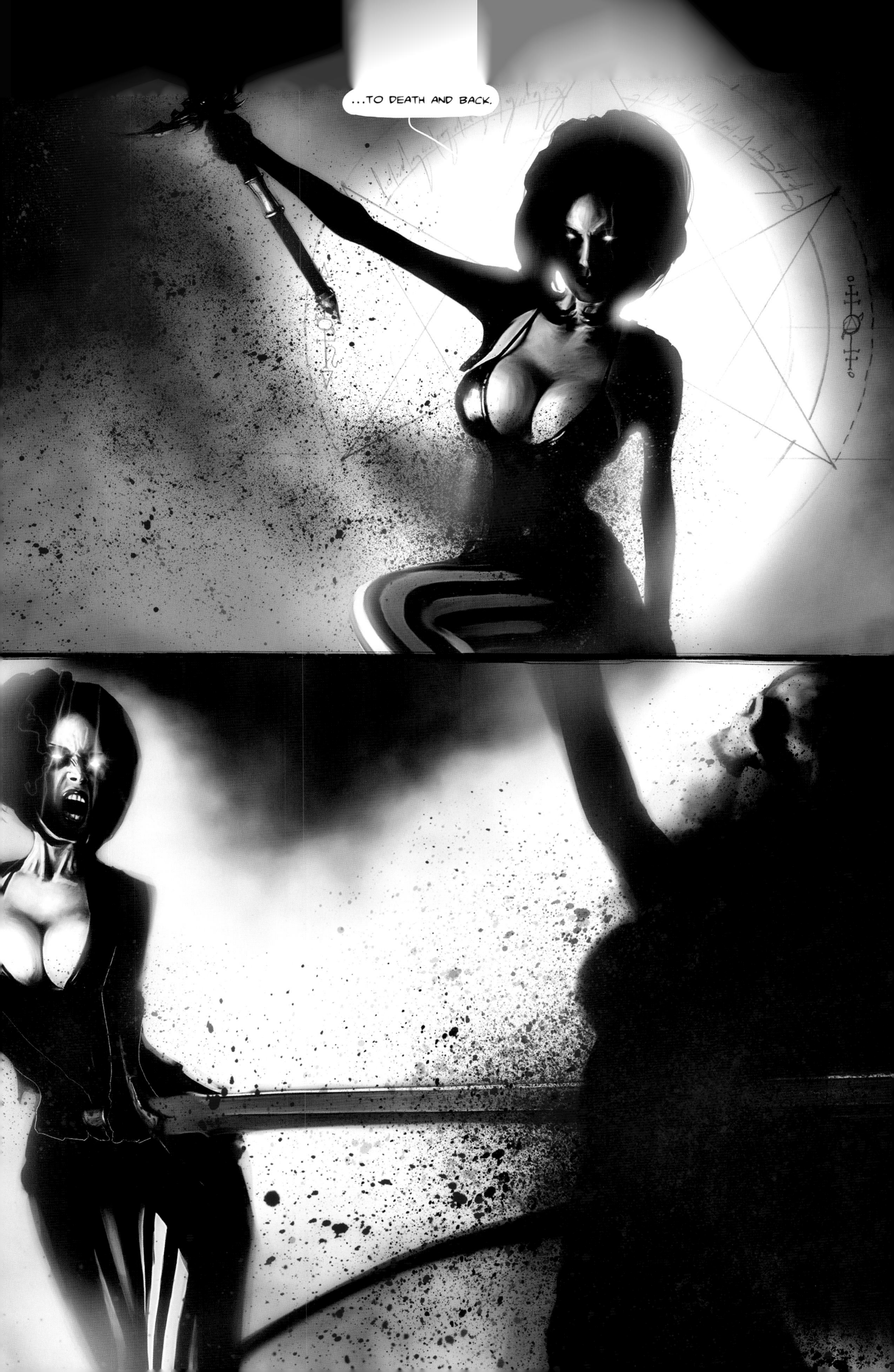
...TO DEATH AND BACK.

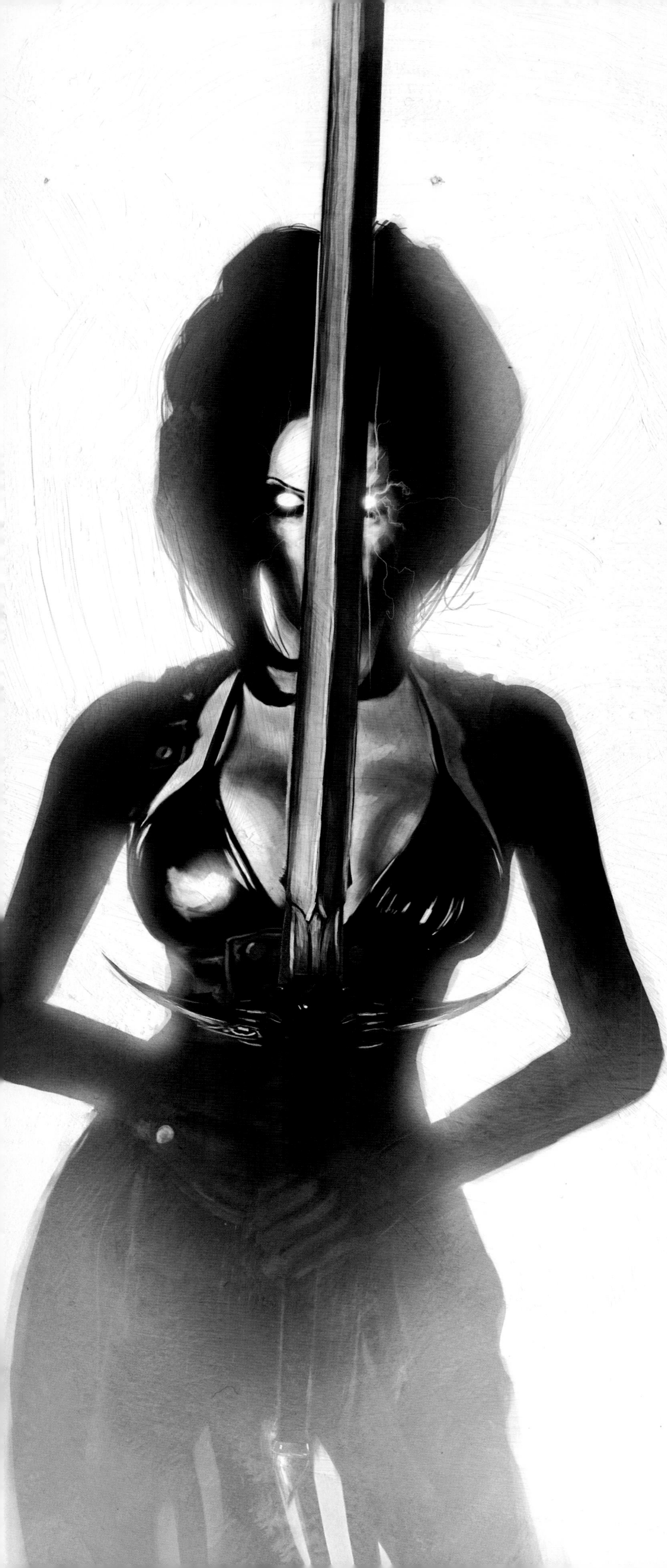

The field was covered in Magdalena and Glamour's blood. Edith stood with her head down and eyes closed not wanting to admit to herself what had just happened. Any sense of safety now that Glamour was dead was completely overcome by the horror of what she just watched Beatrice do. The two stood there for quite some time, Edith not wanting to speak and Beatrice allowing her to have time to contemplate. Edith did all she could to calm herself, but the same sentence kept looping in her mind, and she already knew the answer to it.

"What have you done? What have you done? What have you done?" Edith whispered over and over.

"You know the answer: What I had to do," Beatrice interrupted.

"You are now one of them—do I hunt you now? Do you hunt me? Will you change or take my memories? I would have followed you anywhere. I would have even died for you. How do I follow you now? What becomes of us?" Edith said with tears not even having time to rest on her eyes.

"I am not just one of them, I am more then that. I am now Magdalena's memories and everything she was. I am also Glamour's memories now. I know where her master is, but I am still Beatrice. You can trust me now as you always have. We are still sisters in this together," Beatrice said.

"No, you are not the same, I cannot see you. How do I trust you when you are the very thing I wish to kill? Our group is lost, and I am the only one standing. You died Beatrice, I watched you. Who will you now feed on for your memories? Me? Mother? How I do fight and kill these things with one standing next to me? Am I to become like you now? I refuse! You are what I hunt," Edith said.

Beatrice walked over to hold Edith, Edith allowed it with the same expression you would see in a suicide.

"Nothing was left for us to do my friend. This was the only thing that could have been done. I do not have all the answers right now, but it was the only way of saving Mother. I may not look the same, but I tell you my heart is the same. You would not flee, so I had to act. I need your help now more than ever to understand what I have become and how to deal with it. But above all things, know I only did this to save you and Mother," Beatrice said.

"You do not know that Mother needed our help. You have no way of knowing that. If you did it to save anyone, you did it to save me. I can see that. I will still follow you, but I cannot trust you till we understand this. If Magdalena's memories and life force were going to get taken, I would rather have you take them than the thing that was here. But know this, I will never become what you are," Edith said while pushing Beatrice away.

"What would you have done? Just lie down and die? Allow me to die? Have both of our memories and life stolen by that thing? No, I do not know if it could hurt Mother or not, but should my dying thoughts be in the wonder of that threat? There was no other way, and I take your condemnation of me and I wear it like a badge. I saved us, and possibly Mother. Whatever it is that was controlling Glamour is much larger, and I can now see it was hunting Mother. I need time to work out this information from Glamour's memories. There are hundreds of lifetimes in there. I need to meditate, I need to go somewhere safe, and we don't have time to get all the way back to Mother right now," Beatrice said.

"How will you know what are Glamour's memories and what are the ones she has fed on?" Edith asked.

"I do not know! I need time to work it out. My head is flooded with memories. I'm… trying to… w…" Beatrice said, falling to the ground.

Panic flew though every part of Edith. She looked and saw Beatrice was not dead, just in a coma-like state, and fell to her knees and began to weep. Hours she sat there, running from every thought in her mind. She was completely alone. Over time she was able to get control of herself.

"I need to get us somewhere safe, but I don't even know what that means right now." Edith went over to what was left of Magdalena, bowed her head, then picked up Beatrice and began to walk.

Hours and hours Edith walked till she came upon a cabin in the middle of nowhere. This would have to do. As she approached the cabin, it first looked like someone was inside, but as she got closer she could see it was empty. It appeared to have been abandoned for quite a while. Opossum shit was everywhere, and the wood furniture was more or less rotten. She did the best she could to make a bed for Beatrice, laying her down in it when done. It was then she heard a noise near the door, it sounded like a laugh of some kind. She stood up, looking with her mind's eye, and saw nothing.

It was unnerving, but there was not much Edith could do about it. Hours passed and she eventually fell asleep. Morning came and Beatrice was still unconscious. Edith then decided to give Beatrice a full 24 hours of rest and would wait for night—it would be better to travel then anyway. She spent the day meditating and trying to work out her feelings as much as should could, but really the death of Magdalena and the rebirth of Beatrice was too much to take. So most of the time was just spent trying to calm down.

Day turned into night. "Just a few more hours and I am going to take Beatrice back to Mother. There is no other choice, it must be done."

It was then Edith saw something in her mind's eye—something was in the corner watching her, something that could truly hide. She could not make out what it was, and as she was trying to focus, it then spoke.

"It is so amusing to see dead bitches end up in ditches."

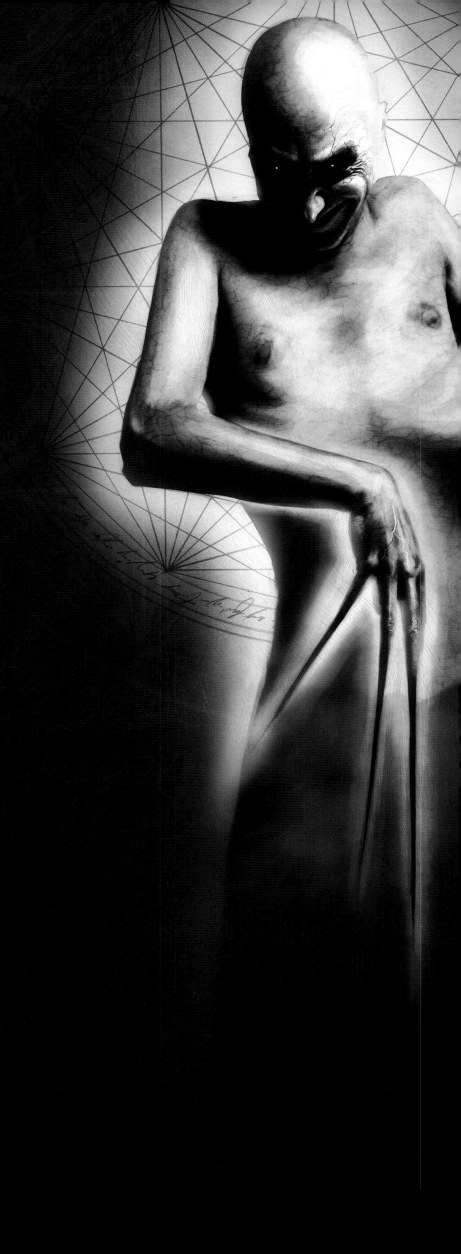

There in the corner of the room it stood smiling, tiny little beacons of light for its eyes locked on Edith. She looked with middle-focus meditation trying to see what she was looking at. She had no definition for what this was, but she knew two things, one: it was not a memory collector, two: she was only able to see it because it allowed her to see it. In pure reaction she pulled out her blades and swung both in places that would be kill shots. The thing did nothing to defend itself, which was strange until Edith realized the blades had met nothing—there was no effect. It just stood there smiling, waiting patiently for her to come to terms with the fact that she had no course of action against it. They both stood there for a moment staring at each other. She knew she would have to break the silence.

"What do you want?" Edith asked in her best monotone voice.

"Oh, there are so many things flesh can steal, but in the end what does this pleasure truly reveal? We are looking for the dance my dear," it said in an almost singing, high-pitched tone.

"You can't possibly think I understand what you're talking about. Who are you?" Edith asked, still trying to keep clam.

"A name? My name? A name that can be spoken from your lips cannot be the eternal name—that was here long before your language came. But, as I always like to say, if you insist, I will allow you to call me Lapis."

Lapis sang, his voice raising in pitch. He bent over, sticking his nose right on the tip of Edith's nose. "You do interest me strangely, little killer of memories. Glamour did not quite know what she was walking into, did she? Before you act, know that I am the sleep inside your hasty little friend over there, and there are so few actions you could take that would pleasure me."

"You are causing Beatrice to sleep in this way?" Edith asked.

Lapis set straight up and just looked at Edith, allowing her to realize the question she just asked she already knew the answer to. She did feel silly and naked. Whatever this thing was, he could see right through her. His words and mannerisms mocked her in every way

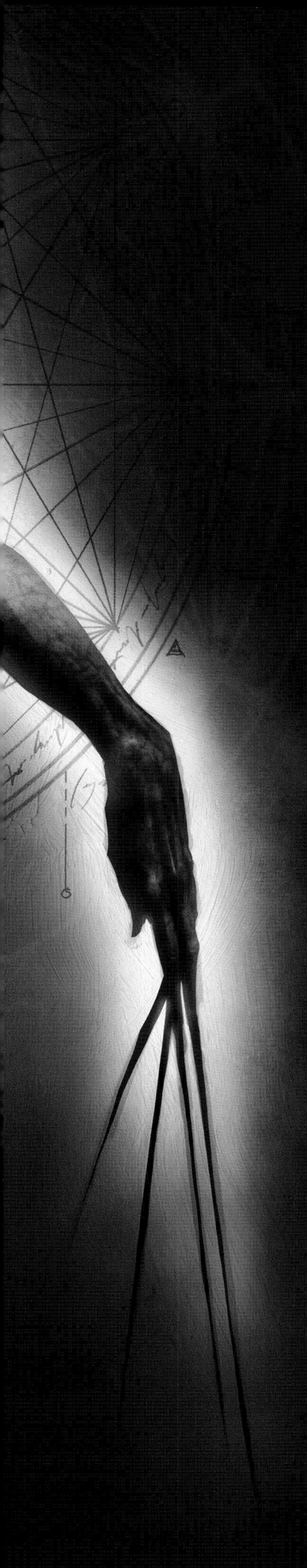

"You are part of Glamour! You're a friend? Her protector? You have come to avenge her death?" Edith asked.

An eruption of laughter raged out like too many ambulance sirens driving right at you, causing Edith to recoil. "Oh, sweet little thing, you will bring me much game. I am no friend to Glamour—she was not much more than a plaything to me in my plans. Glamour never even knew of my presence. These little memory collectors are so fragile when you know what you're looking at, something you know too well. I knew Glamour would lead me to something, and I am guessing that something is your beloved Beatrice. When she took all the memories of Glamour, she allowed me access to her as well," Lapis said.

"YOU WILL LEAVE BEATRICE! YOU WILL NOT HURT HER!" Edith screamed, losing her temper and trying to will it into motion.

Lapis's smile finally dropped, and a very deep voice boomed out that seemed to move the air around them. "You tell me nothing! What control of this do you really think you have, silly fetish model? A little girl in a world you have no idea how really works. You have had a brush with true reality, and you think memory collectors are the biggest secret. You have no idea what true reality is. I will do what I will and you can do so very little to affect me. But I do not wish to harm you or your pretty friend. You will aid me in my game. When you look into the abyss, the abyss looks back."

"I will aid you in no way that hurts Mother or Beatrice," Edith said.

"See, you still think everything is about you. I wish no ill will to your leader, or your sister. I have my own game. Just like any other model, you still believe the whole of the world revolves around you," Lapis said moving back into the darkness of the room.

"If you needed help with something, I would try and help. If it involves the death of memory collectors, I would aid in anyway I can." Edith said.

"There you go again, thinking everything is about you. There will be the

"Do I really have a choice?" Edith asked. She began to see Lapis was not insane, he knew too much and she could feel his spirit moving at times. He did want something for himself, but she could see in him some truth. He was so much larger than even Glamour, and there was wisdom here of a kind. Something in her started to like him. There was also something very familiar about him, something that reminded her of Mother.

"My sweet dear, if you ever learn anything from me it is that choice is the only thing to own. You help me now regardless of what you do because of what has been set in motion. But choice is all we have. There is someone coming after you. It was the master of Glamour, and it is not, shall we say, happy. I will give you the tools to defeat it, but you must vow to me. You owe me a favor. Without my help, this thing that is coming will end you and Beatrice. If this thing ends you, that helps my game, and if you defeat it, then that aids me as well. I win both ways. What is your choice?" Lapis asked.

"I choose to end this thing coming for me and Beatrice," Edith said.

"Grand! Then it shall be so. I have planted all the information needed to kill this thing into Beatrice—she will know it when she wakes. Now, she will not be powerful enough to do this alone, you will have to help her. In order to help her, I will have to change you... a little," Lapis sang.

"Change me how? Into what? What are you talking about? How am I to believe you?" Edith asked.

"There you go again thinking you're the center of the universe. Do you accept this or not?" Lapis sang.

"How do I accept that when I know nothing of you or this change?" Edith yelled.

The deep voice booming out of Lapis again, "DO YOU ACCEPT THIS?! Yes or No? Yes, and you live to try and kill this thing coming for you. No, and you and your Beatrice die from it. Choose."

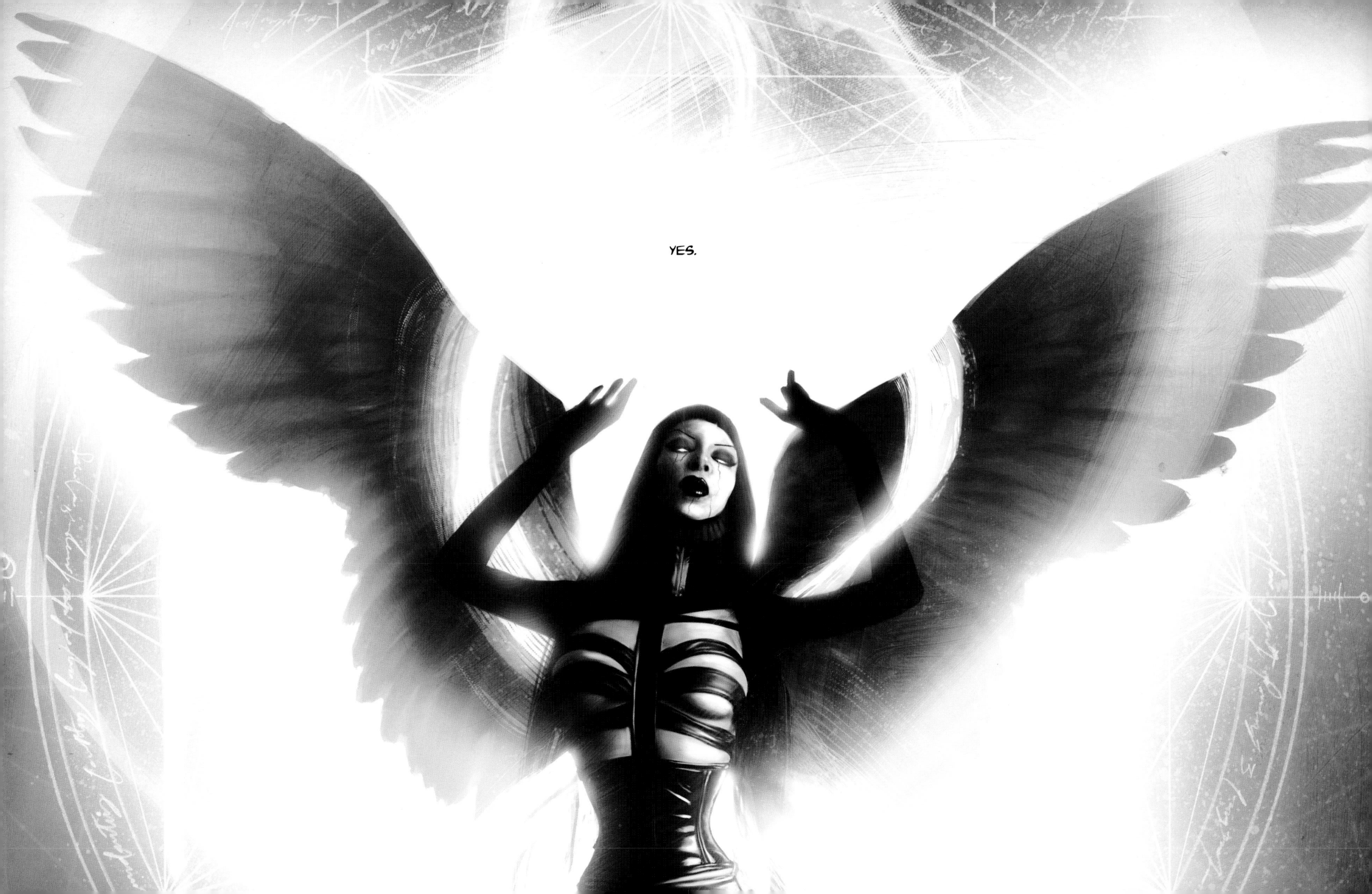
YES.

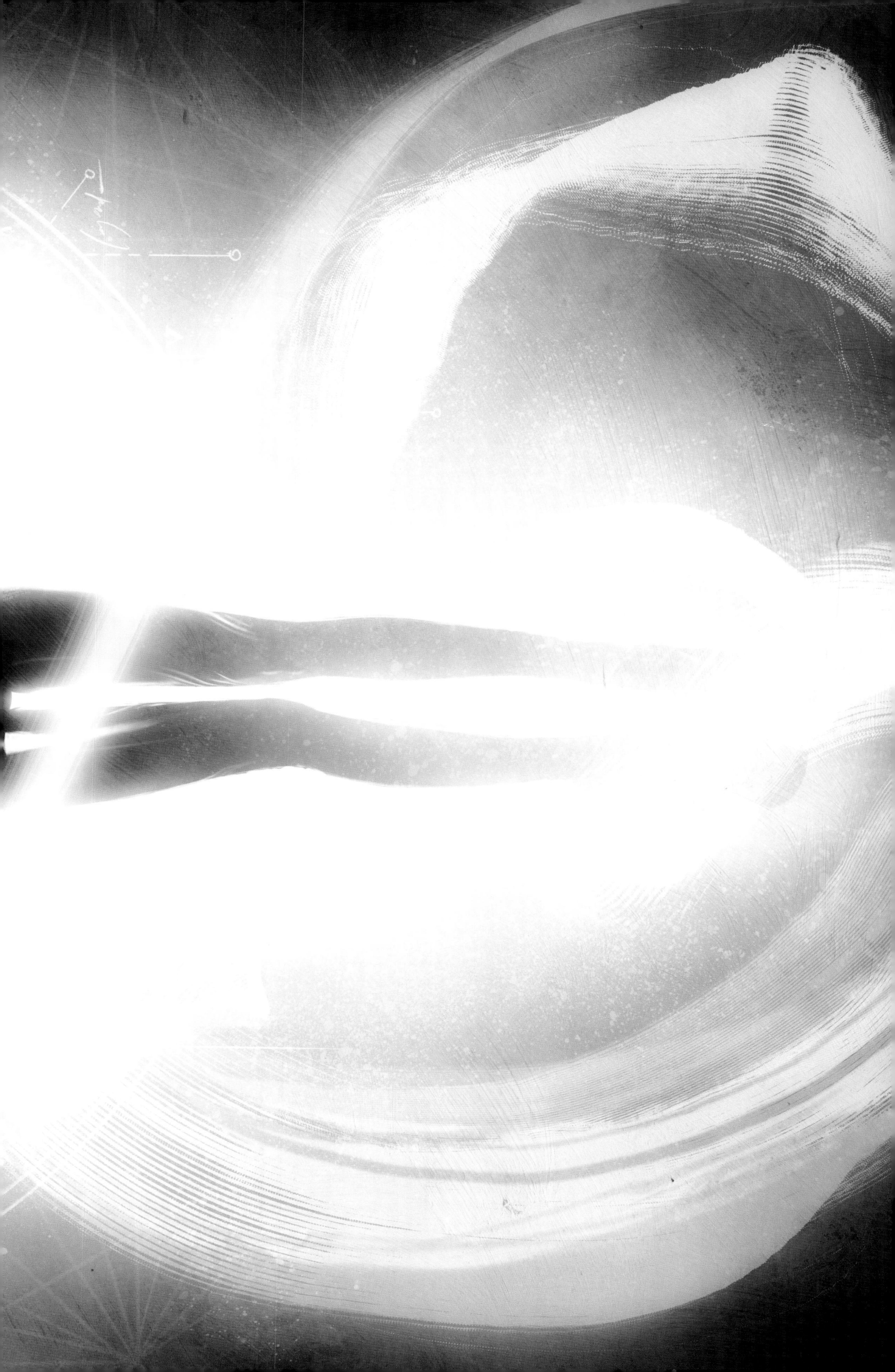

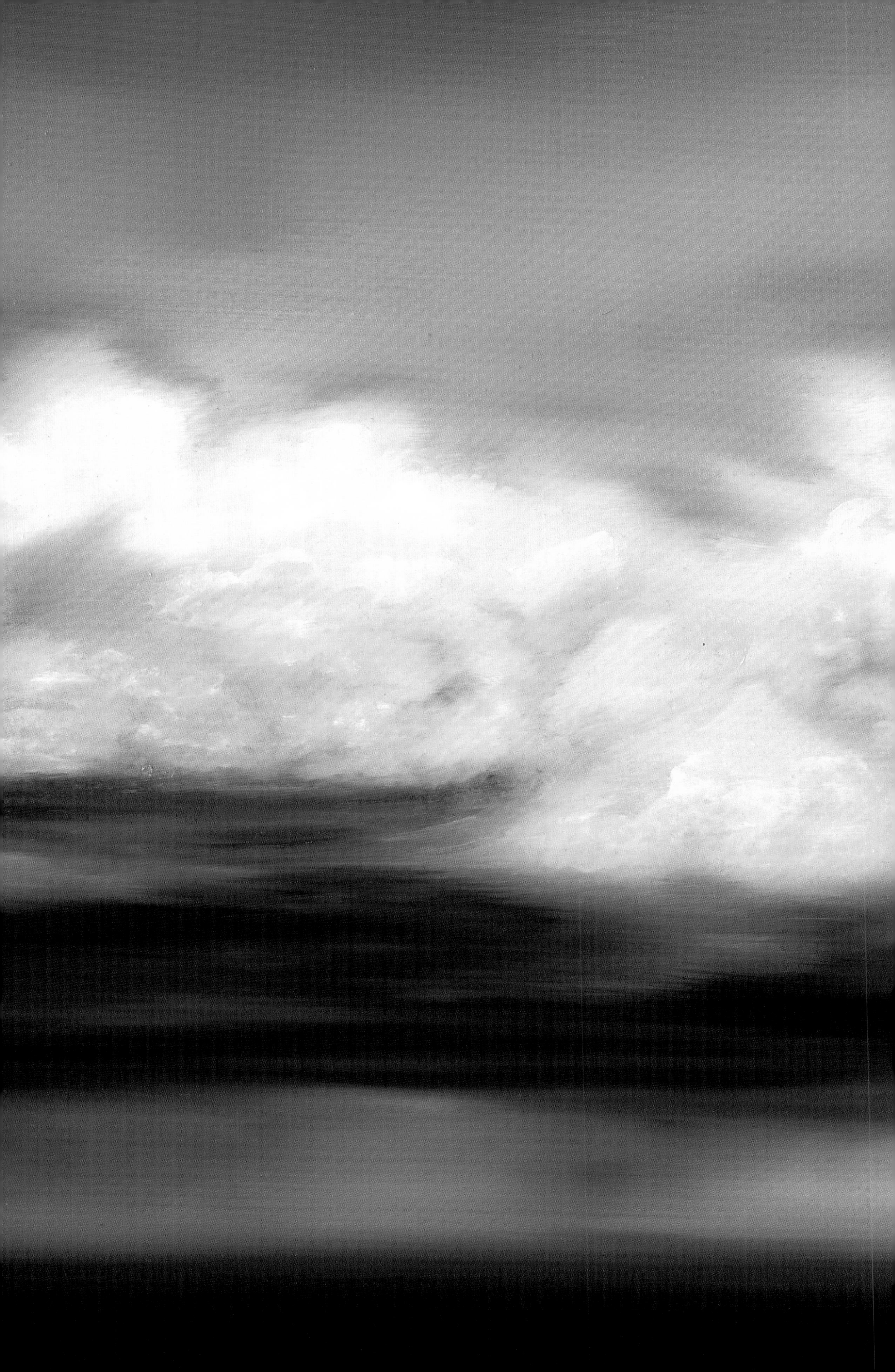

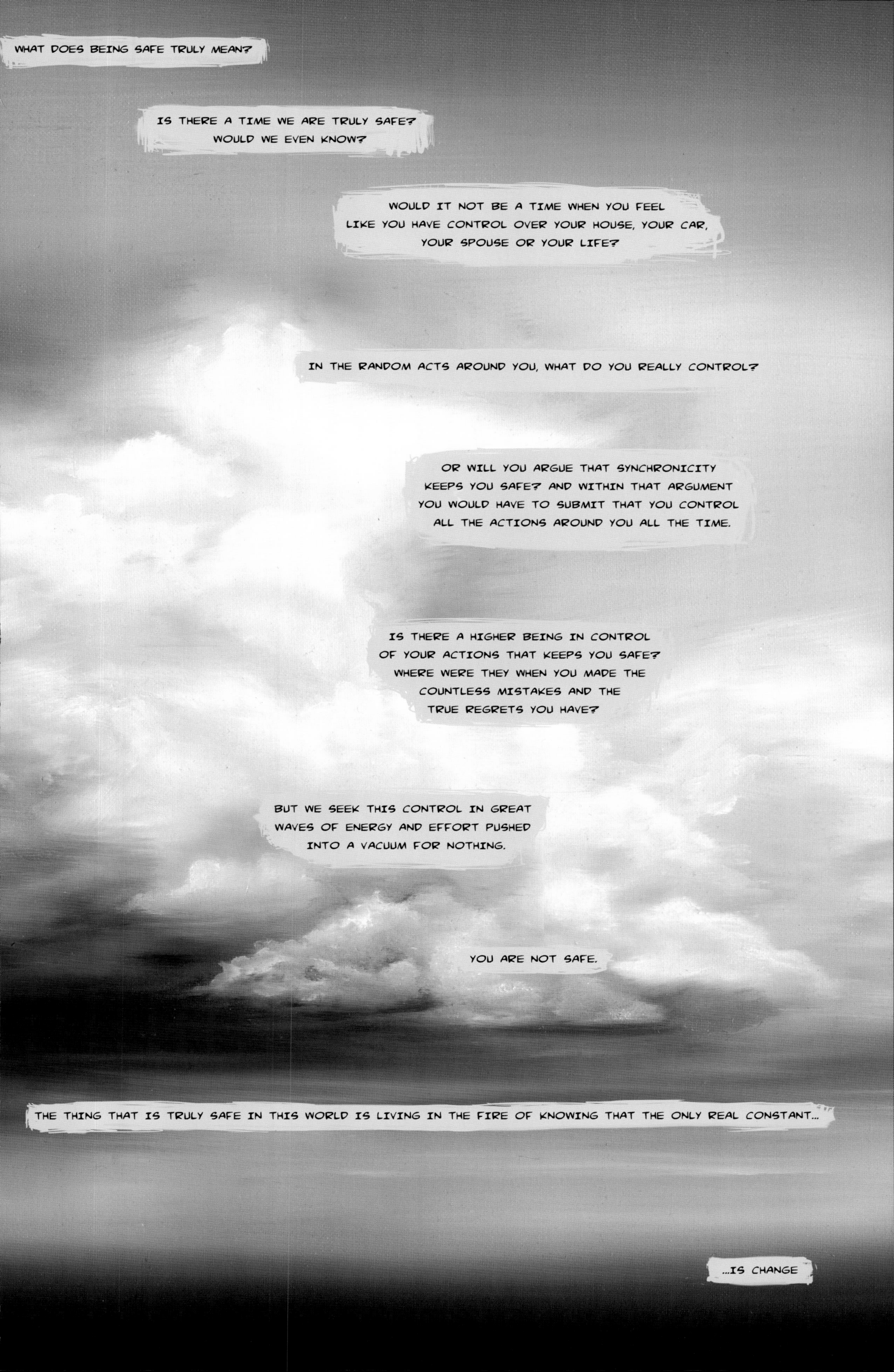
WHAT DOES BEING SAFE TRULY MEAN?
IS THERE A TIME WE ARE TRULY SAFE? WOULD WE EVEN KNOW?
WOULD IT NOT BE A TIME WHEN YOU FEEL LIKE YOU HAVE CONTROL OVER YOUR HOUSE, YOUR CAR, YOUR SPOUSE OR YOUR LIFE?
IN THE RANDOM ACTS AROUND YOU, WHAT DO YOU REALLY CONTROL?
OR WILL YOU ARGUE THAT SYNCHRONICITY KEEPS YOU SAFE? AND WITHIN THAT ARGUMENT YOU WOULD HAVE TO SUBMIT THAT YOU CONTROL ALL THE ACTIONS AROUND YOU ALL THE TIME.
IS THERE A HIGHER BEING IN CONTROL OF YOUR ACTIONS THAT KEEPS YOU SAFE? WHERE WERE THEY WHEN YOU MADE THE COUNTLESS MISTAKES AND THE TRUE REGRETS YOU HAVE?
BUT WE SEEK THIS CONTROL IN GREAT WAVES OF ENERGY AND EFFORT PUSHED INTO A VACUUM FOR NOTHING.
YOU ARE NOT SAFE.
THE THING THAT IS TRULY SAFE IN THIS WORLD IS LIVING IN THE FIRE OF KNOWING THAT THE ONLY REAL CONSTANT...
...IS CHANGE

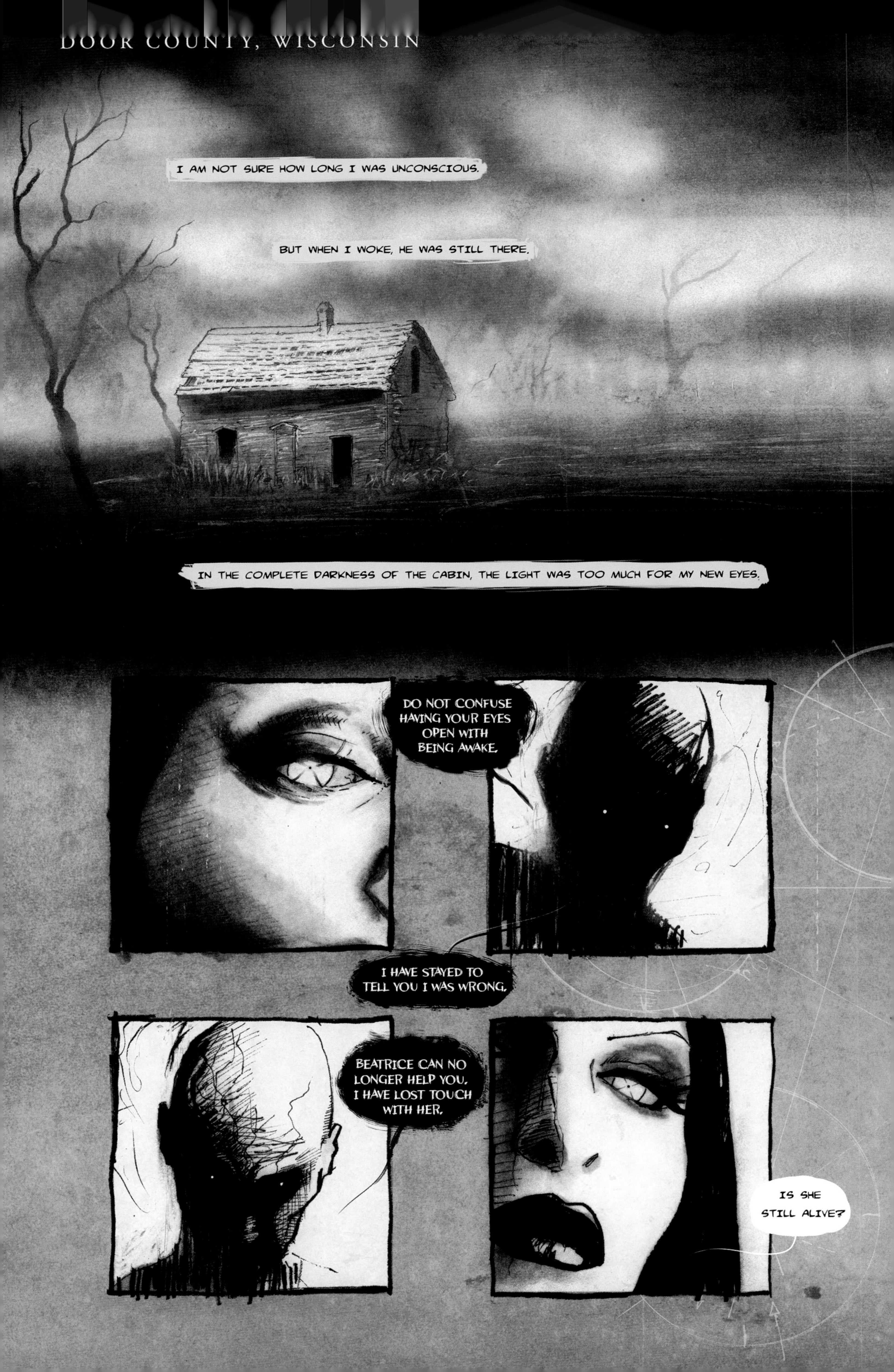
DOOR COUNTY, WISCONSIN
I AM NOT SURE HOW LONG I WAS UNCONSCIOUS.
BUT WHEN I WOKE, HE WAS STILL THERE.
IN THE COMPLETE DARKNESS OF THE CABIN, THE LIGHT WAS TOO MUCH FOR MY NEW EYES.
DO NOT CONFUSE HAVING YOUR EYES OPEN WITH BEING AWAKE.
I HAVE STAYED TO TELL YOU I WAS WRONG.
BEATRICE CAN NO LONGER HELP YOU. I HAVE LOST TOUCH WITH HER.
IS SHE STILL ALIVE?

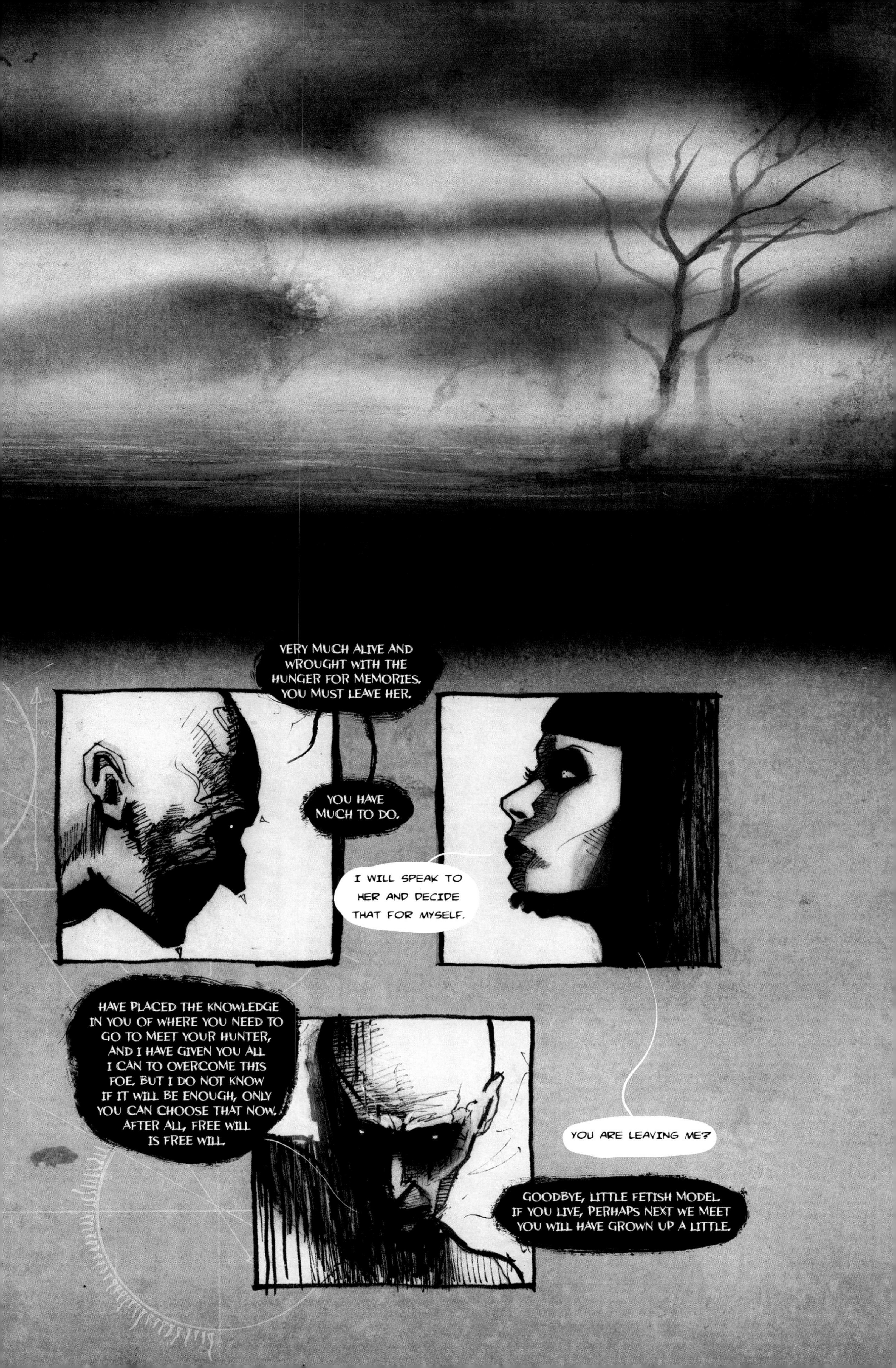
VERY MUCH ALIVE AND WROUGHT WITH THE HUNGER FOR MEMORIES. YOU MUST LEAVE HER.
YOU HAVE MUCH TO DO.
I WILL SPEAK TO HER AND DECIDE THAT FOR MYSELF.
HAVE PLACED THE KNOWLEDGE IN YOU OF WHERE YOU NEED TO GO TO MEET YOUR HUNTER, AND I HAVE GIVEN YOU ALL I CAN TO OVERCOME THIS FOE. BUT I DO NOT KNOW IF IT WILL BE ENOUGH, ONLY YOU CAN CHOOSE THAT NOW. AFTER ALL, FREE WILL IS FREE WILL.
YOU ARE LEAVING ME?
GOODBYE, LITTLE FETISH MODEL. IF YOU LIVE, PERHAPS NEXT WE MEET YOU WILL HAVE GROWN UP A LITTLE.

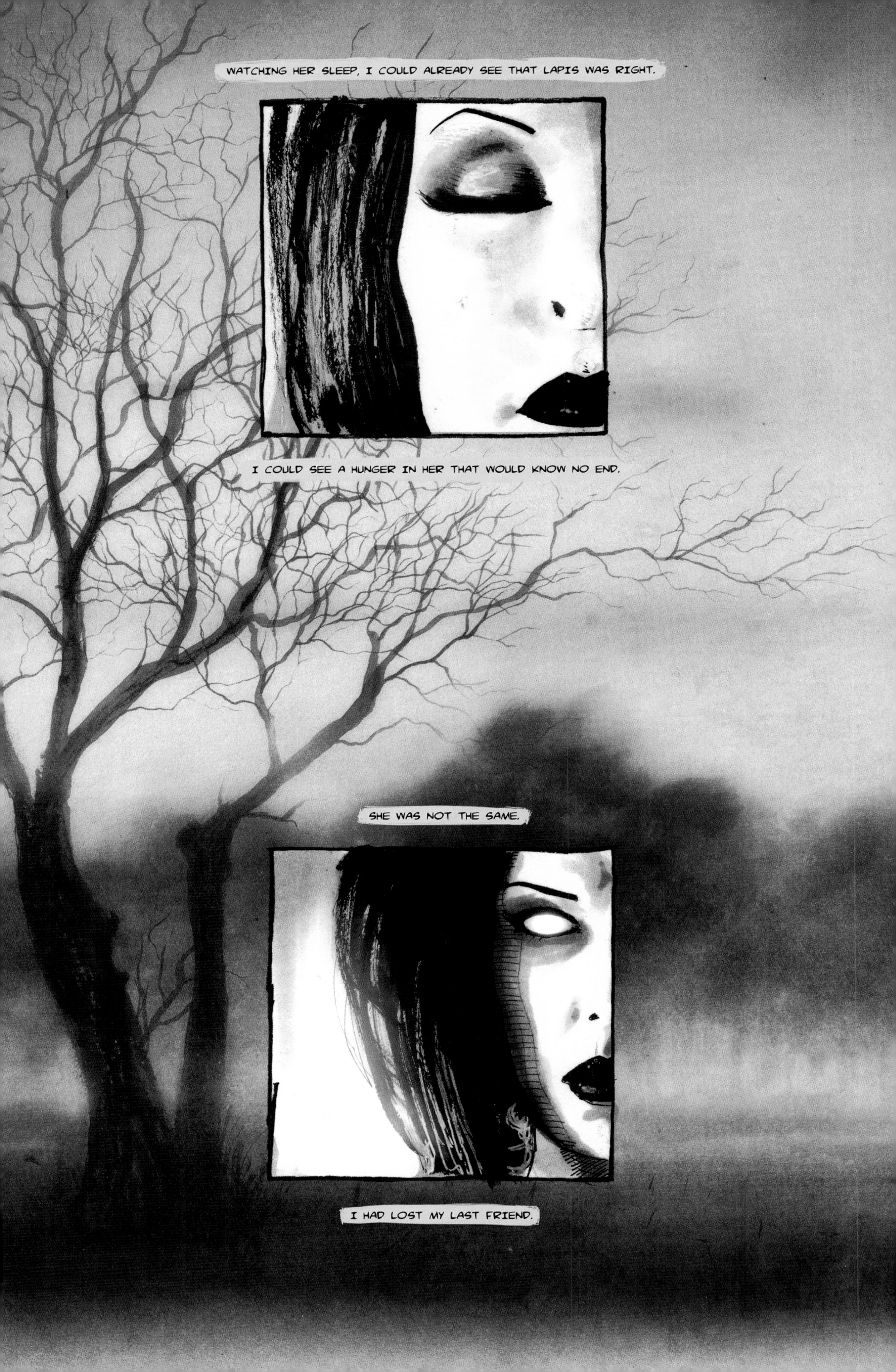
WATCHING HER SLEEP, I COULD ALREADY SEE THAT LAPIS WAS RIGHT.
I COULD SEE A HUNGER IN HER THAT WOULD KNOW NO END.
SHE WAS NOT THE SAME.
I HAD LOST MY LAST FRIEND.

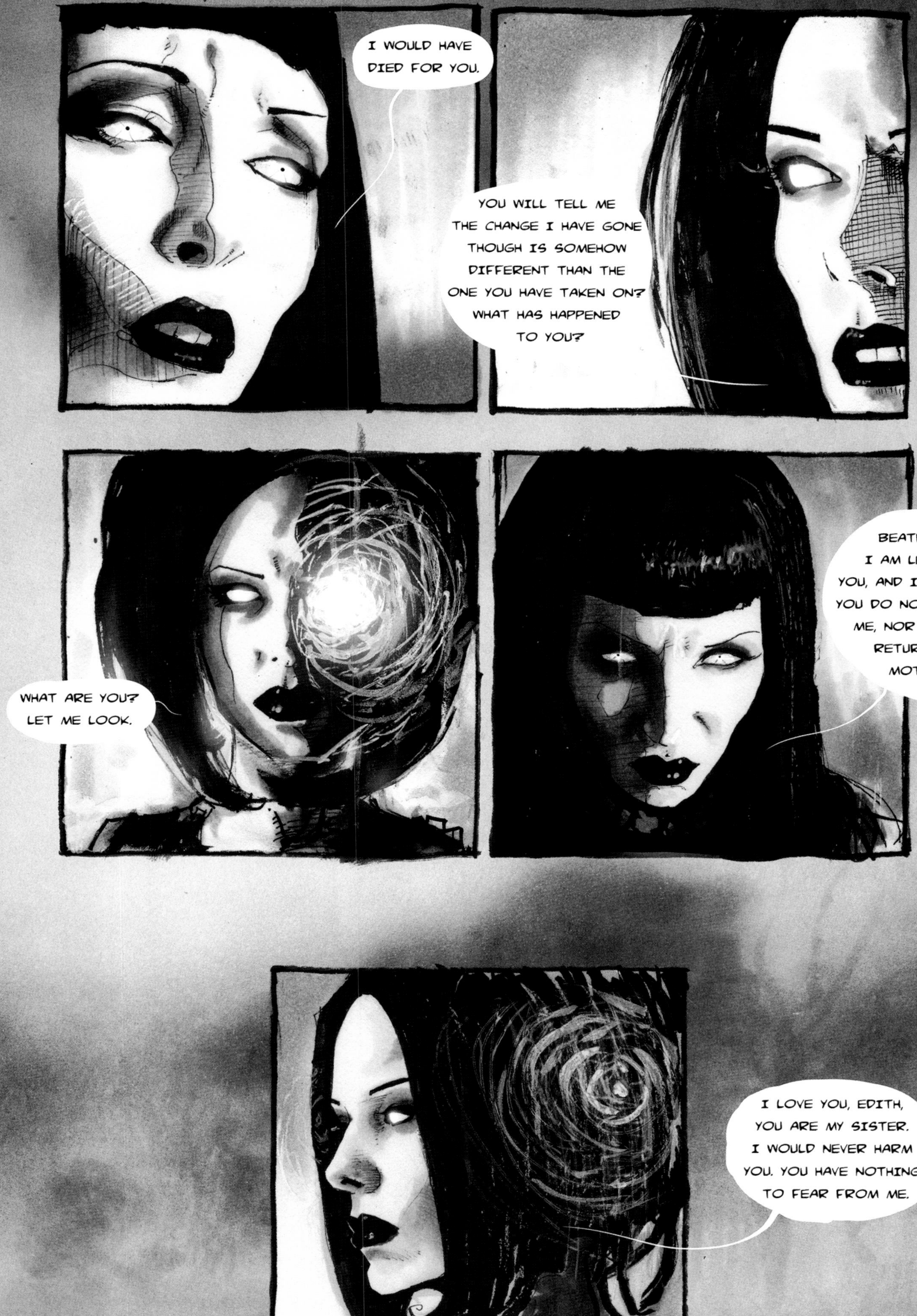
I WOULD HAVE DIED FOR YOU.
YOU WILL TELL ME THE CHANGE I HAVE GONE THOUGH IS SOMEHOW DIFFERENT THAN THE ONE YOU HAVE TAKEN ON? WHAT HAS HAPPENED TO YOU?
WHAT ARE YOU? LET ME LOOK.
BEATRICE, I AM LEAVING YOU, AND I WILL ASK YOU DO NOT FOLLOW ME, NOR DO YOU RETURN TO MOTHER.
I LOVE YOU, EDITH, YOU ARE MY SISTER. I WOULD NEVER HARM YOU. YOU HAVE NOTHING TO FEAR FROM ME.

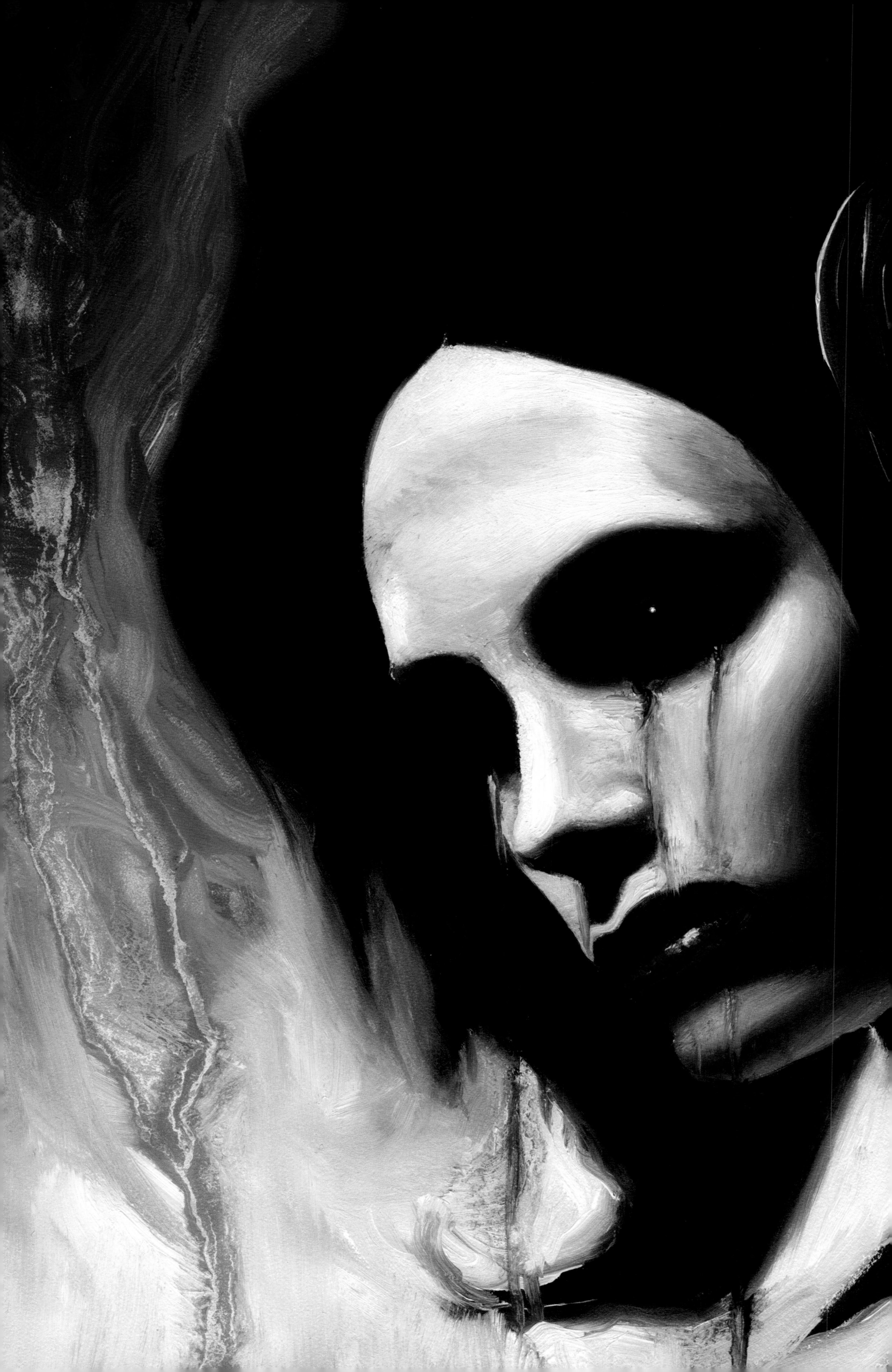

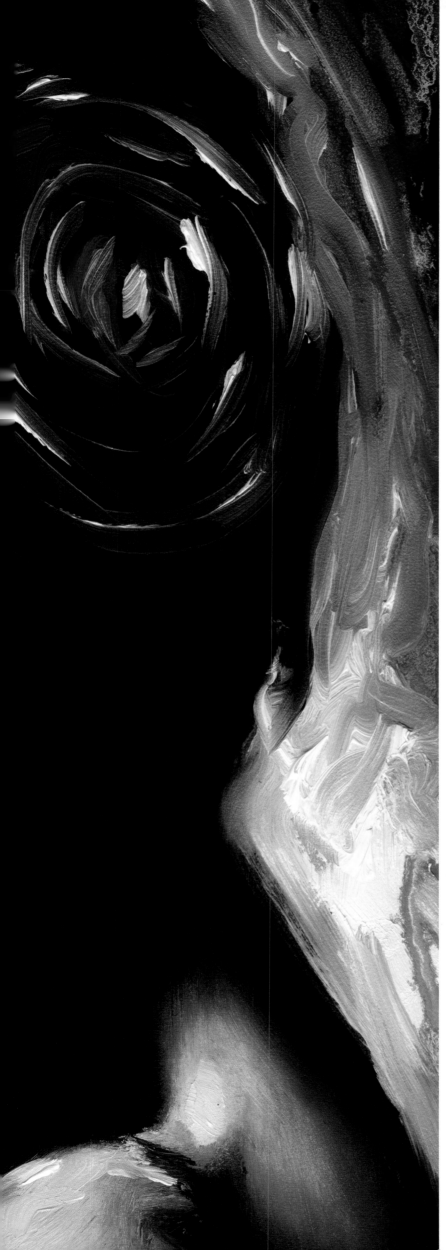

EDITH FELL TO HER KNEES, CLOSING HER EYES. THOSE WORDS AND THE SMALL AMOUNT OF LIGHT IN THE ROOM WERE TOO MUCH FOR HER. THE LIGHT WAS NOW PIERCING. IT WAS AS IF ALL THE WAVES OF LIGHT NEVER STOPPED MOVING. SHE WAS EVEN ABLE TO SEE WHAT THE LIGHT WAS GOING TO DO BEFORE THE MOVEMENT OF THE LIGHT, EVEN WHERE HER EYES CLOSED SHE COULD SEE THIS, BUT AT LEAST WITH CLOSED EYES IT DID NOT HURT ANYMORE. THERE WERE WHOLE WORLDS, IT SEEMED, IN EVERY WAVE OF LIGHT, CONTRACTING AND EXPANDING AT THE SAME TIME.

BEATRICE STOOD THERE ABLE TO SENSE WHAT WAS GOING ON WITH EDITH. SHE KNEW IF SHE TRIED TO HOLD HER OR TO COMFORT HER, SHE WOULD JUST BE PUSHED AWAY. THE TWO OF THEM STARTED TO COMMUNICATE IN PURE EMOTION. THEY BOTH TRULY DID NOT HAVE TO SPEAK, BUT OUT OF RESPECT BEATRICE SAID, "I DON'T KNOW WHAT YOU HAVE BECOME. I DO NOT UNDERSTAND WHAT I AM SEEING. I CAN SEE WE ARE NOW TOO DIFFERENT FROM EACH OTHER. I UNDERSTAND WHY WE HAVE TO LEAVE ONE ANOTHER, BUT PLEASE KNOW I LOVE YOU AND I WILL ALWAYS LOVE YOU. IF I CAN EVER HELP YOU IN ANY WAY, CALL FOR ME, AND I WILL DO EVERYTHING TO GET TO YOU."

EDITH STOOD UP AND COULD FEEL THAT BEATRICE WAS BEING AS HONEST AS SHE COULD BE. SHE DID UNDERSTAND SOME PART OF THIS. SHE COULD SENSE THE WISDOM IN BEATRICE THAT HAD ALWAYS MADE HER FEEL SAFE. IT WAS SUCH AN AMAZING FEELING TO KNOW THAT PART OF HER WAS STILL THERE. "I HAVE MADE A PACT WITH SOMETHING I DO NOT UNDERSTAND, AND I DO NOT KNOW HOW FAR THAT RABBIT HOLE GOES," EDITH SAID. "I AM IN OVER MY HEAD. BUT HEAR ME, YOU HAVE BEEN MY TEACHER AND MY SISTER. I HAVE LEARNED FROM YOU EVERYTHING I KNOW. YOU SAVED ME THE NIGHT WE MET, AND YOU CHANGED INTO WHAT WE HUNT TO SAVE ME AGAIN. LOVE IS TOO SMALL A WORD FOR WHAT I FEEL TOWARD YOU." EDITH WALKED OVER AND HUGGED BEATRICE.

THEY STOOD THERE FOR A FEW MOMENTS BOTH FEELING THAT EMOTION WHEN YOU KNOW YOU HAVE TO LEAVE SOMETHING BEHIND, WHEN SLOWLY, EVER SO GENTLY, EDITH COULD FEEL BEATRICE STARTING TO FEED OFF THE MEMORIES THIS MOMENT WAS CREATING. EDITH PUSHED BEATRICE BACK, SHOCK RAN THOUGH THEM BOTH, AND NEITHER COULD HOLD BACK THE TEARS THAT WERE NOW MAKING SOUNDS FROM HITTING THE WOODEN FLOORBOARDS.

THEY BOTH STOOD THERE IN SILENCE, NOT WANTING TO WALK AWAY FROM ONE ANOTHER, BUT BEATRICE SLOWLY AND QUIETLY WALKED OUT THE DOOR AND KEPT WALKING. EDITH HAD NEVER FELT ANY PAIN LIKE THIS IN HER LIFE—FOR HOURS SHE STOOD THERE WITH HER EYES CLOSED, WEEPING.

EDITH COULD FEEL BEATRICE MOVING FARTHER AND FARTHER AWAY AS HER EMOTIONS SPIRALED OUT OF HER CONTROL. RAGE TOOK OVER, AND THEN INSTINCT. EDITH RAISED HER ARM AND REACHED OUT FOR THE DOOR, GRASPING FOR THE HUMANITY SHE WAS LOSING. AND ALTHOUGH SHE HAD NOT MOVED, THE DOOR GREW CLOSER TO HER FINGERTIPS UNTIL IT WAS WITHIN HER GRASP. EDITH COULD FEEL HERSELF CHANGING. IT WAS THEN THAT SHE COULD SEE THE DOOR HAD NOT MOVED. INSTEAD, HER FINGERTIPS HAD GROWN INTO SHARP KNIVES PIERCING THE LIGHT. SHE HAD BECOME A WEAPON, AND IT WAS NOT HER HUMANITY SHE WAS GRASPING FOR, THAT HAD BEEN REPLACED. SHE WAS ABLE TO MANIFEST ANYTHING SHE SAW IN HER MIND'S EYE. WHATEVER LAPIS HAD DONE TO HER ALLOWED THIS, AND SHE COULD ALREADY SENSE THERE WAS MORE. SOMETHING HAD TO BE DONE ABOUT THE LIGHT THAT HER EYES WERE TAKING IN.

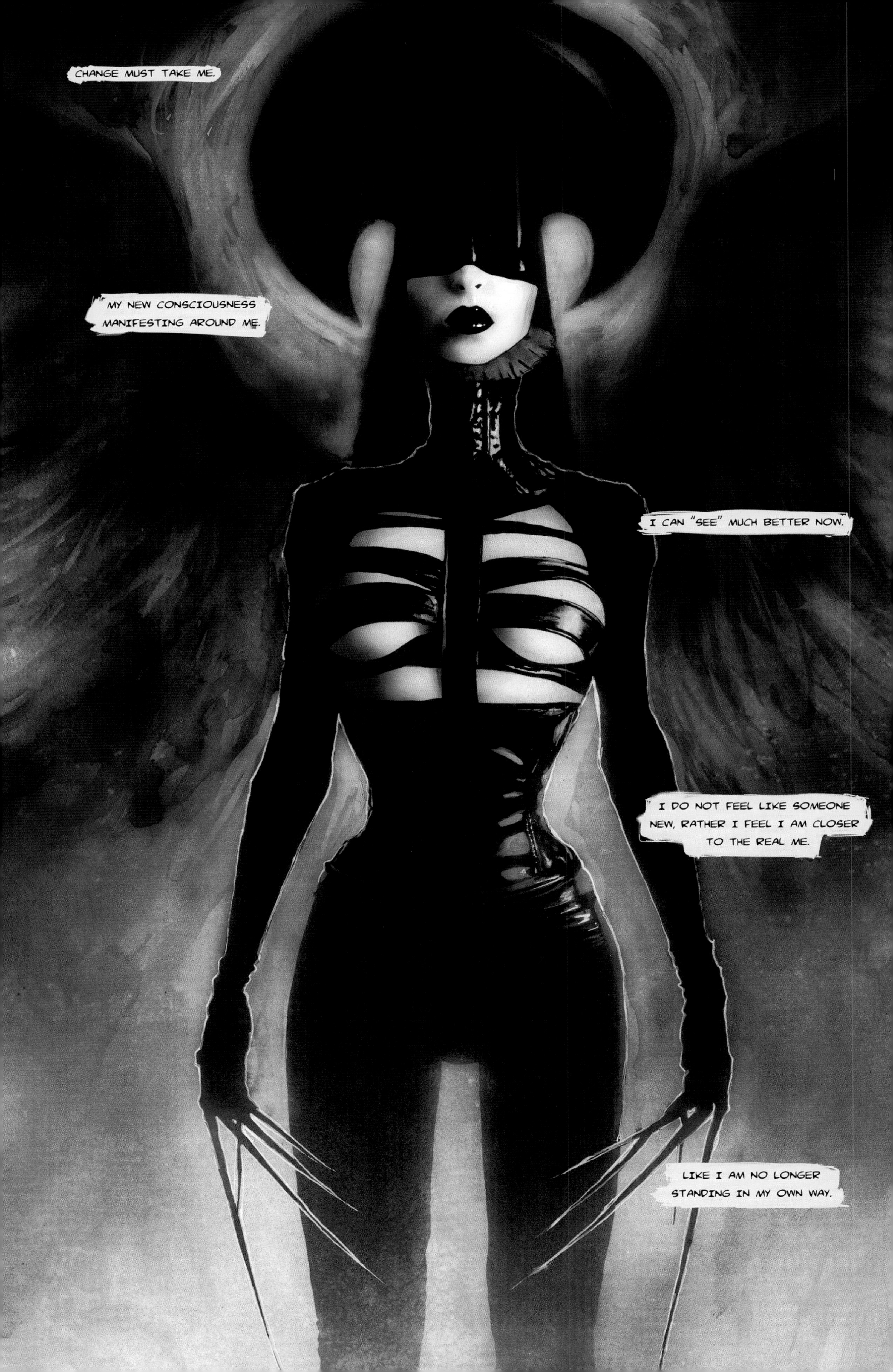
CHANGE MUST TAKE ME.
MY NEW CONSCIOUSNESS MANIFESTING AROUND ME.
I CAN "SEE" MUCH BETTER NOW.
I DO NOT FEEL LIKE SOMEONE NEW, RATHER I FEEL I AM CLOSER TO THE REAL ME.
LIKE I AM NO LONGER STANDING IN MY OWN WAY.

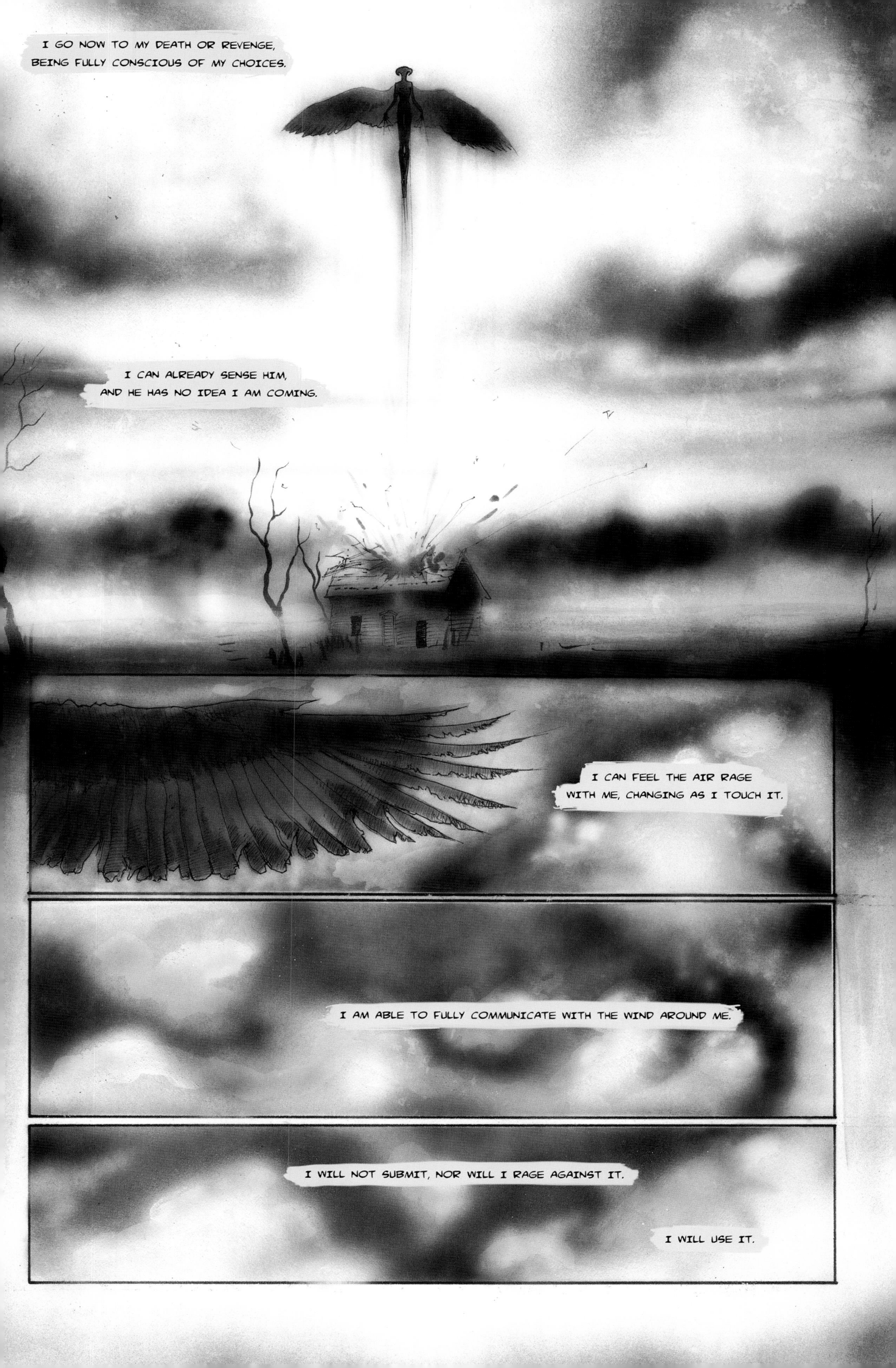
I GO NOW TO MY DEATH OR REVENGE, BEING FULLY CONSCIOUS OF MY CHOICES.
I CAN ALREADY SENSE HIM, AND HE HAS NO IDEA I AM COMING.
I CAN FEEL THE AIR RAGE WITH ME, CHANGING AS I TOUCH IT.
I AM ABLE TO FULLY COMMUNICATE WITH THE WIND AROUND ME.
I WILL NOT SUBMIT, NOR WILL I RAGE AGAINST IT.
I WILL USE IT.

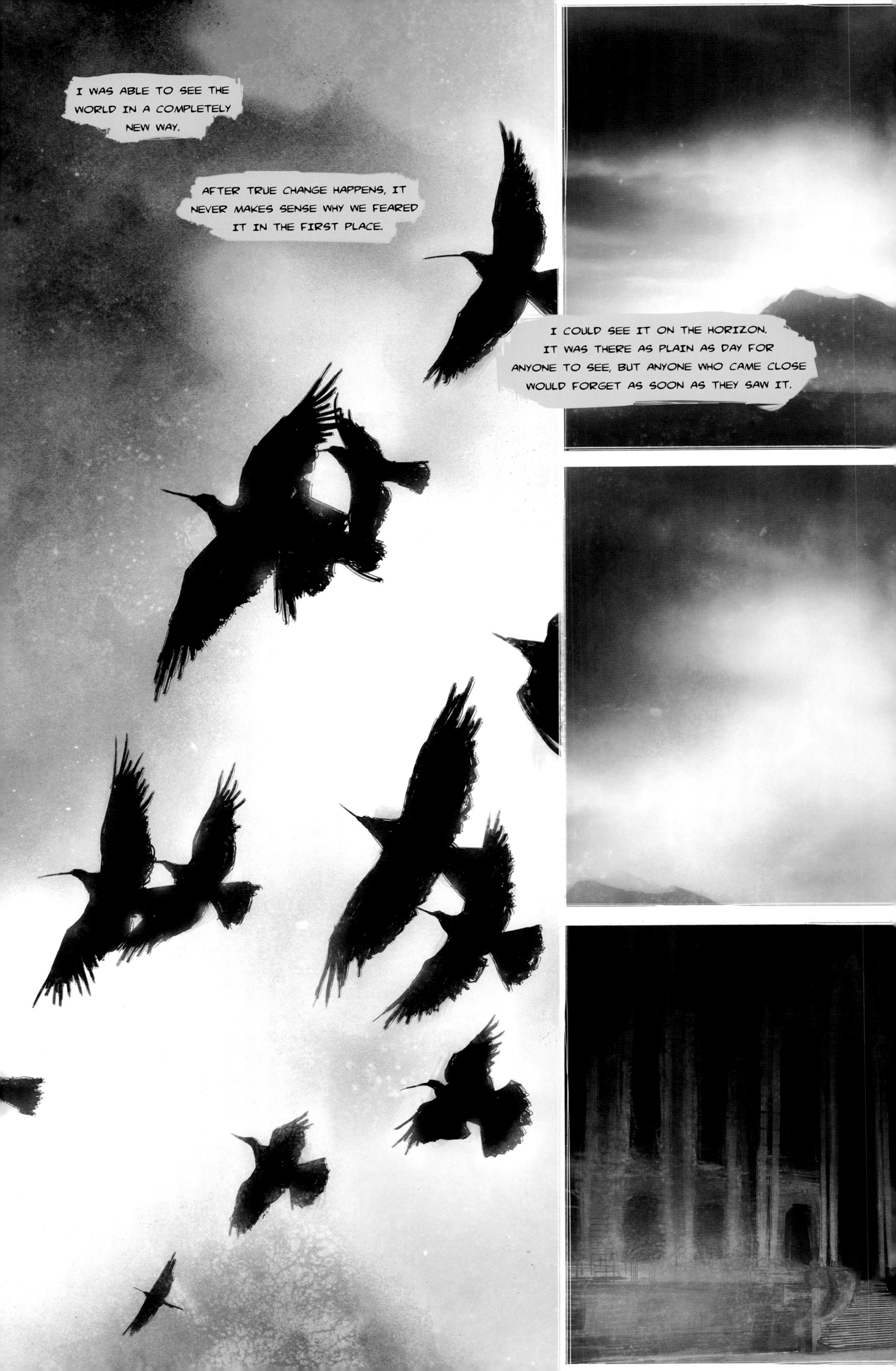
I WAS ABLE TO SEE THE WORLD IN A COMPLETELY NEW WAY.
AFTER TRUE CHANGE HAPPENS, IT NEVER MAKES SENSE WHY WE FEARED IT IN THE FIRST PLACE.
I COULD SEE IT ON THE HORIZON. IT WAS THERE AS PLAIN AS DAY FOR ANYONE TO SEE, BUT ANYONE WHO CAME CLOSE WOULD FORGET AS SOON AS THEY SAW IT.

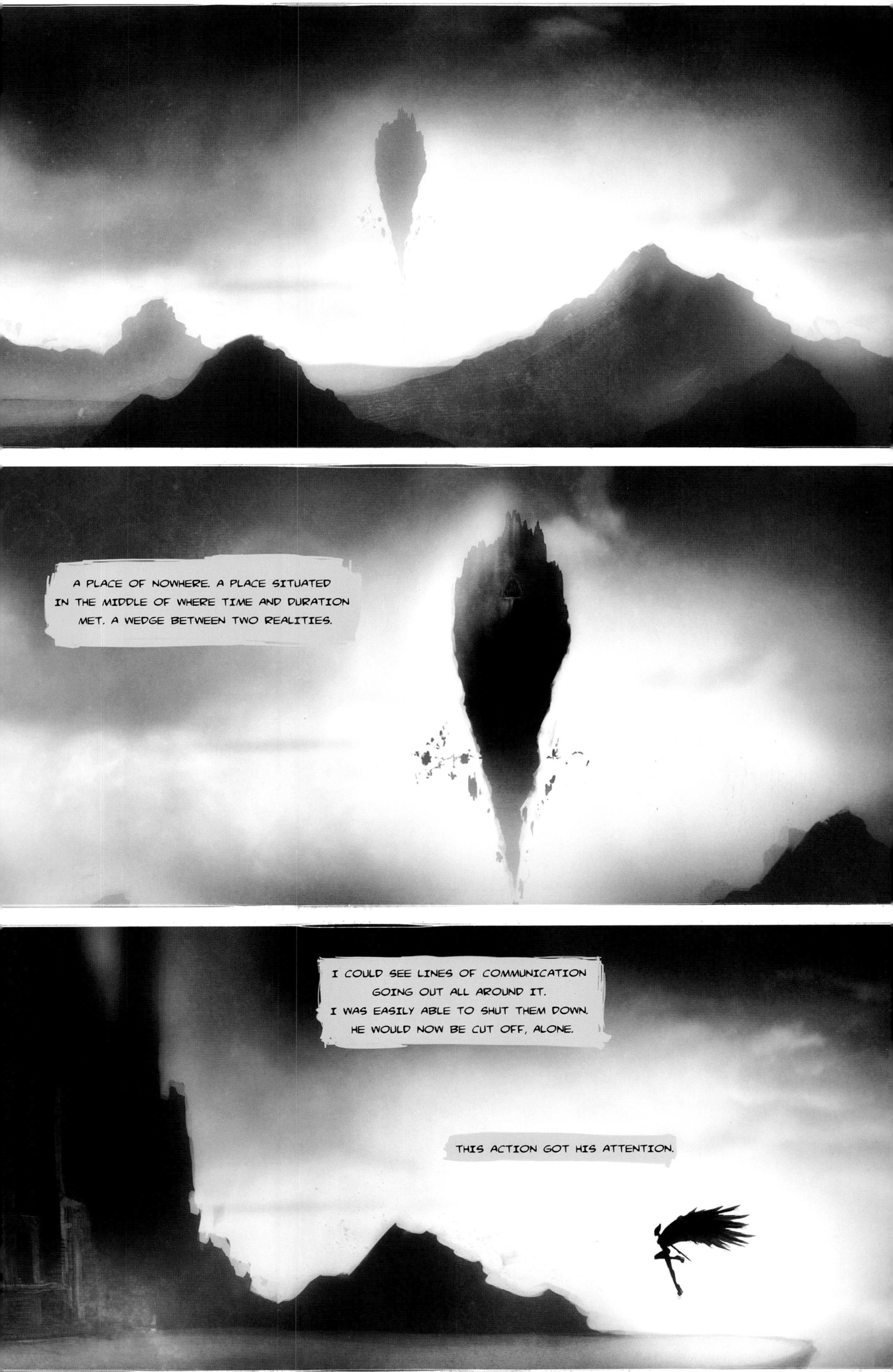
A PLACE OF NOWHERE. A PLACE SITUATED IN THE MIDDLE OF WHERE TIME AND DURATION MET. A WEDGE BETWEEN TWO REALITIES.
I COULD SEE LINES OF COMMUNICATION GOING OUT ALL AROUND IT. I WAS EASILY ABLE TO SHUT THEM DOWN. HE WOULD NOW BE CUT OFF, ALONE.
THIS ACTION GOT HIS ATTENTION.

HE NOW SENSED I WAS THERE.

SEEMS YOUR SISTERS-IN-ARMS COULD NOT MAKE IT, BUT SOMEHOW YOU DID. A MYSTERY FOR ME?

IT HAS BEEN AN AGE SINCE SOMETHING HAS SURPRISED ME I WOULD HAVE WELCOMED YOU HERE WERE IT NOT FOR YOUR INTENT.

THIS HERALD OF MISUNDERSTANDING, THIS WHORE OF FLESH...

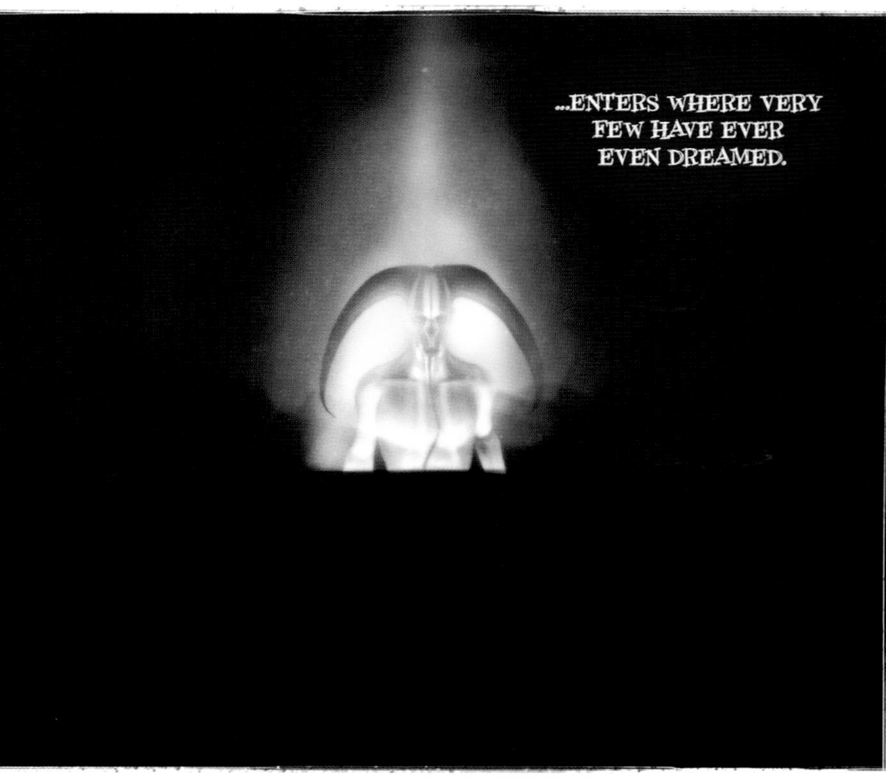

...ENTERS WHERE VERY FEW HAVE EVER EVEN DREAMED.

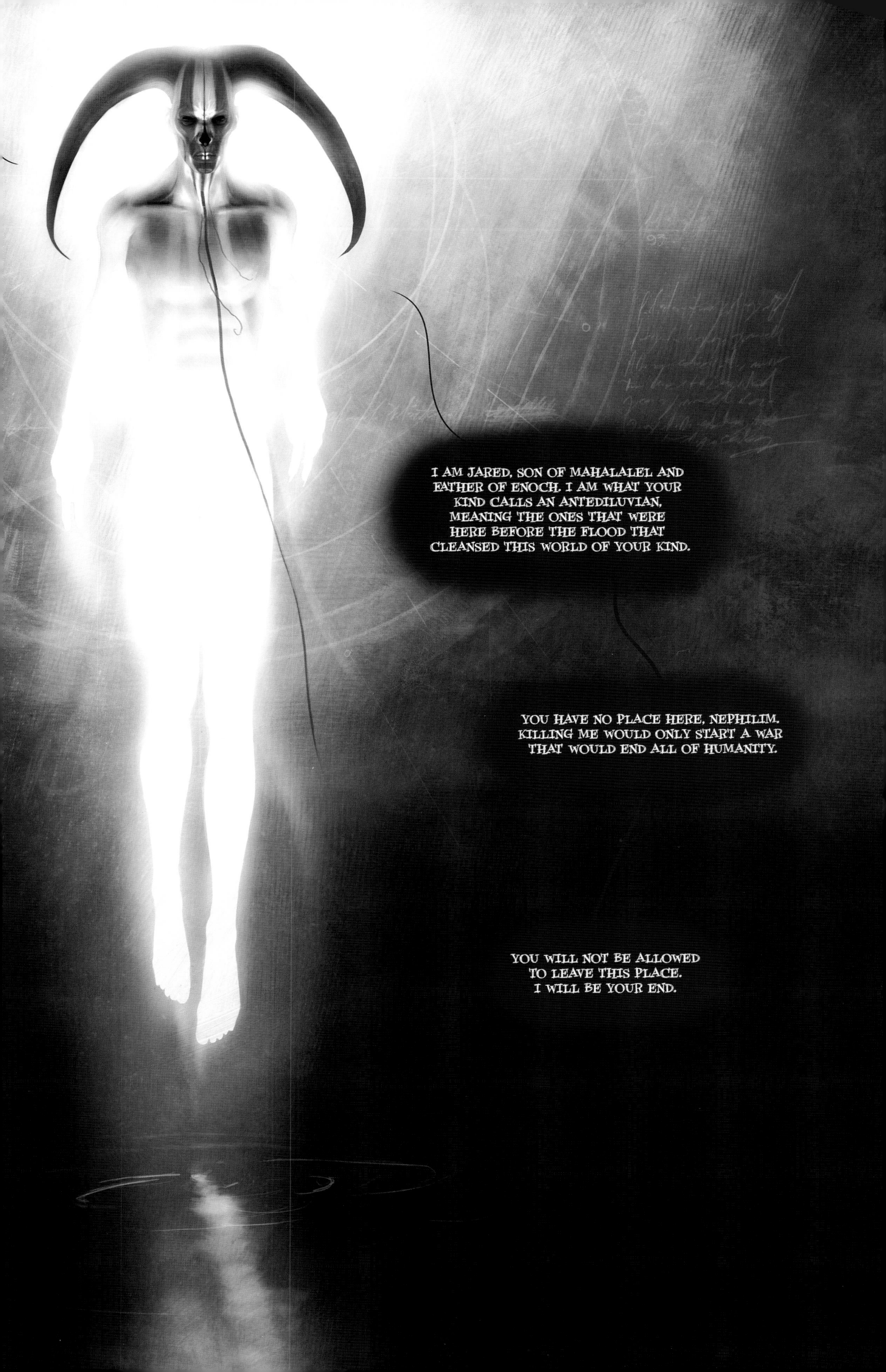
I AM JARED, SON OF MAHALALEL AND FATHER OF ENOCH. I AM WHAT YOUR KIND CALLS AN ANTEDILUVIAN, MEANING THE ONES THAT WERE HERE BEFORE THE FLOOD THAT CLEANSED THIS WORLD OF YOUR KIND.
YOU HAVE NO PLACE HERE, NEPHILIM. KILLING ME WOULD ONLY START A WAR THAT WOULD END ALL OF HUMANITY.
YOU WILL NOT BE ALLOWED TO LEAVE THIS PLACE. I WILL BE YOUR END.

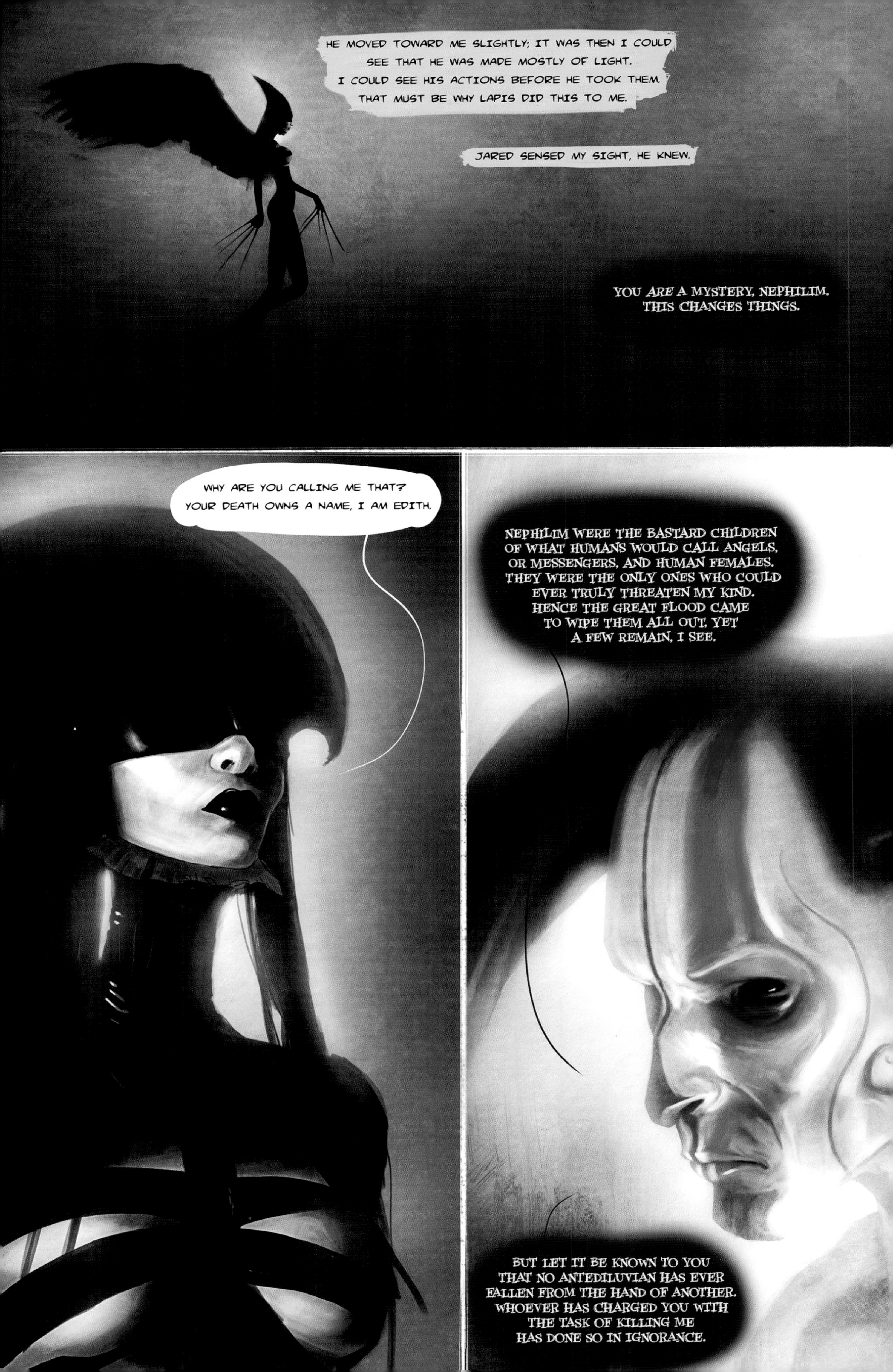

HE MOVED TOWARD ME SLIGHTLY; IT WAS THEN I COULD SEE THAT HE WAS MADE MOSTLY OF LIGHT. I COULD SEE HIS ACTIONS BEFORE HE TOOK THEM. THAT MUST BE WHY LAPIS DID THIS TO ME.
JARED SENSED MY SIGHT, HE KNEW.
YOU *ARE* A MYSTERY, NEPHILIM. THIS CHANGES THINGS.
WHY ARE YOU CALLING ME THAT? YOUR DEATH OWNS A NAME, I AM EDITH.
NEPHILIM WERE THE BASTARD CHILDREN OF WHAT HUMANS WOULD CALL ANGELS, OR MESSENGERS, AND HUMAN FEMALES. THEY WERE THE ONLY ONES WHO COULD EVER TRULY THREATEN MY KIND. HENCE THE GREAT FLOOD CAME TO WIPE THEM ALL OUT, YET A FEW REMAIN, I SEE.
BUT LET IT BE KNOWN TO YOU THAT NO ANTEDILUVIAN HAS EVER FALLEN FROM THE HAND OF ANOTHER. WHOEVER HAS CHARGED YOU WITH THE TASK OF KILLING ME HAS DONE SO IN IGNORANCE.

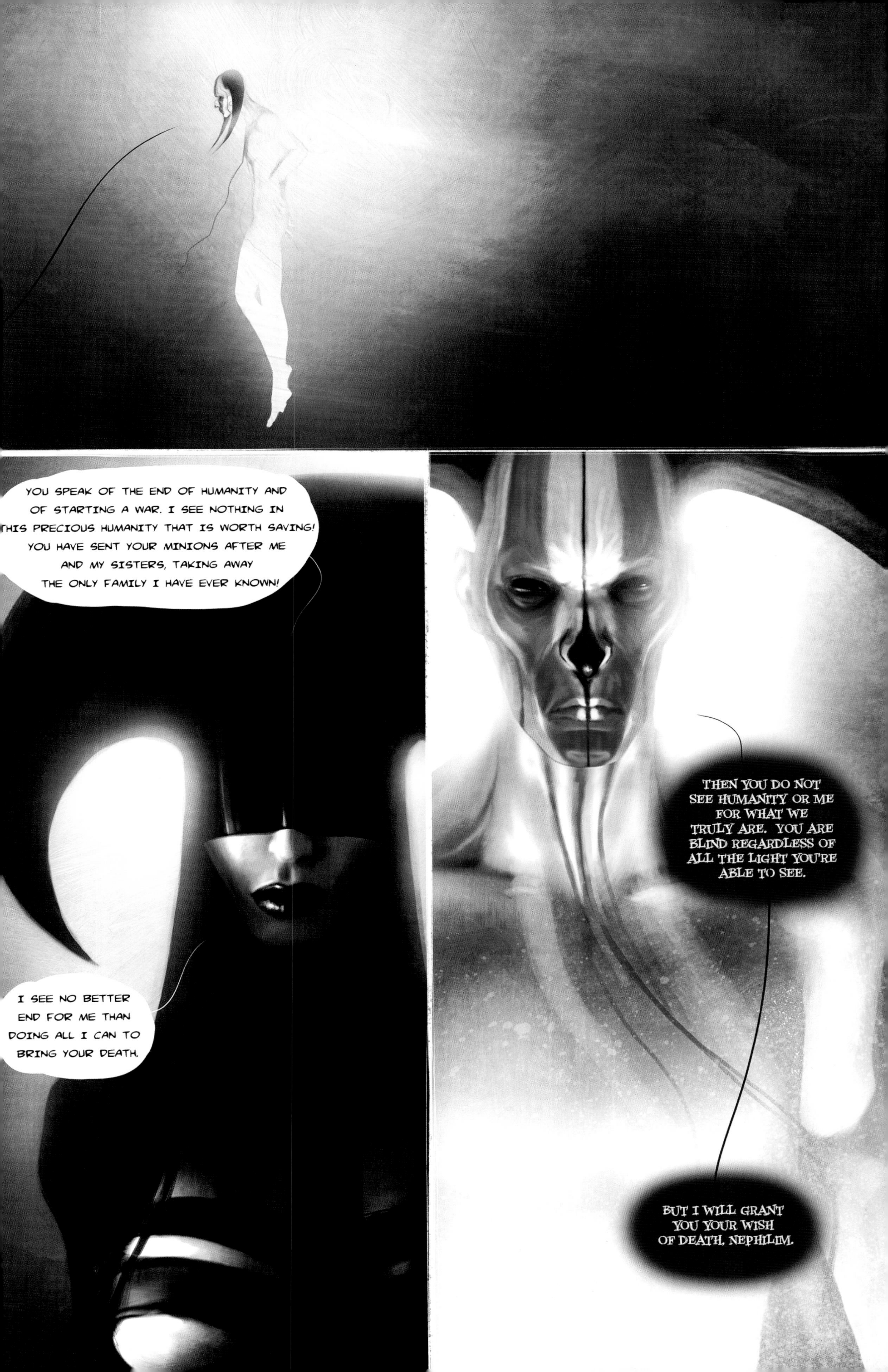
YOU SPEAK OF THE END OF HUMANITY AND OF STARTING A WAR. I SEE NOTHING IN THIS PRECIOUS HUMANITY THAT IS WORTH SAVING! YOU HAVE SENT YOUR MINIONS AFTER ME AND MY SISTERS, TAKING AWAY THE ONLY FAMILY I HAVE EVER KNOWN!
I SEE NO BETTER END FOR ME THAN DOING ALL I CAN TO BRING YOUR DEATH.
THEN YOU DO NOT SEE HUMANITY OR ME FOR WHAT WE TRULY ARE. YOU ARE BLIND REGARDLESS OF ALL THE LIGHT YOU'RE ABLE TO SEE.
BUT I WILL GRANT YOU YOUR WISH OF DEATH, NEPHILIM.

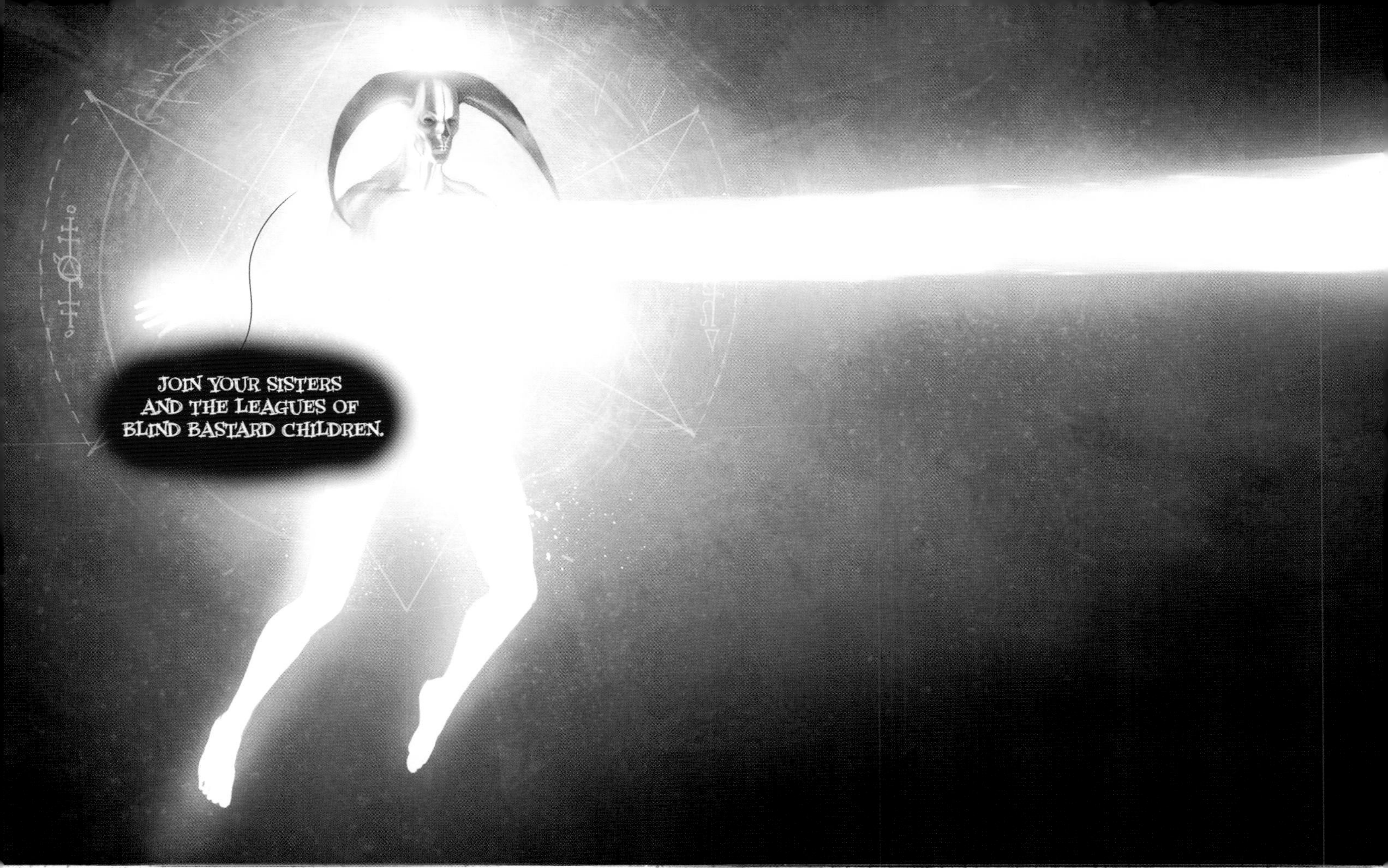
JOIN YOUR SISTERS
AND THE LEAGUES OF
BLIND BASTARD CHILDREN.

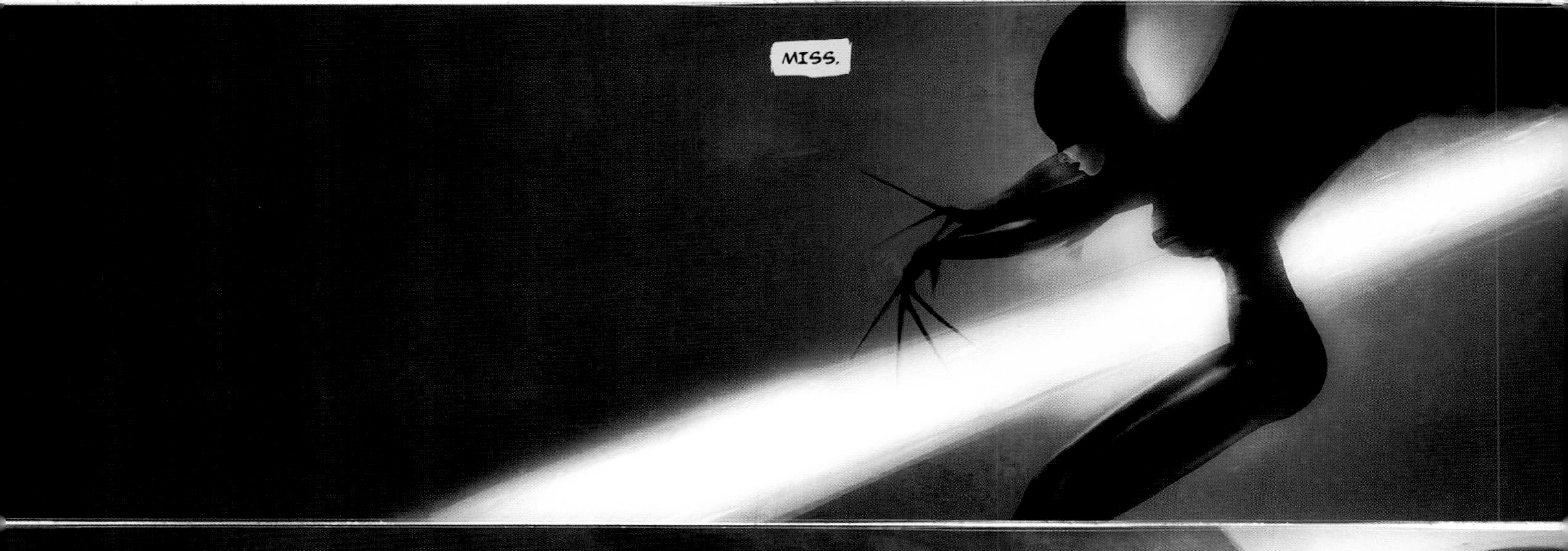
MISS.

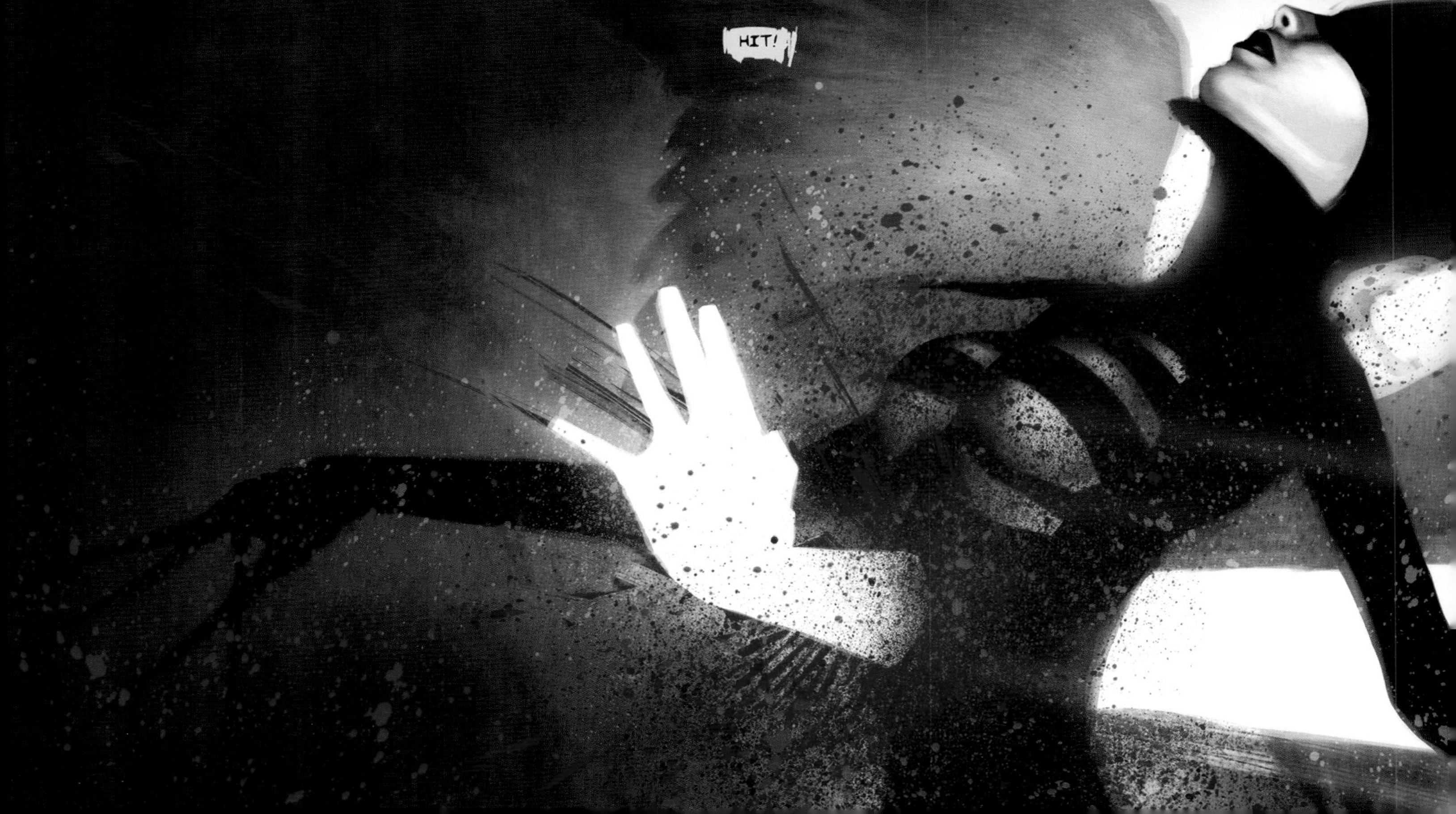
HIT!

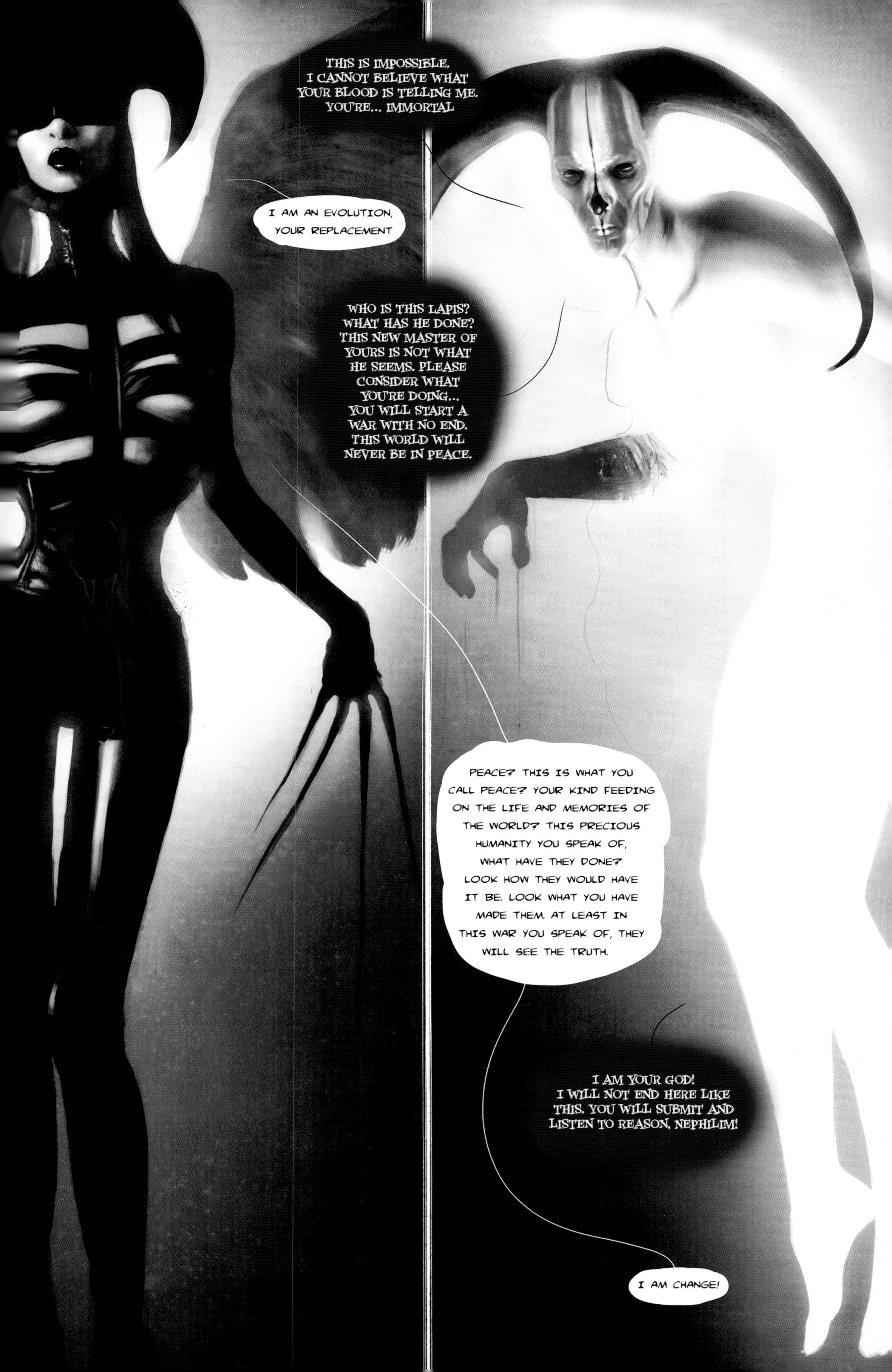
THIS IS IMPOSSIBLE. I CANNOT BELIEVE WHAT YOUR BLOOD IS TELLING ME. YOU'RE... IMMORTAL
I AM AN EVOLUTION, YOUR REPLACEMENT
WHO IS THIS LAPIS? WHAT HAS HE DONE? THIS NEW MASTER OF YOURS IS NOT WHAT HE SEEMS. PLEASE CONSIDER WHAT YOU'RE DOING... YOU WILL START A WAR WITH NO END. THIS WORLD WILL NEVER BE IN PEACE.
PEACE? THIS IS WHAT YOU CALL PEACE? YOUR KIND FEEDING ON THE LIFE AND MEMORIES OF THE WORLD? THIS PRECIOUS HUMANITY YOU SPEAK OF, WHAT HAVE THEY DONE? LOOK HOW THEY WOULD HAVE IT BE. LOOK WHAT YOU HAVE MADE THEM. AT LEAST IN THIS WAR YOU SPEAK OF, THEY WILL SEE THE TRUTH.
I AM YOUR GOD! I WILL NOT END HERE LIKE THIS. YOU WILL SUBMIT AND LISTEN TO REASON, NEPHILIM!
I AM CHANGE!

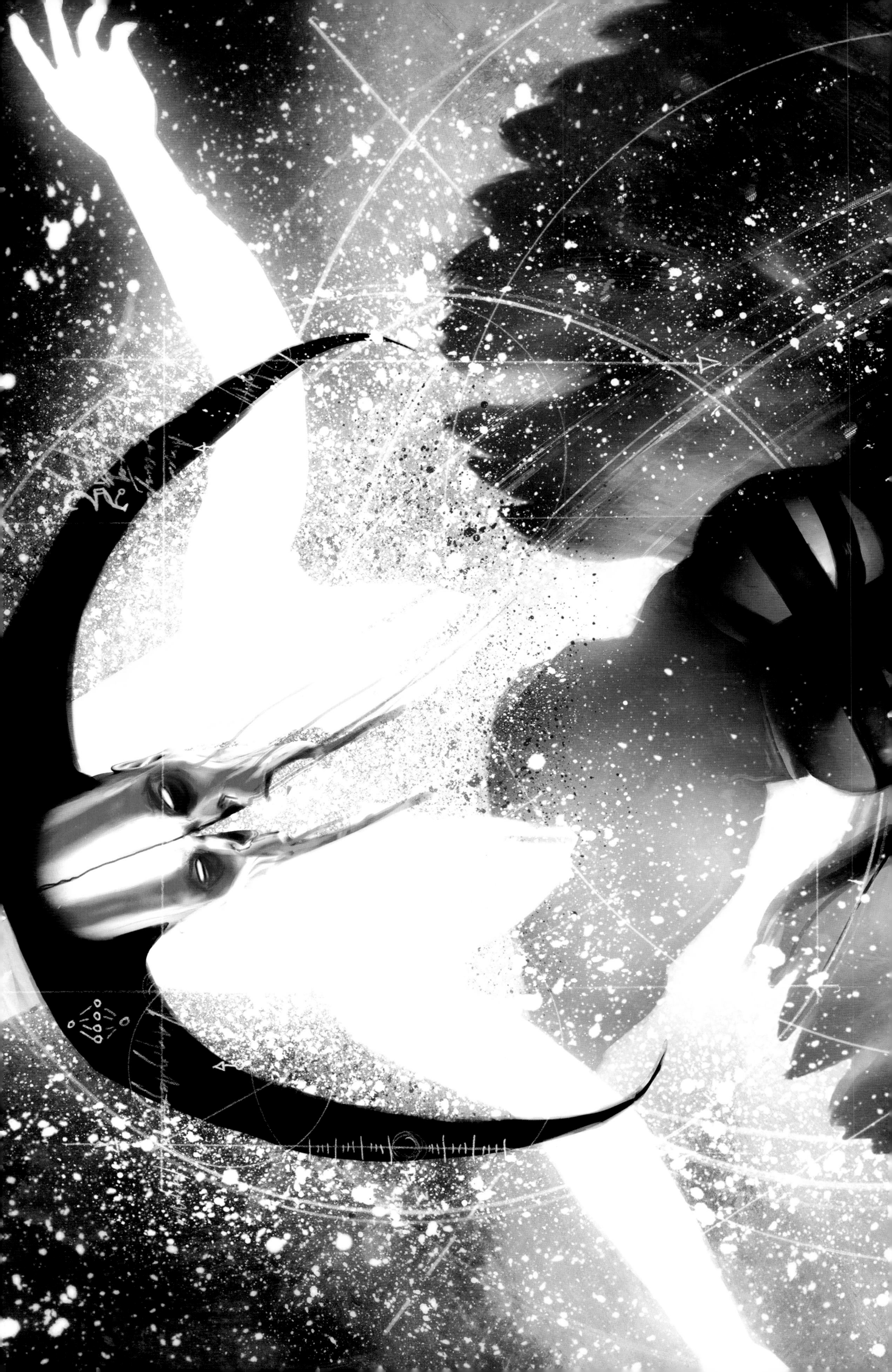

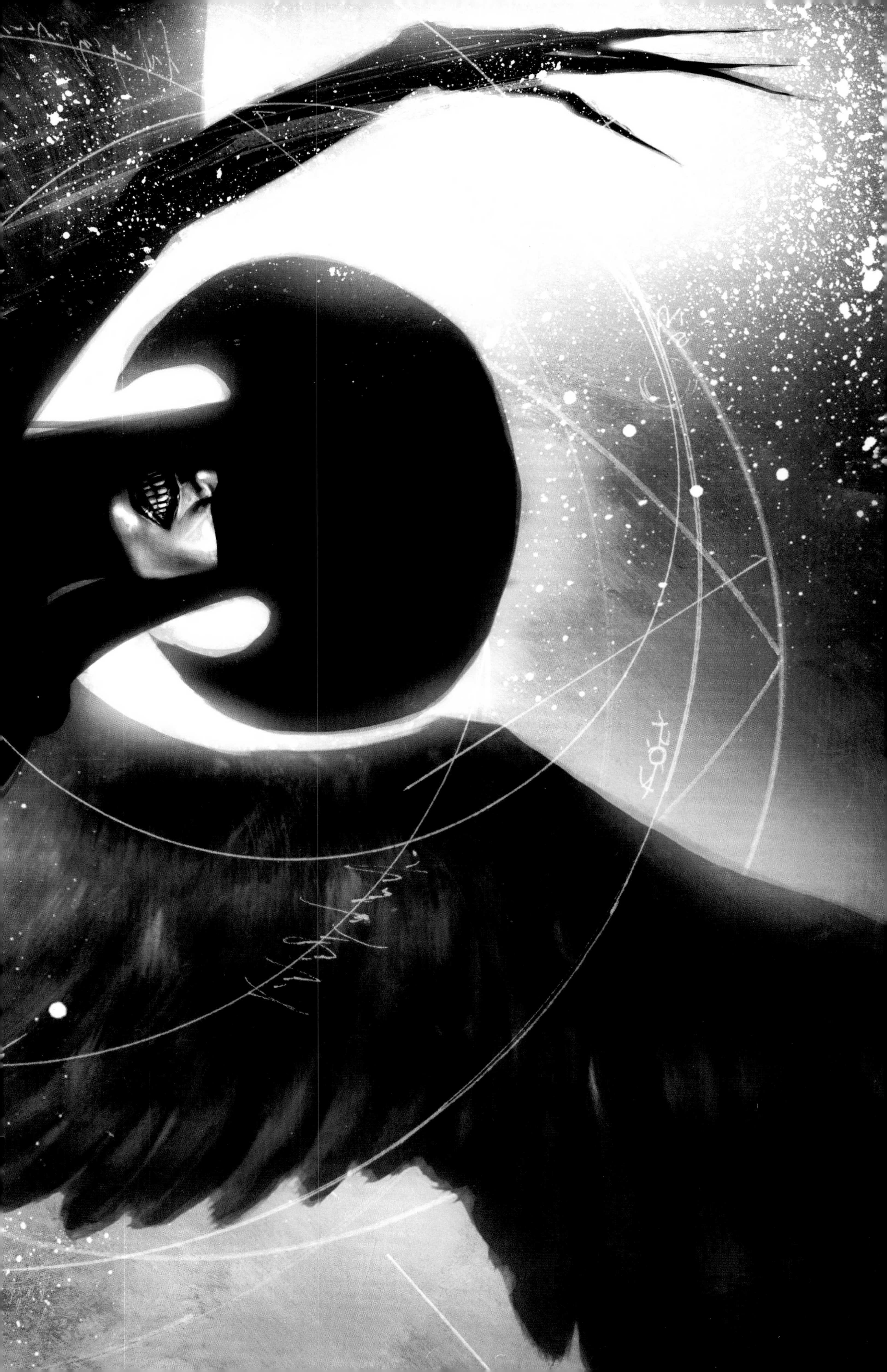

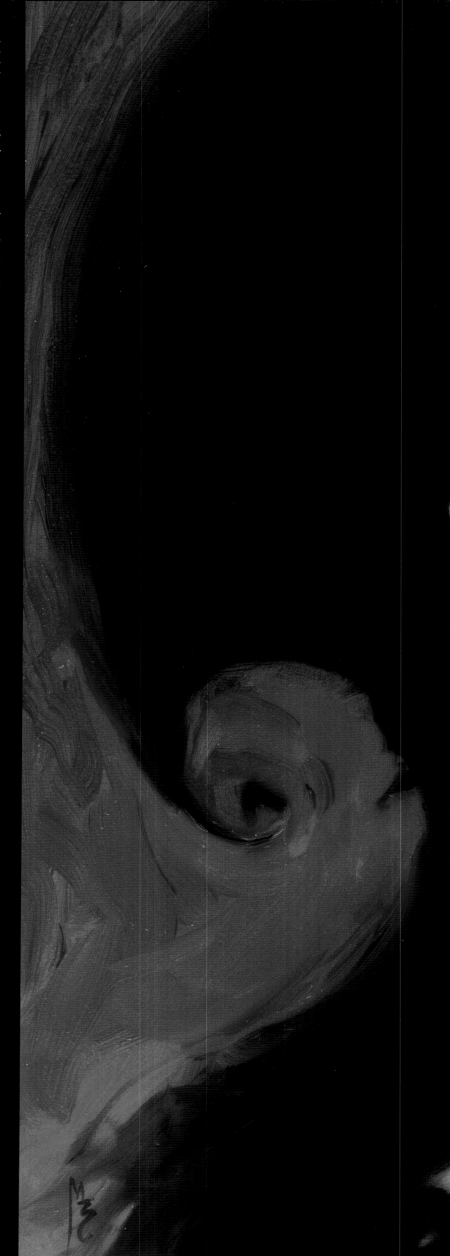

Killing Jared transformed me even more. I do not fully understand what I am, but I know what I must do.

There are many like Jared all around the world. I see their hiding places, I know what they fear.

To be quite honest, they are extremely vulnerable if you know what you're doing. I intend on hunting them, soliciting the debt that the Antediluvians have incurred over the full history of human civilization.

They feed off the whole of the world, using us like cattle. They use our greed and vices against us, allowing it to shape how we see reality, but very few ever see past the illusion. The few that do get dead or become so rich and successful they forget about their ideals.

They truly control us with the ideal weapon, our own free will.

They make themselves out to be gods to us, so even if we were to get close to one, we would just think we are having some religious revelation.

I see now how they use the memories and energy that humankind creates. I see how easily they have done this to us. I see we have never truly been allowed to be what we could be.

I will not collect memories.

I will collect Gods.

End chapter one.

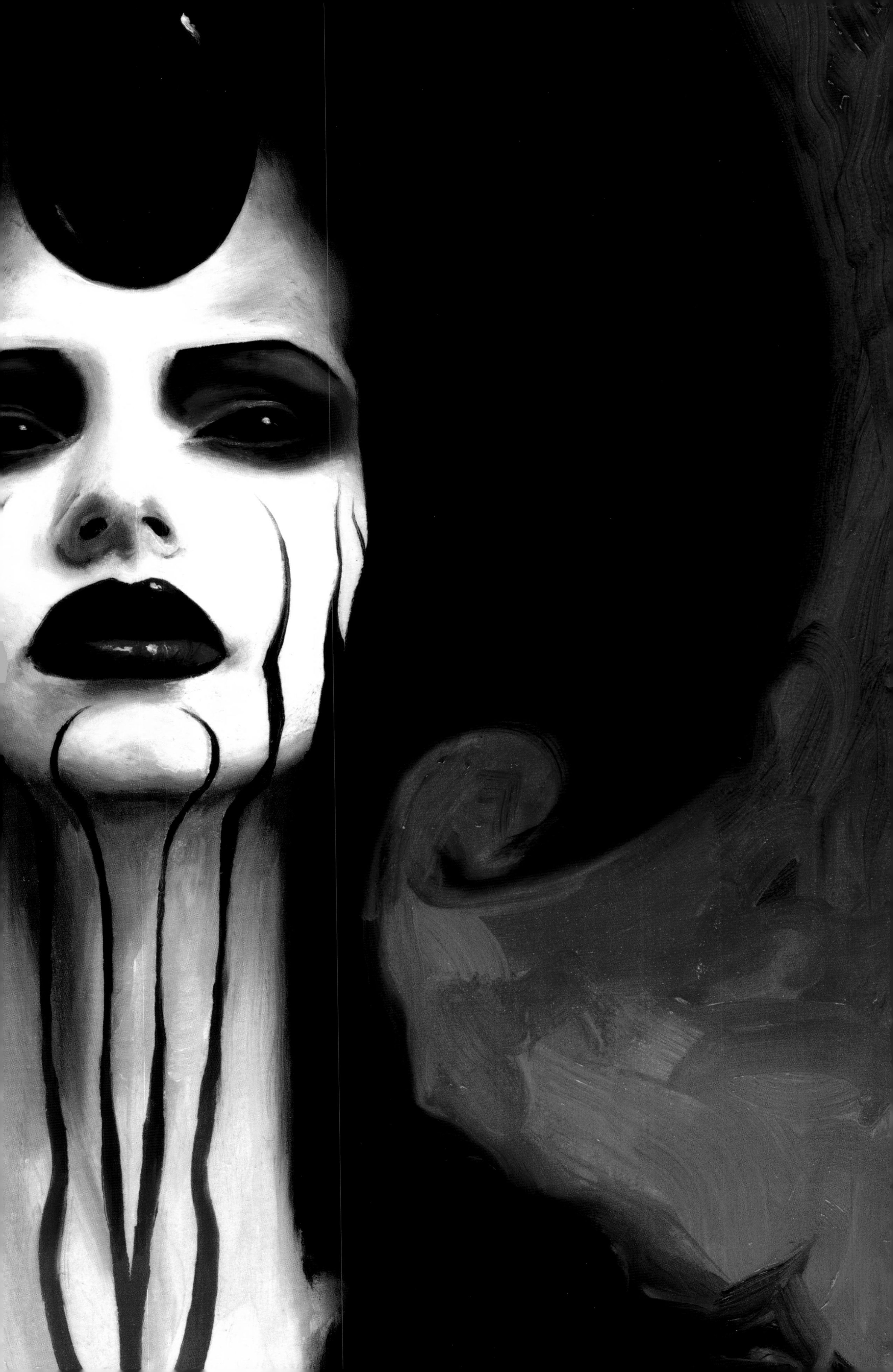

FOR SOME SMALL PART OF THE MEMORY

STORY BY MENTON3 ART BY TONY MOY

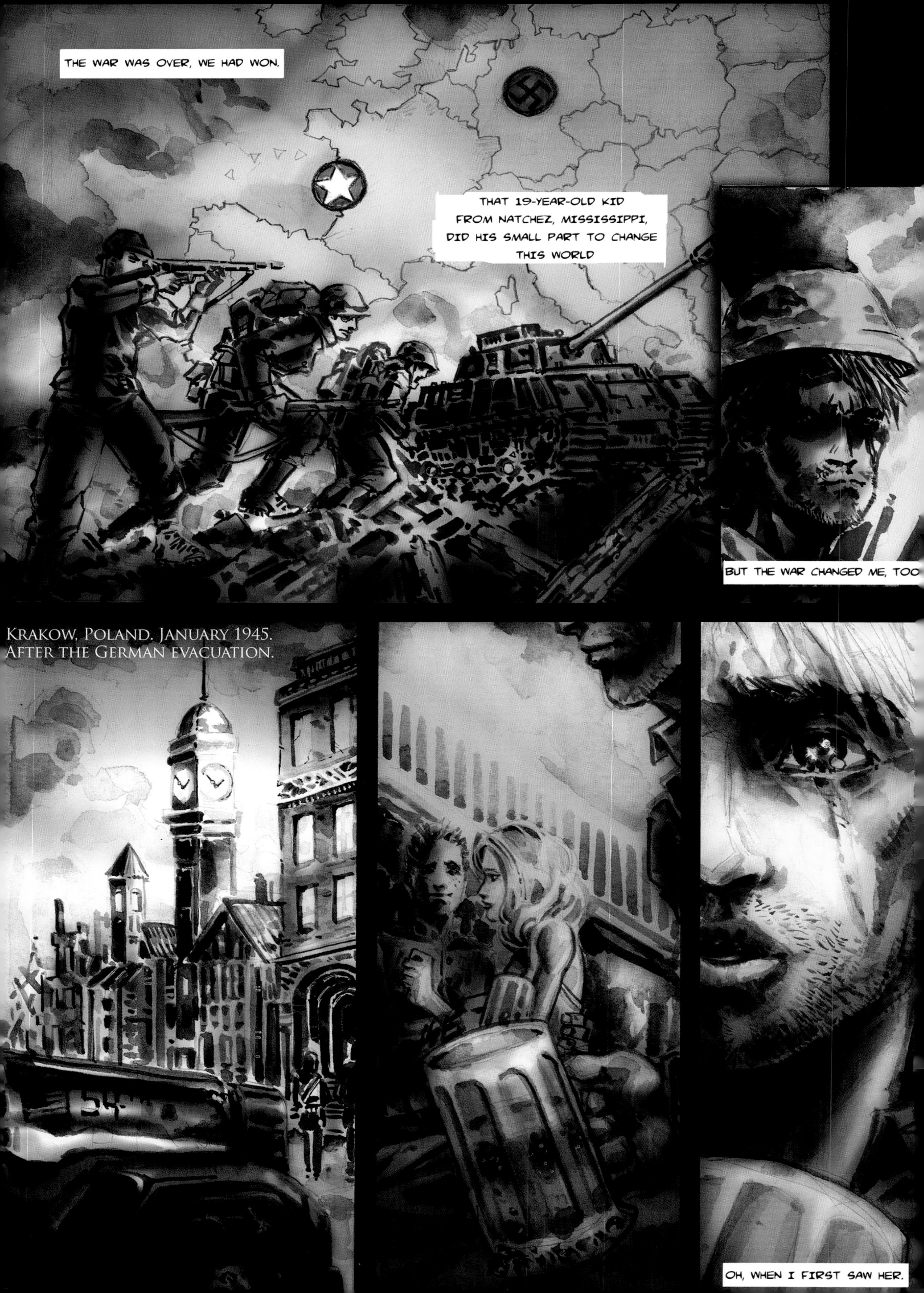
THE WAR WAS OVER, WE HAD WON.
THAT 19-YEAR-OLD KID FROM NATCHEZ, MISSISSIPPI, DID HIS SMALL PART TO CHANGE THIS WORLD
BUT THE WAR CHANGED ME, TOO
KRAKOW, POLAND. JANUARY 1945. AFTER THE GERMAN EVACUATION.
OH, WHEN I FIRST SAW HER.

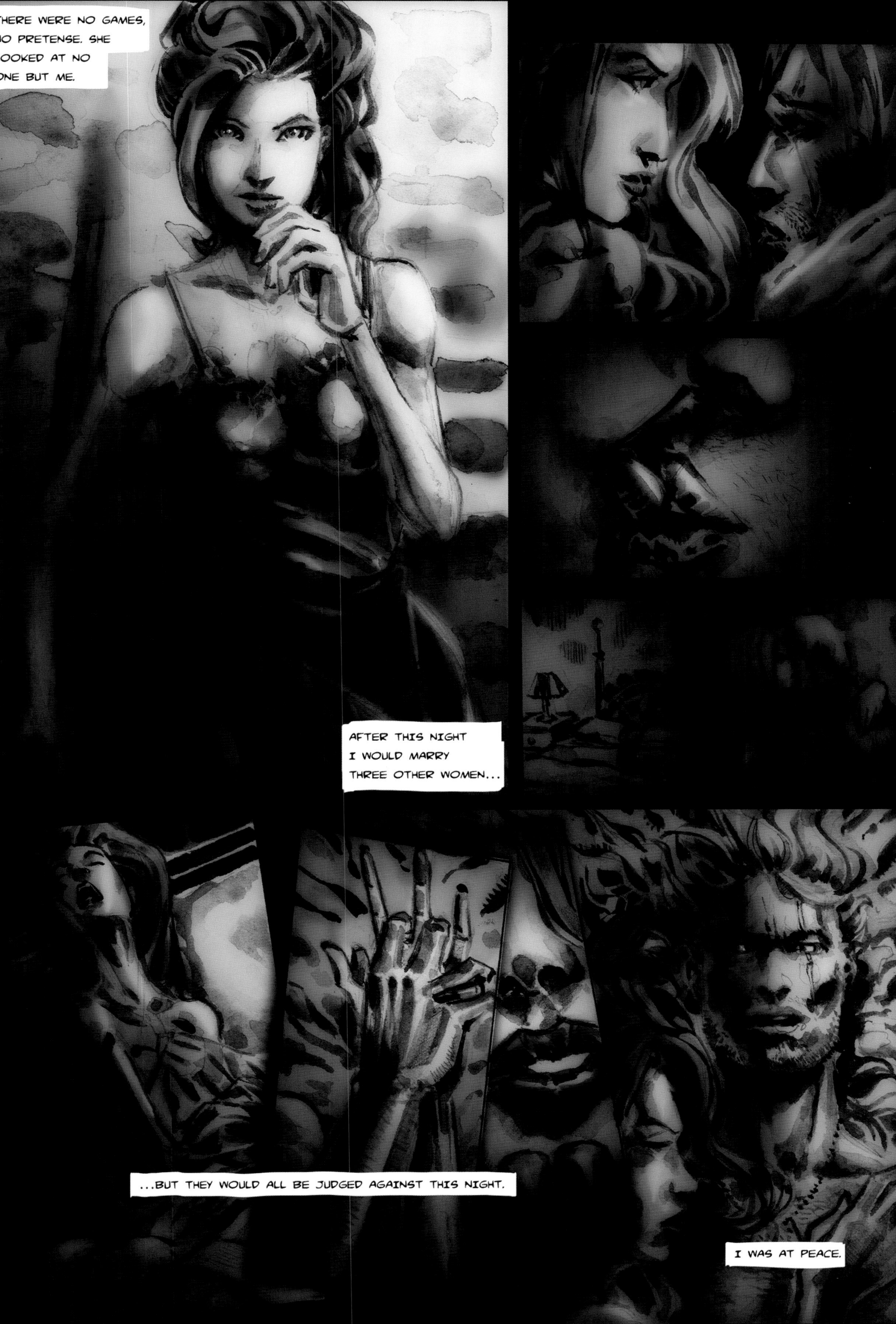
THERE WERE NO GAMES, NO PRETENSE. SHE LOOKED AT NO ONE BUT ME.
AFTER THIS NIGHT I WOULD MARRY THREE OTHER WOMEN...
...BUT THEY WOULD ALL BE JUDGED AGAINST THIS NIGHT.
I WAS AT PEACE.

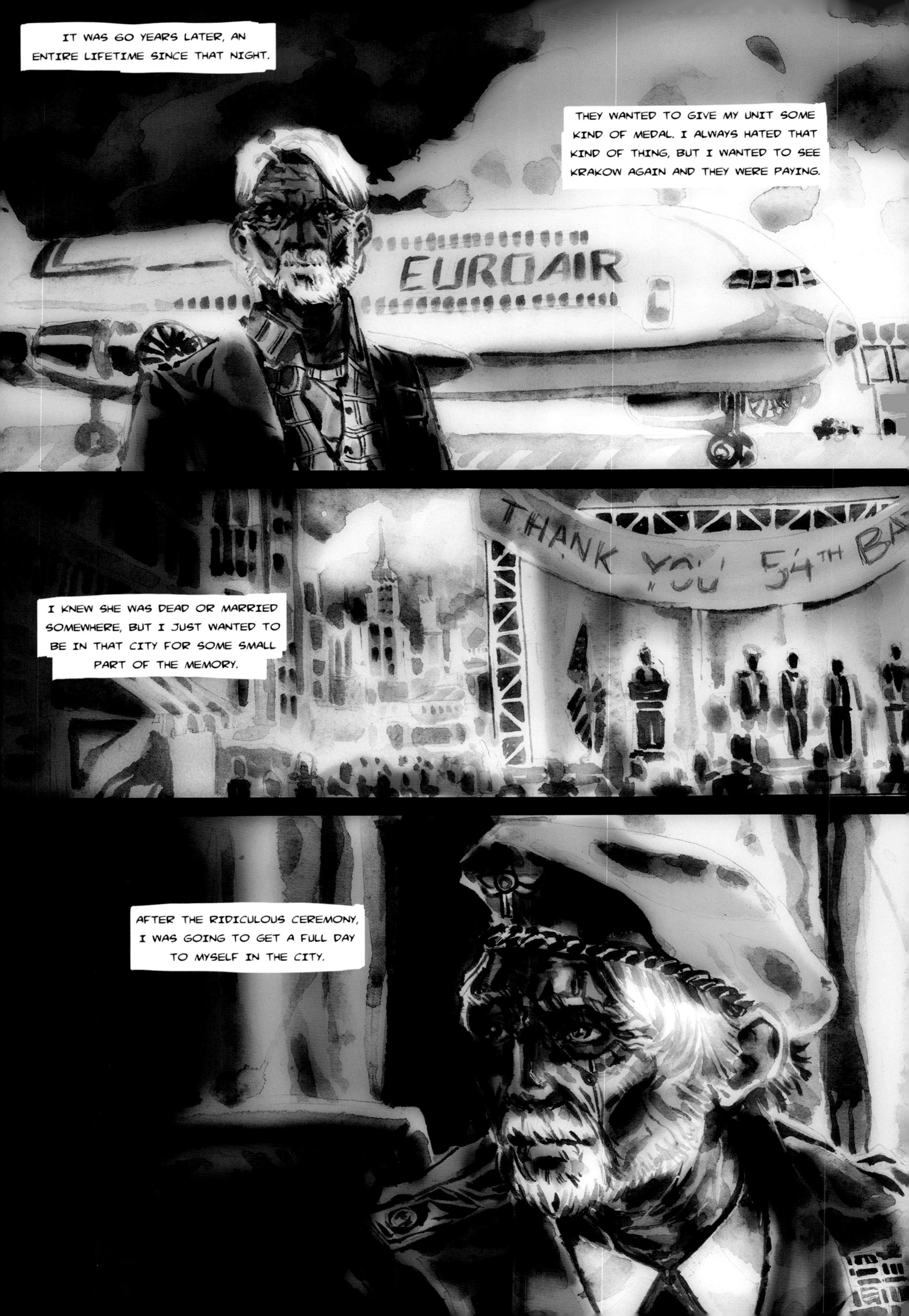
IT WAS 60 YEARS LATER, AN ENTIRE LIFETIME SINCE THAT NIGHT.
THEY WANTED TO GIVE MY UNIT SOME KIND OF MEDAL. I ALWAYS HATED THAT KIND OF THING, BUT I WANTED TO SEE KRAKOW AGAIN AND THEY WERE PAYING.
EUROAIR
THANK YOU 54TH
I KNEW SHE WAS DEAD OR MARRIED SOMEWHERE, BUT I JUST WANTED TO BE IN THAT CITY FOR SOME SMALL PART OF THE MEMORY.
AFTER THE RIDICULOUS CEREMONY, I WAS GOING TO GET A FULL DAY TO MYSELF IN THE CITY.

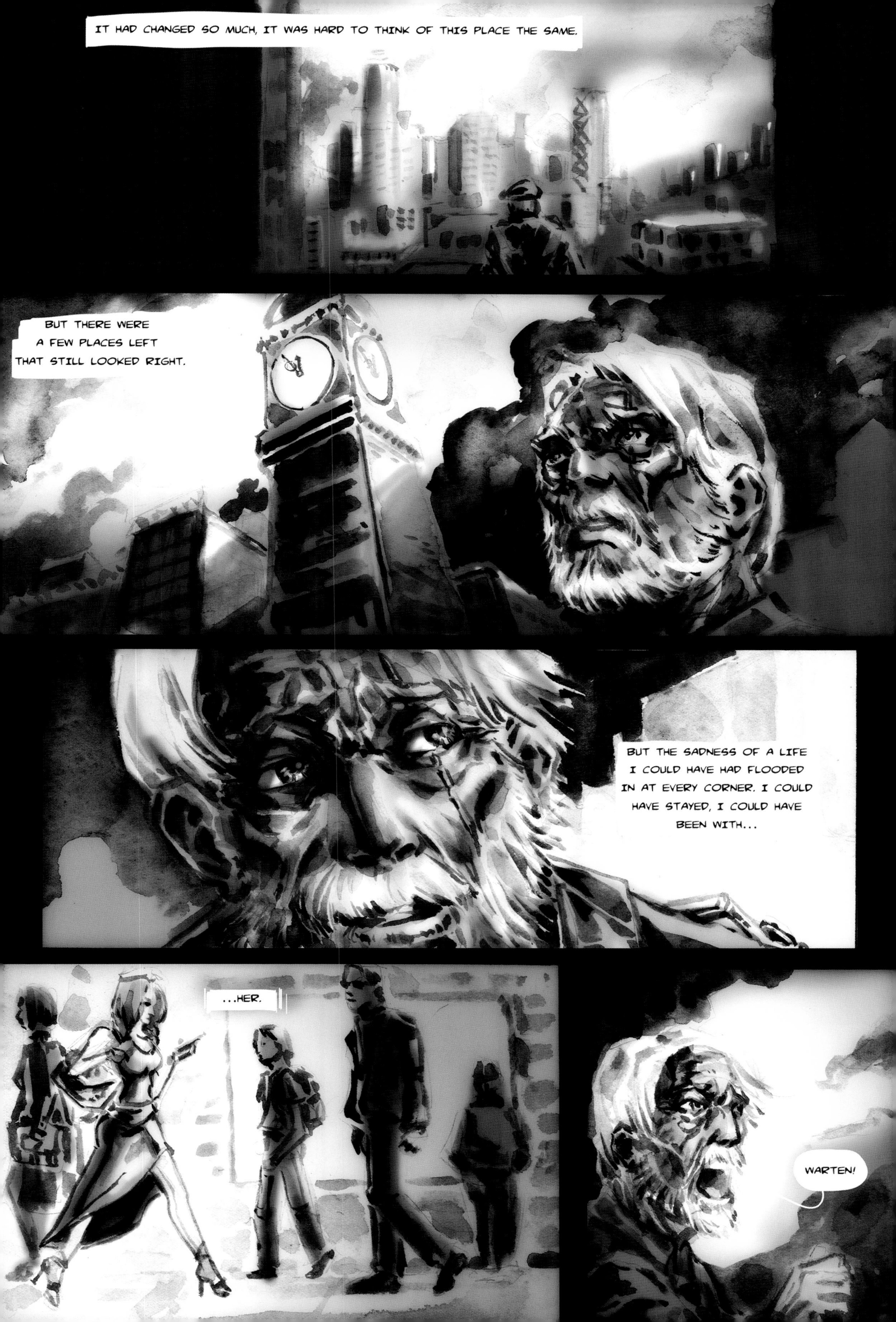
IT HAD CHANGED SO MUCH, IT WAS HARD TO THINK OF THIS PLACE THE SAME.
BUT THERE WERE A FEW PLACES LEFT THAT STILL LOOKED RIGHT.
BUT THE SADNESS OF A LIFE I COULD HAVE HAD FLOODED IN AT EVERY CORNER. I COULD HAVE STAYED, I COULD HAVE BEEN WITH...
...HER.
WARTEN!

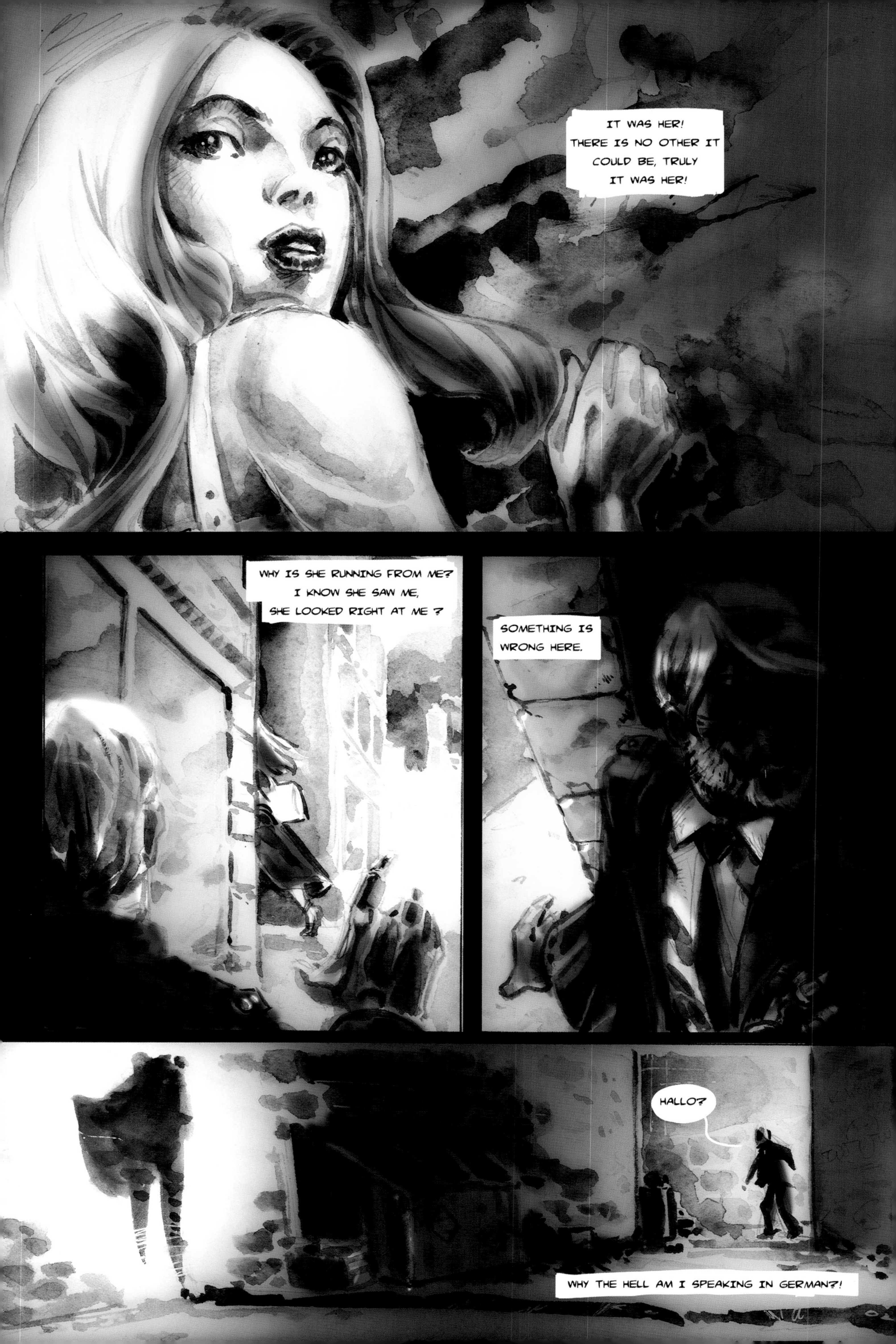
IT WAS HER!
THERE IS NO OTHER IT COULD BE, TRULY IT WAS HER!
WHY IS SHE RUNNING FROM ME? I KNOW SHE SAW ME, SHE LOOKED RIGHT AT ME ?
SOMETHING IS WRONG HERE.
HALLO?
WHY THE HELL AM I SPEAKING IN GERMAN?!

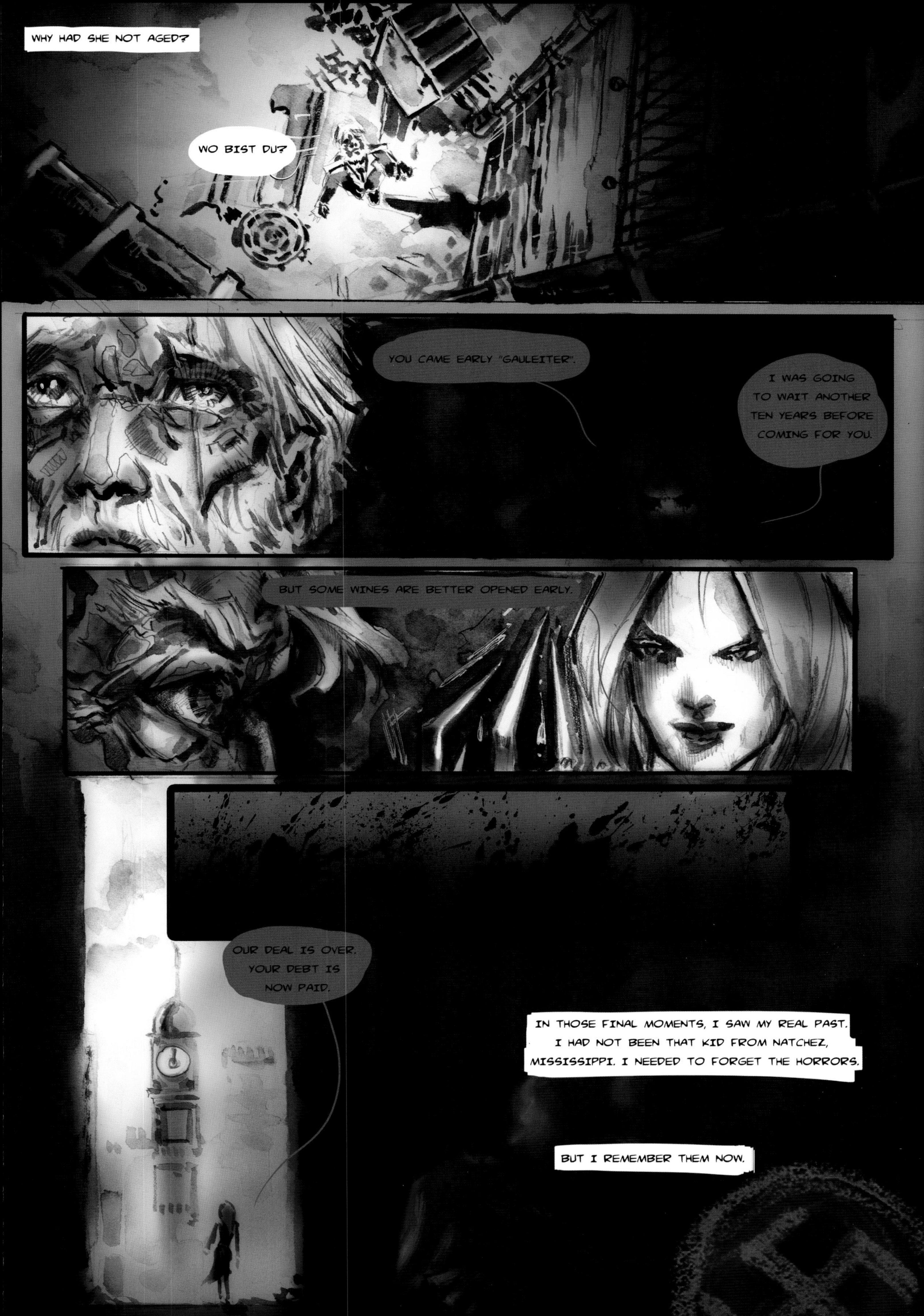
WHY HAD SHE NOT AGED?
WO BIST DU?
YOU CAME EARLY "GAULEITER".
I WAS GOING TO WAIT ANOTHER TEN YEARS BEFORE COMING FOR YOU.
BUT SOME WINES ARE BETTER OPENED EARLY.
OUR DEAL IS OVER. YOUR DEBT IS NOW PAID.
IN THOSE FINAL MOMENTS, I SAW MY REAL PAST. I HAD NOT BEEN THAT KID FROM NATCHEZ, MISSISSIPPI. I NEEDED TO FORGET THE HORRORS.
BUT I REMEMBER THEM NOW.

STORY & ART BY BEN TEMPLESMITH

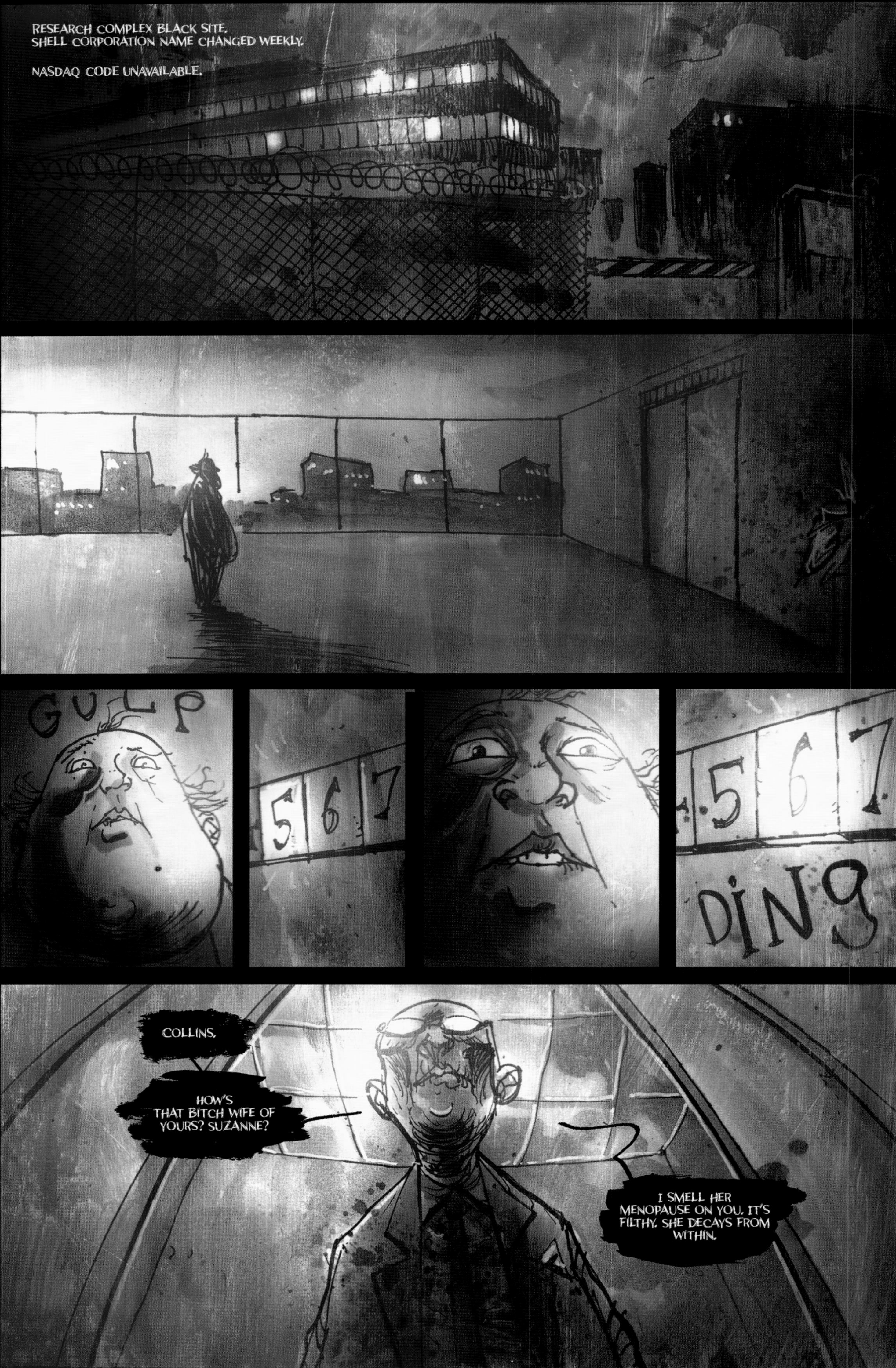
RESEARCH COMPLEX BLACK SITE.
SHELL CORPORATION NAME CHANGED WEEKLY.
NASDAQ CODE UNAVAILABLE.
GULP
567
567
DING
COLLINS.
HOW'S THAT BITCH WIFE OF YOURS? SUZANNE?
I SMELL HER MENOPAUSE ON YOU. IT'S FILTHY. SHE DECAYS FROM WITHIN.

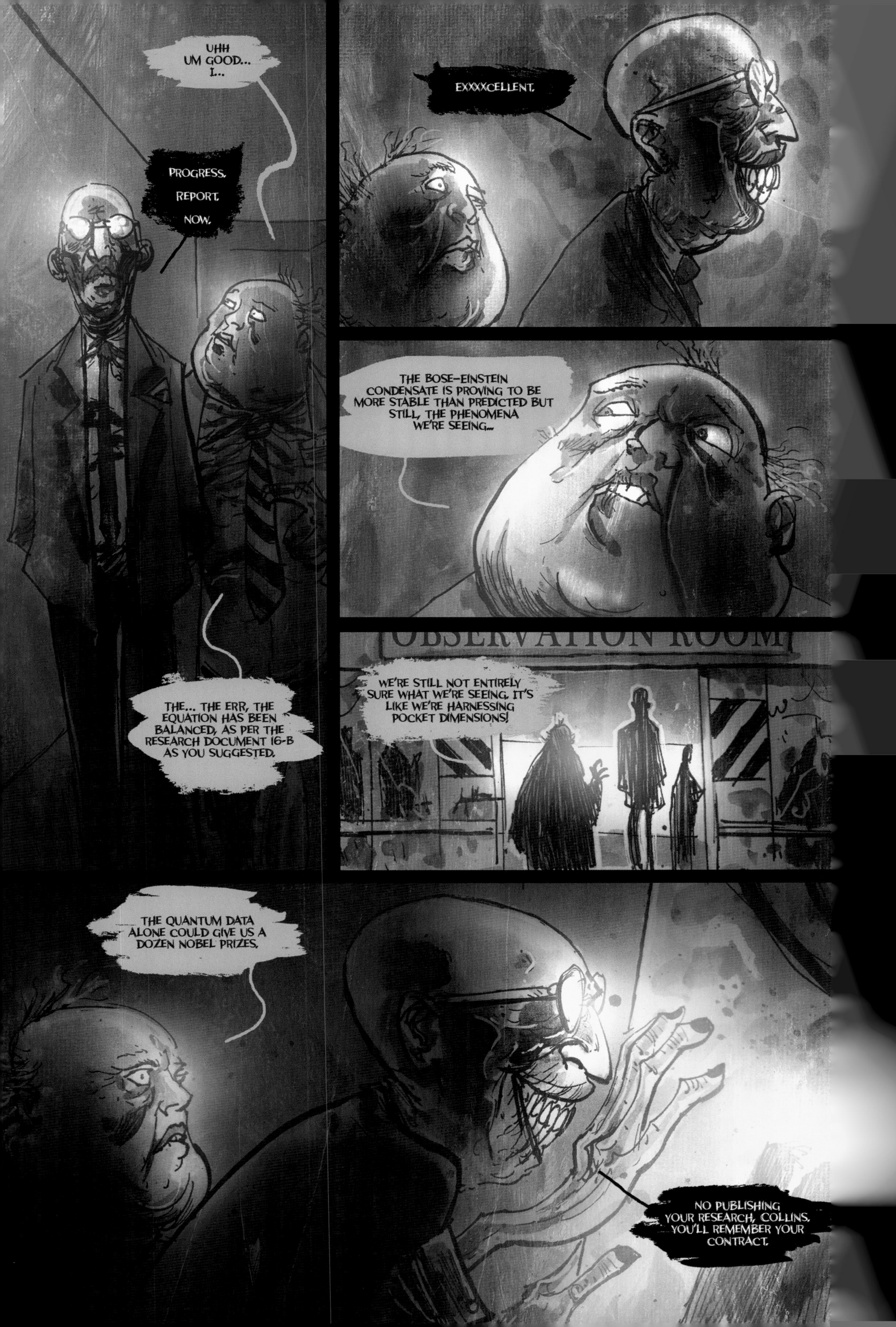

PROGRESS. REPORT. NOW.
UHH UM GOOD... I...
THE... THE ERR, THE EQUATION HAS BEEN BALANCED, AS PER THE RESEARCH DOCUMENT 16-B AS YOU SUGGESTED.
EXXXXCELLENT.
THE BOSE-EINSTEIN CONDENSATE IS PROVING TO BE MORE STABLE THAN PREDICTED BUT STILL, THE PHENOMENA WE'RE SEEING...
OBSERVATION ROOM
WE'RE STILL NOT ENTIRELY SURE WHAT WE'RE SEEING. IT'S LIKE WE'RE HARNESSING POCKET DIMENSIONS!
THE QUANTUM DATA ALONE COULD GIVE US A DOZEN NOBEL PRIZES.
NO PUBLISHING YOUR RESEARCH, COLLINS. YOU'LL REMEMBER YOUR CONTRACT.

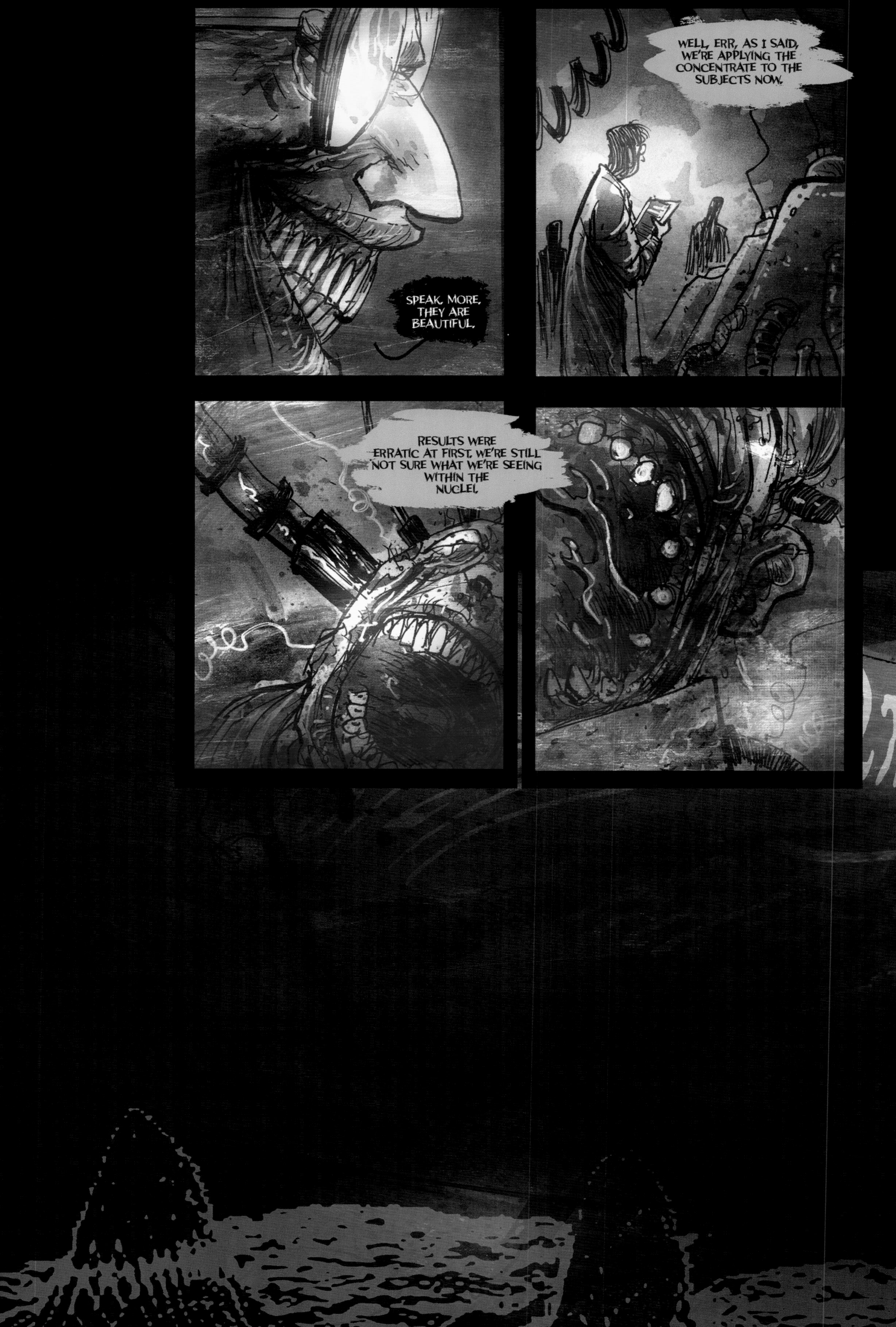
SPEAK, MORE, THEY ARE BEAUTIFUL.
WELL, ERR, AS I SAID, WE'RE APPLYING THE CONCENTRATE TO THE SUBJECTS NOW.
RESULTS WERE ERRATIC AT FIRST. WE'RE STILL NOT SURE WHAT WE'RE SEEING WITHIN THE NUCLEI.

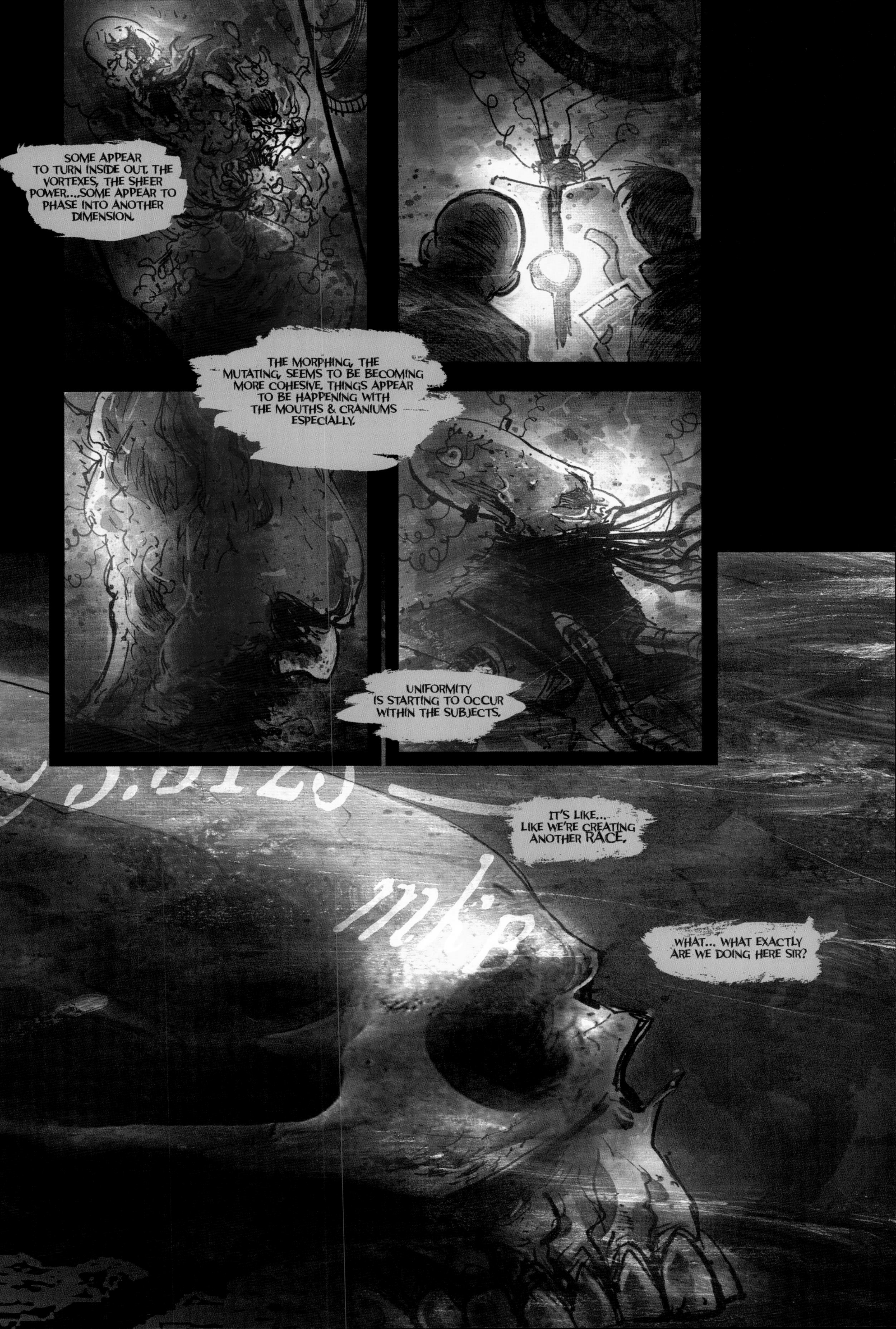
SOME APPEAR TO TURN INSIDE OUT. THE VORTEXES, THE SHEER POWER....SOME APPEAR TO PHASE INTO ANOTHER DIMENSION.
THE MORPHING, THE MUTATING, SEEMS TO BE BECOMING MORE COHESIVE. THINGS APPEAR TO BE HAPPENING WITH THE MOUTHS & CRANIUMS ESPECIALLY.
UNIFORMITY IS STARTING TO OCCUR WITHIN THE SUBJECTS.
IT'S LIKE... LIKE WE'RE CREATING ANOTHER RACE.
WHAT... WHAT EXACTLY ARE WE DOING HERE SIR?

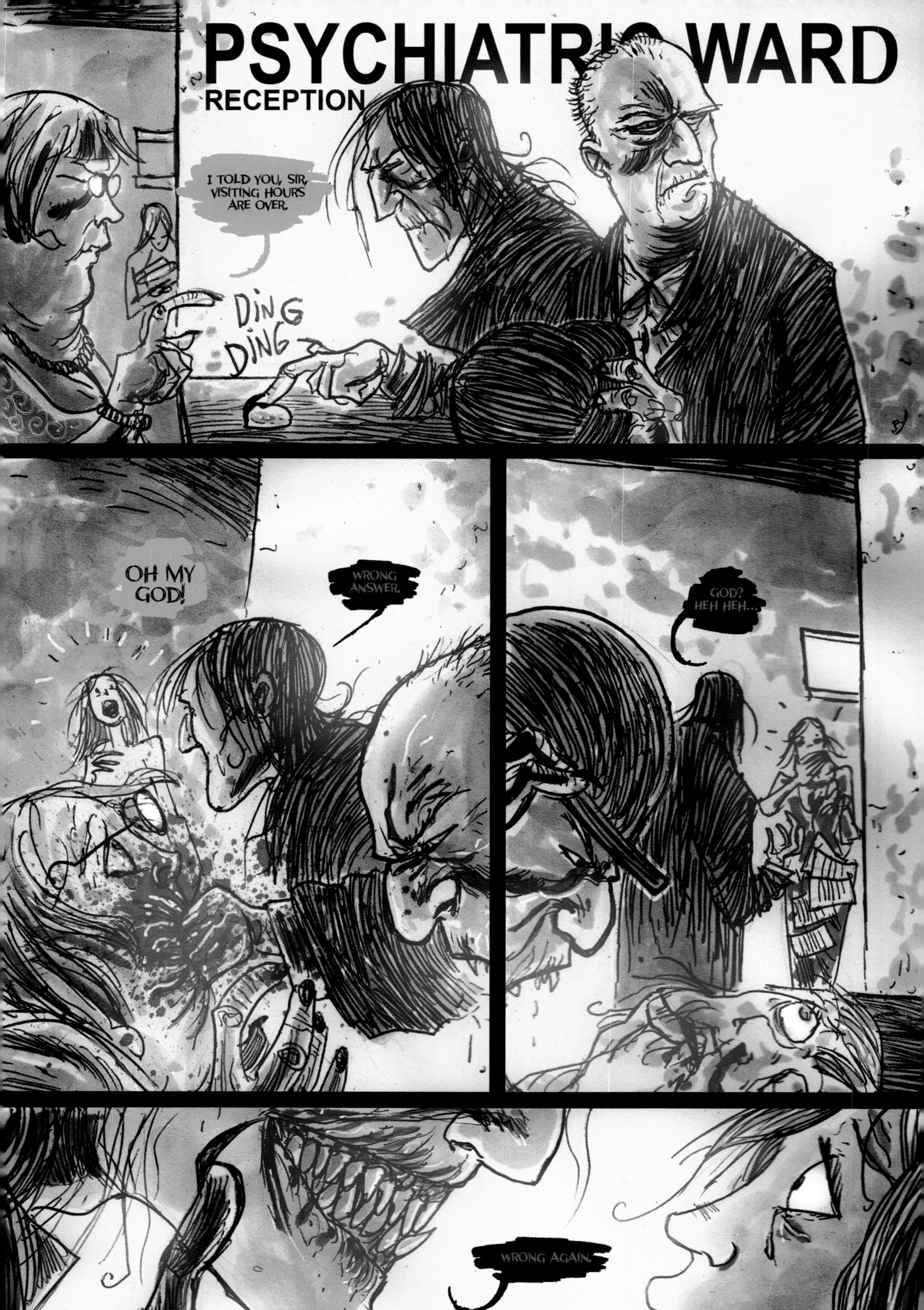

PSYCHIATRIC WARD
RECEPTION
I TOLD YOU, SIR, VISITING HOURS ARE OVER.
DING DING
OH MY GOD!
WRONG ANSWER.
GOD? HEH HEH...
WRONG AGAIN.

AN INTERPRETATION OF FORM

WRITTEN BY BEN MURPHY   ART & LETTERS BY BEN TEMPLESMITH

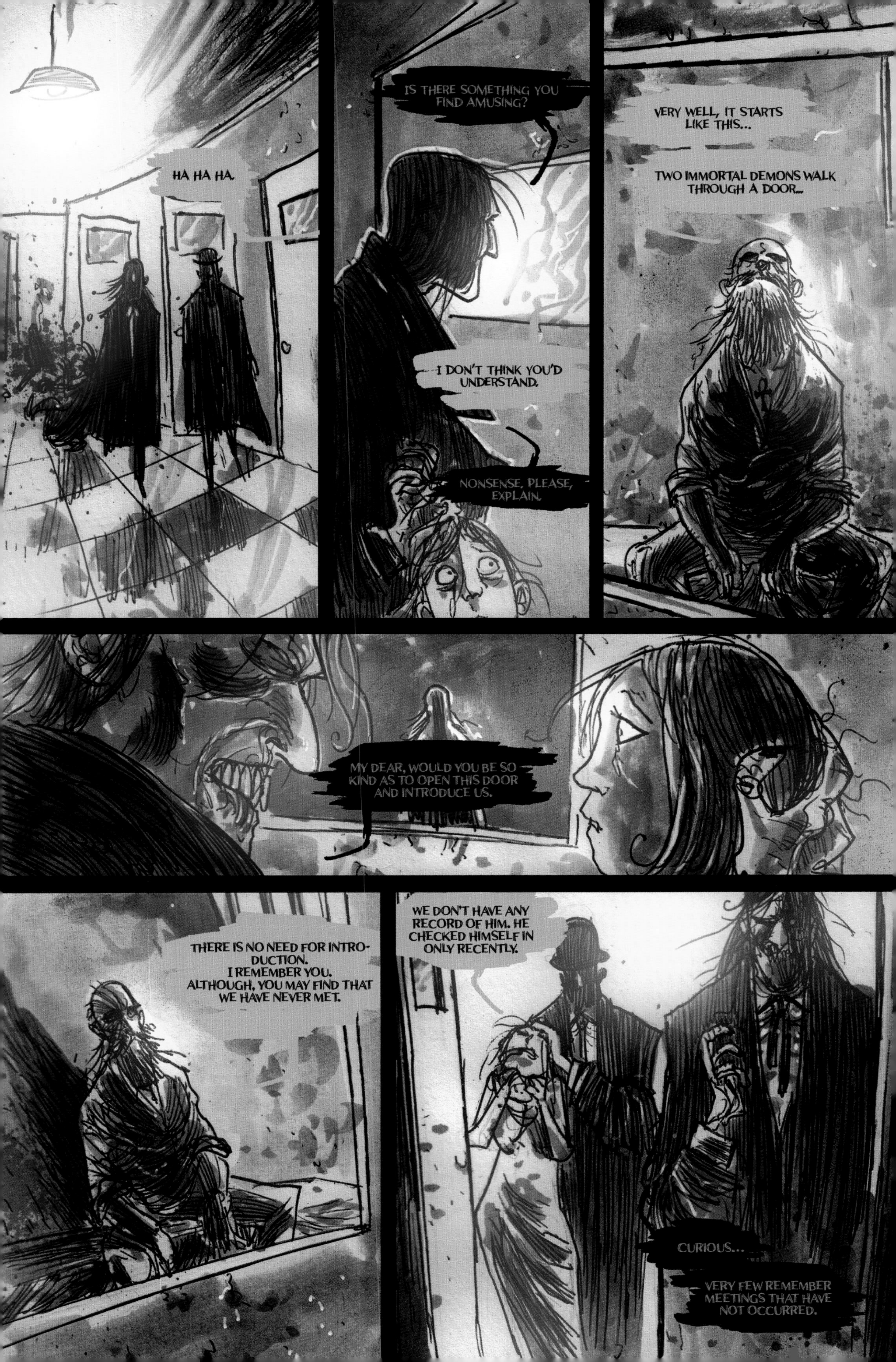
HA HA HA.
IS THERE SOMETHING YOU FIND AMUSING?
I DON'T THINK YOU'D UNDERSTAND.
NONSENSE, PLEASE, EXPLAIN.
VERY WELL, IT STARTS LIKE THIS...
TWO IMMORTAL DEMONS WALK THROUGH A DOOR...
MY DEAR, WOULD YOU BE SO KIND AS TO OPEN THIS DOOR AND INTRODUCE US.
THERE IS NO NEED FOR INTRODUCTION. I REMEMBER YOU. ALTHOUGH, YOU MAY FIND THAT WE HAVE NEVER MET.
WE DON'T HAVE ANY RECORD OF HIM. HE CHECKED HIMSELF IN ONLY RECENTLY.
CURIOUS...
VERY FEW REMEMBER MEETINGS THAT HAVE NOT OCCURRED.

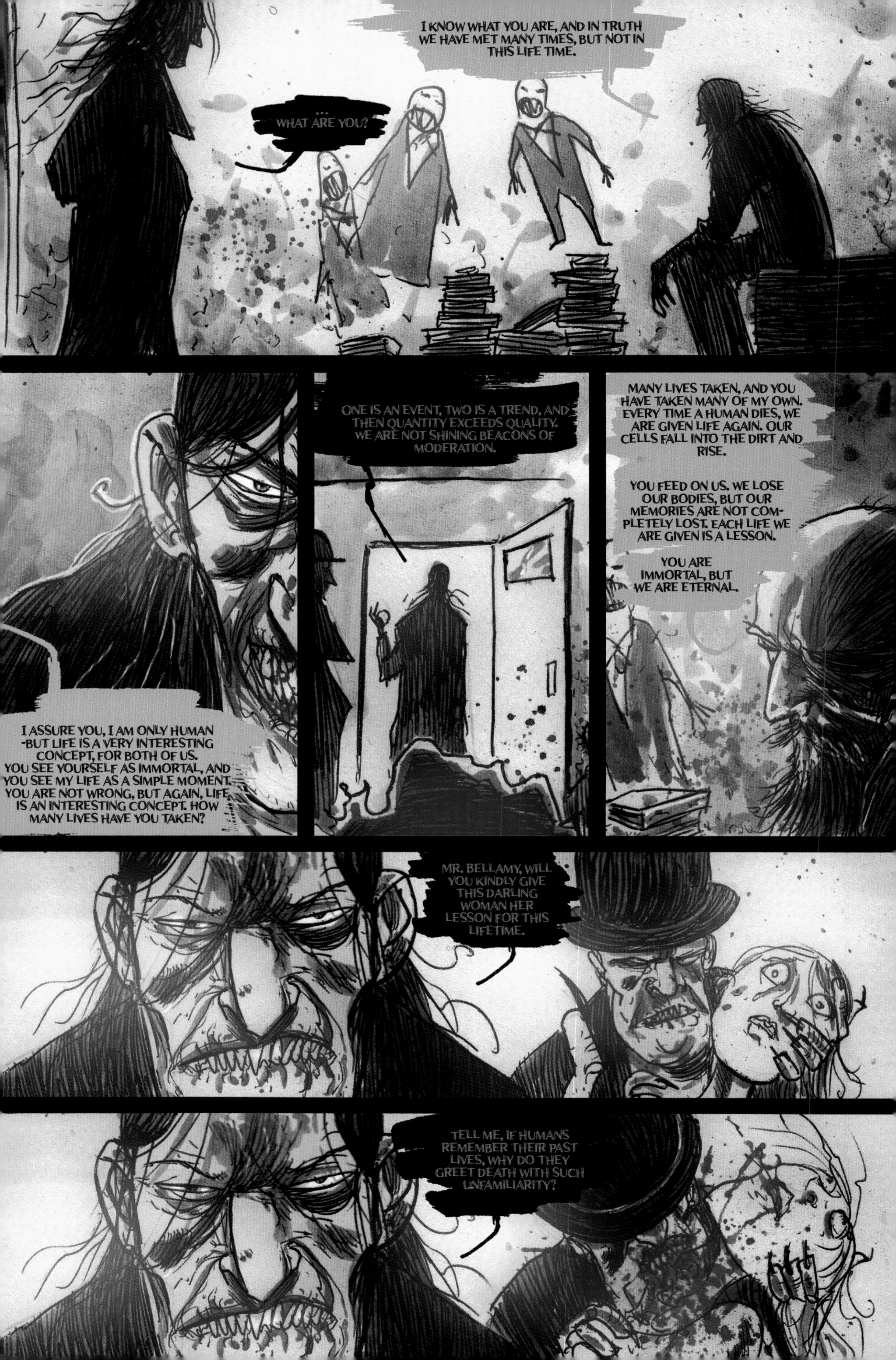
I KNOW WHAT YOU ARE, AND IN TRUTH WE HAVE MET MANY TIMES, BUT NOT IN THIS LIFE TIME.
... WHAT ARE YOU?
I ASSURE YOU, I AM ONLY HUMAN -BUT LIFE IS A VERY INTERESTING CONCEPT, FOR BOTH OF US. YOU SEE YOURSELF AS IMMORTAL, AND YOU SEE MY LIFE AS A SIMPLE MOMENT. YOU ARE NOT WRONG, BUT AGAIN, LIFE IS AN INTERESTING CONCEPT. HOW MANY LIVES HAVE YOU TAKEN?
ONE IS AN EVENT, TWO IS A TREND, AND THEN QUANTITY EXCEEDS QUALITY. WE ARE NOT SHINING BEACONS OF MODERATION.
MANY LIVES TAKEN, AND YOU HAVE TAKEN MANY OF MY OWN. EVERY TIME A HUMAN DIES, WE ARE GIVEN LIFE AGAIN. OUR CELLS FALL INTO THE DIRT AND RISE.
YOU FEED ON US. WE LOSE OUR BODIES, BUT OUR MEMORIES ARE NOT COMPLETELY LOST. EACH LIFE WE ARE GIVEN IS A LESSON.
YOU ARE IMMORTAL, BUT WE ARE ETERNAL.
MR. BELLAMY, WILL YOU KINDLY GIVE THIS DARLING WOMAN HER LESSON FOR THIS LIFETIME.
TELL ME, IF HUMANS REMEMBER THEIR PAST LIVES, WHY DO THEY GREET DEATH WITH SUCH UNFAMILIARITY?

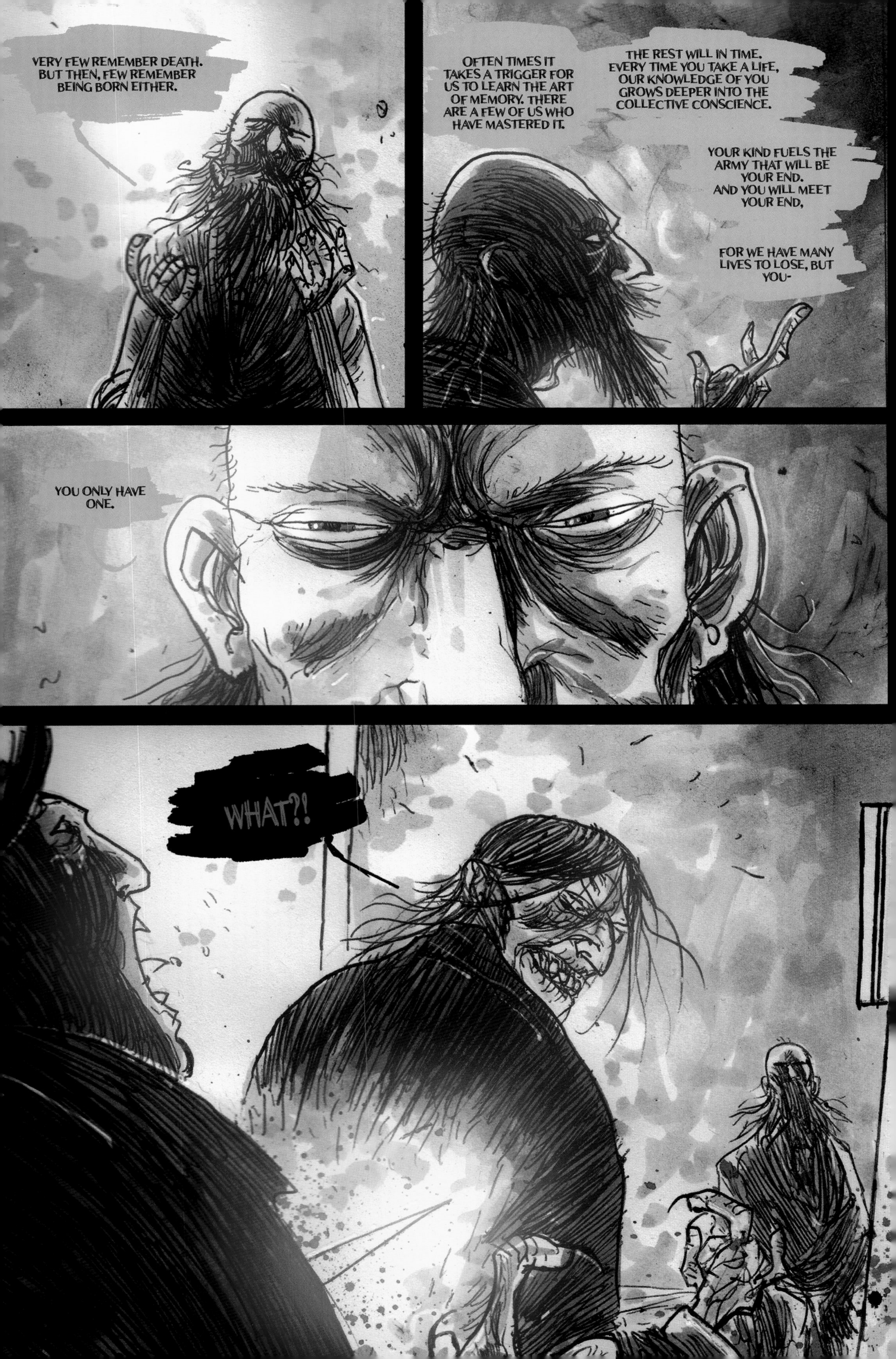
VERY FEW REMEMBER DEATH. BUT THEN, FEW REMEMBER BEING BORN EITHER.
OFTEN TIMES IT TAKES A TRIGGER FOR US TO LEARN THE ART OF MEMORY. THERE ARE A FEW OF US WHO HAVE MASTERED IT.
THE REST WILL IN TIME. EVERY TIME YOU TAKE A LIFE, OUR KNOWLEDGE OF YOU GROWS DEEPER INTO THE COLLECTIVE CONSCIENCE.
YOUR KIND FUELS THE ARMY THAT WILL BE YOUR END. AND YOU WILL MEET YOUR END,
FOR WE HAVE MANY LIVES TO LOSE, BUT YOU-
YOU ONLY HAVE ONE.
WHAT?!

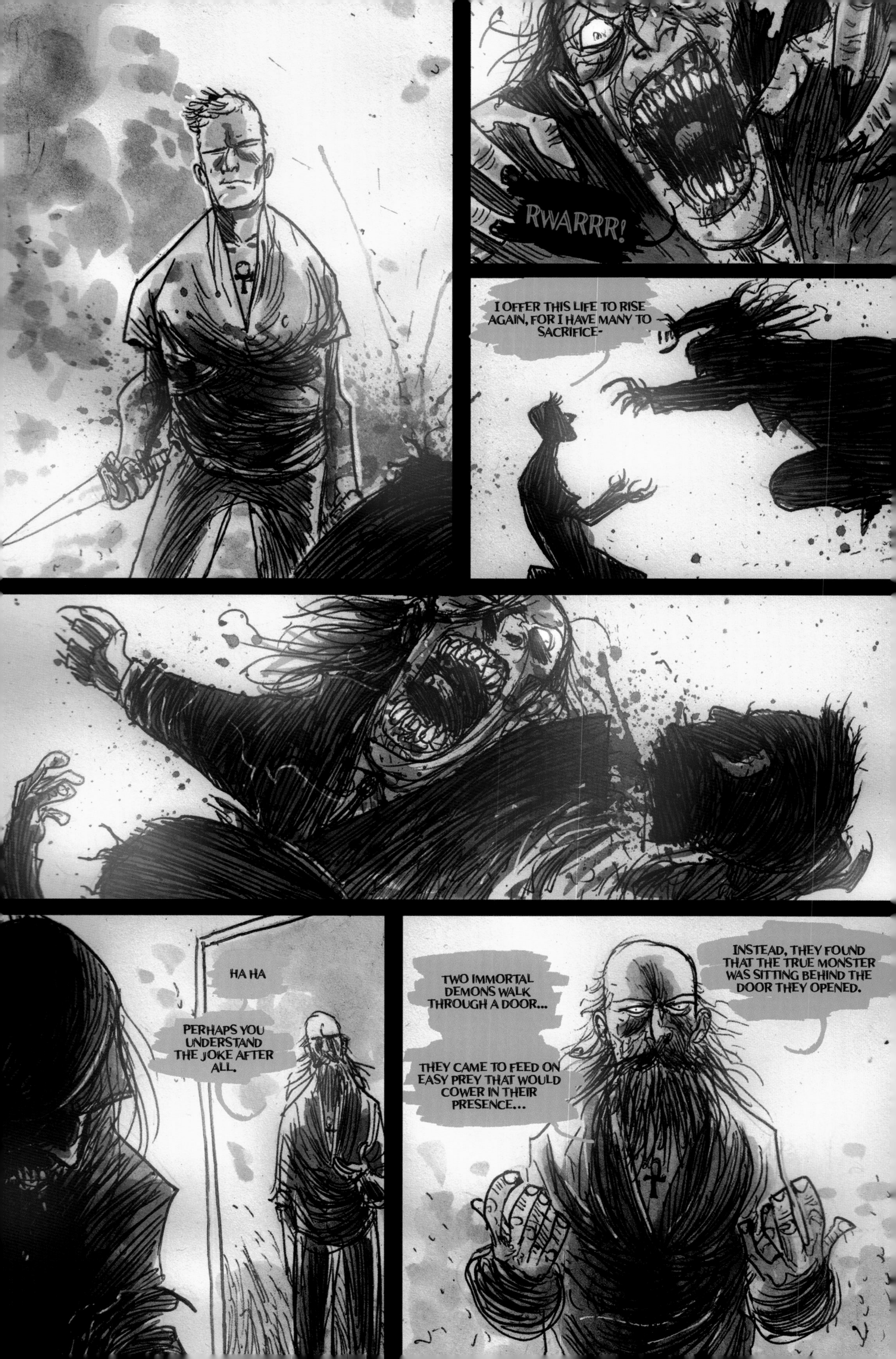
RWARRR!
I OFFER THIS LIFE TO RISE AGAIN, FOR I HAVE MANY TO SACRIFICE-
HA HA
PERHAPS YOU UNDERSTAND THE JOKE AFTER ALL.
TWO IMMORTAL DEMONS WALK THROUGH A DOOR...
THEY CAME TO FEED ON EASY PREY THAT WOULD COWER IN THEIR PRESENCE...
INSTEAD, THEY FOUND THAT THE TRUE MONSTER WAS SITTING BEHIND THE DOOR THEY OPENED.

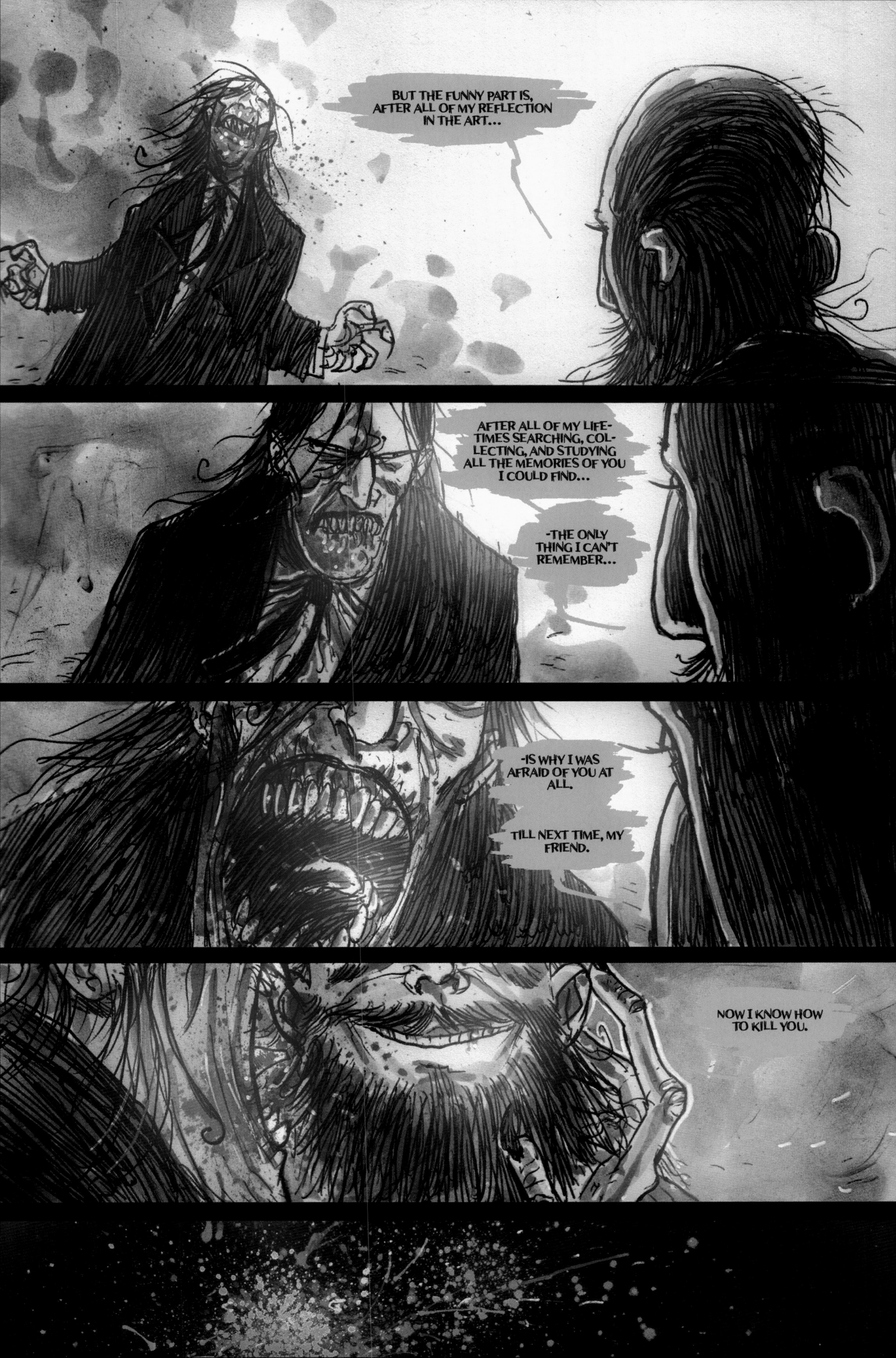

BUT THE FUNNY PART IS, AFTER ALL OF MY REFLECTION IN THE ART...
AFTER ALL OF MY LIFE-TIMES SEARCHING, COL-LECTING, AND STUDYING ALL THE MEMORIES OF YOU I COULD FIND...
-THE ONLY THING I CAN'T REMEMBER...
-IS WHY I WAS AFRAID OF YOU AT ALL.
TILL NEXT TIME, MY FRIEND.
NOW I KNOW HOW TO KILL YOU.

Story by : Jason Mote / Artwork by : Christopher Mitten

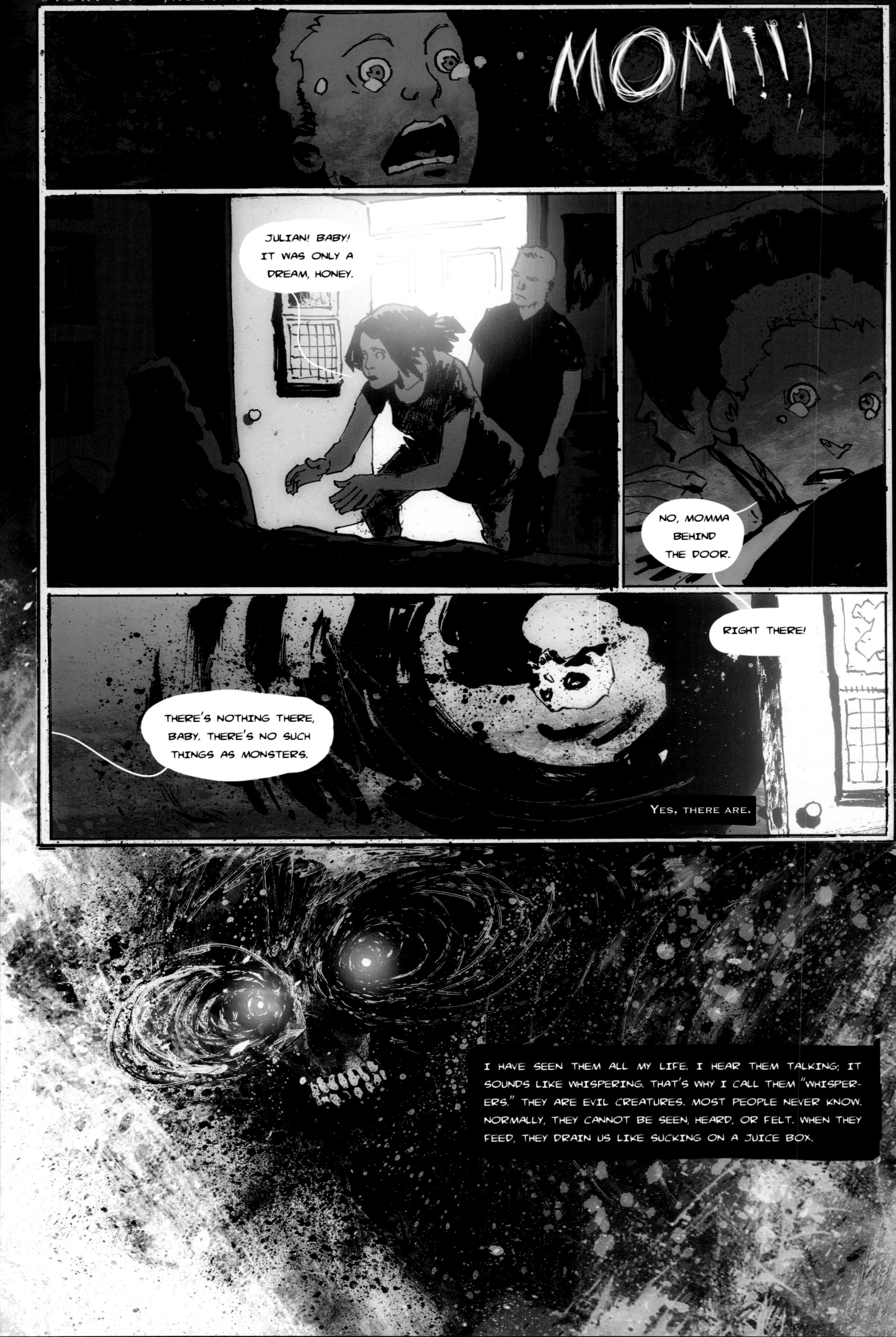
MOM!!!
JULIAN! BABY! IT WAS ONLY A DREAM, HONEY.
NO, MOMMA BEHIND THE DOOR.
RIGHT THERE!
THERE'S NOTHING THERE, BABY. THERE'S NO SUCH THINGS AS MONSTERS.
Yes, there are.
I HAVE SEEN THEM ALL MY LIFE. I HEAR THEM TALKING; IT SOUNDS LIKE WHISPERING. THAT'S WHY I CALL THEM "WHISPERERS." THEY ARE EVIL CREATURES. MOST PEOPLE NEVER KNOW. NORMALLY, THEY CANNOT BE SEEN, HEARD, OR FELT. WHEN THEY FEED, THEY DRAIN US LIKE SUCKING ON A JUICE BOX.

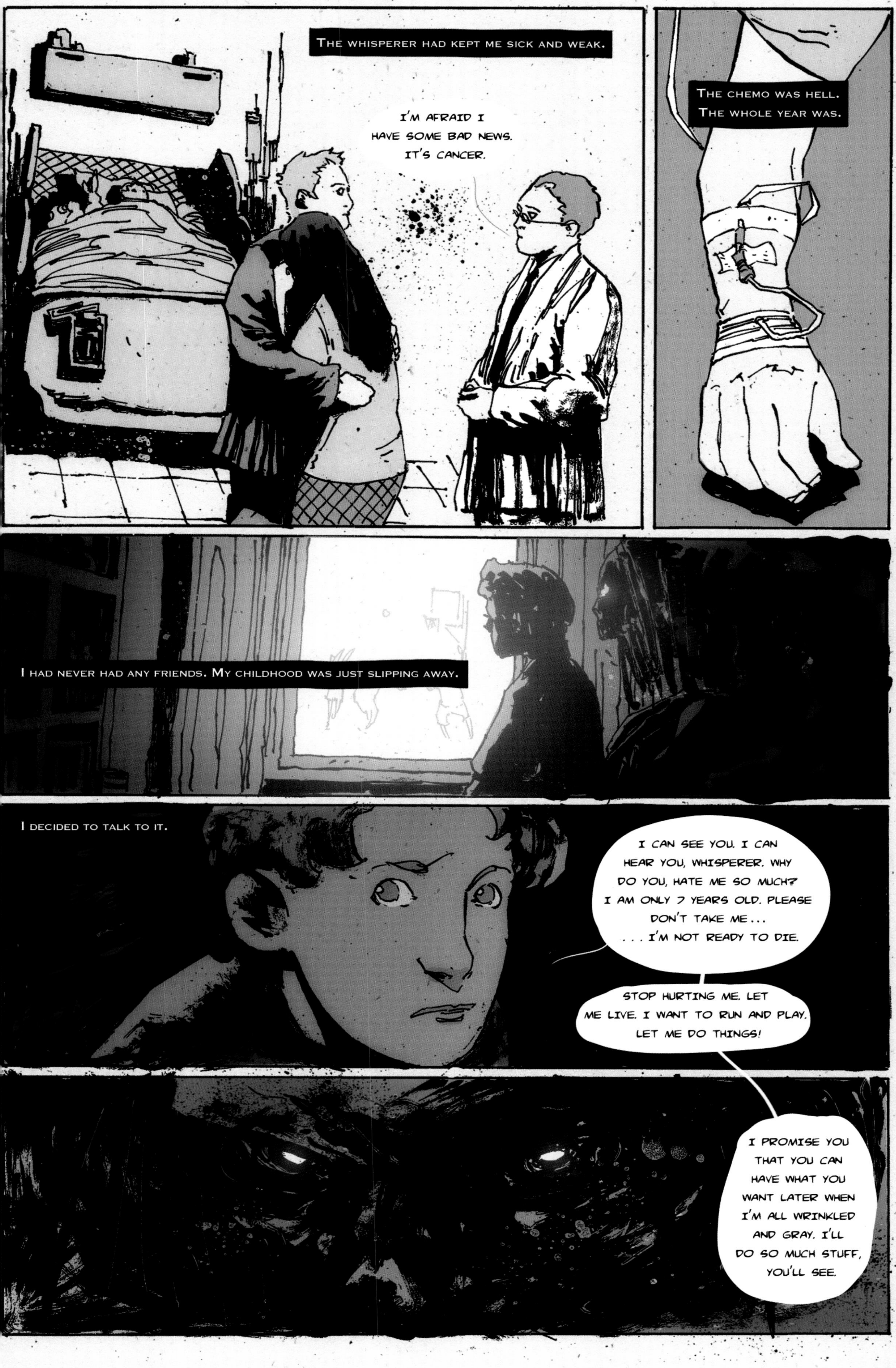
The whisperer had kept me sick and weak.
I'm afraid I have some bad news. It's cancer.
The chemo was hell. The whole year was.
I had never had any friends. My childhood was just slipping away.
I decided to talk to it.
I can see you. I can hear you, whisperer. Why do you, hate me so much? I am only 7 years old. Please don't take me... ...I'm not ready to die.
Stop hurting me. Let me live. I want to run and play. Let me do things!
I promise you that you can have what you want later when I'm all wrinkled and gray. I'll do so much stuff, you'll see.

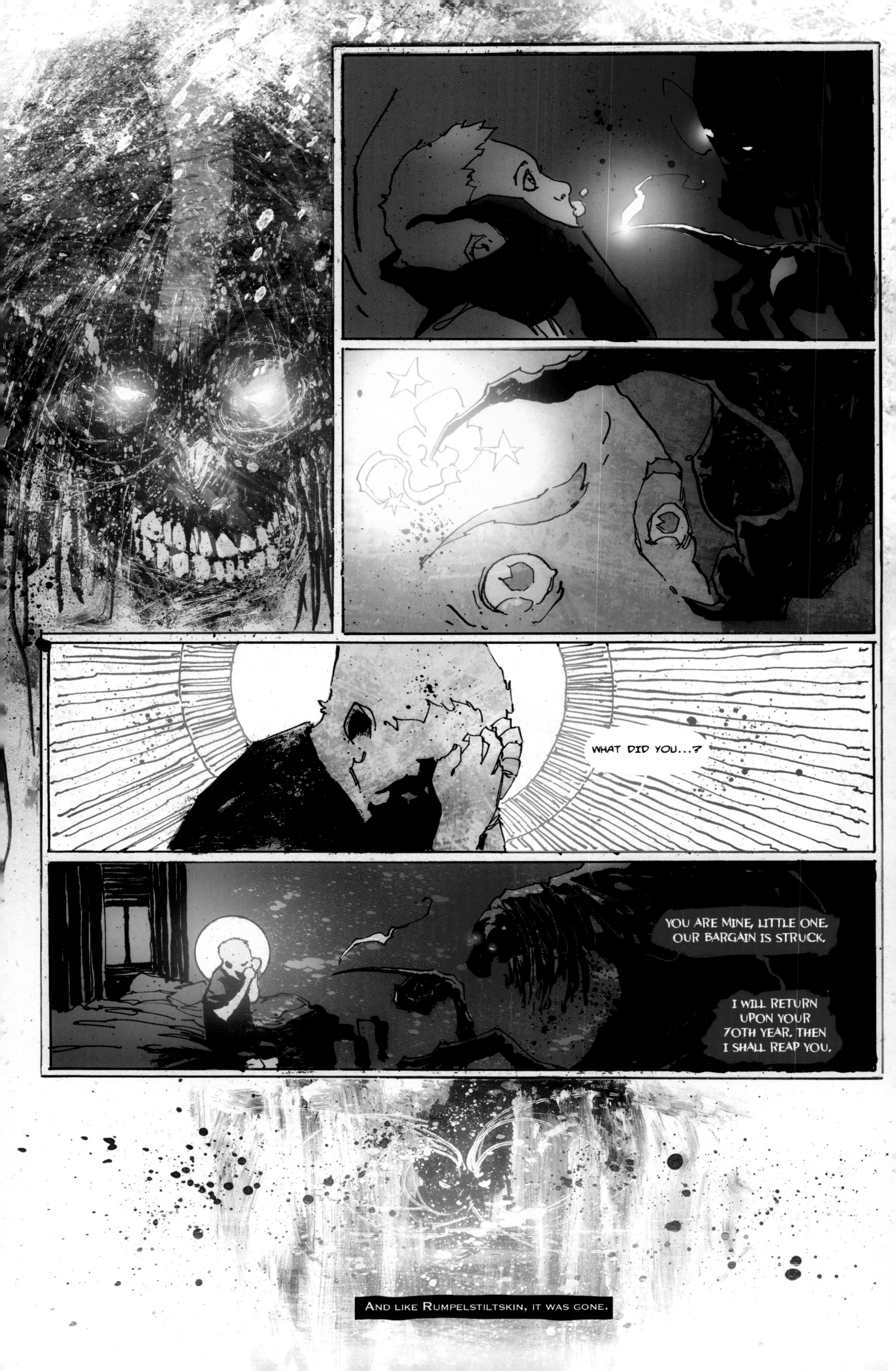
WHAT DID YOU...?
YOU ARE MINE, LITTLE ONE. OUR BARGAIN IS STRUCK.
I WILL RETURN UPON YOUR 70TH YEAR. THEN I SHALL REAP YOU.
And like Rumpelstiltskin, it was gone.

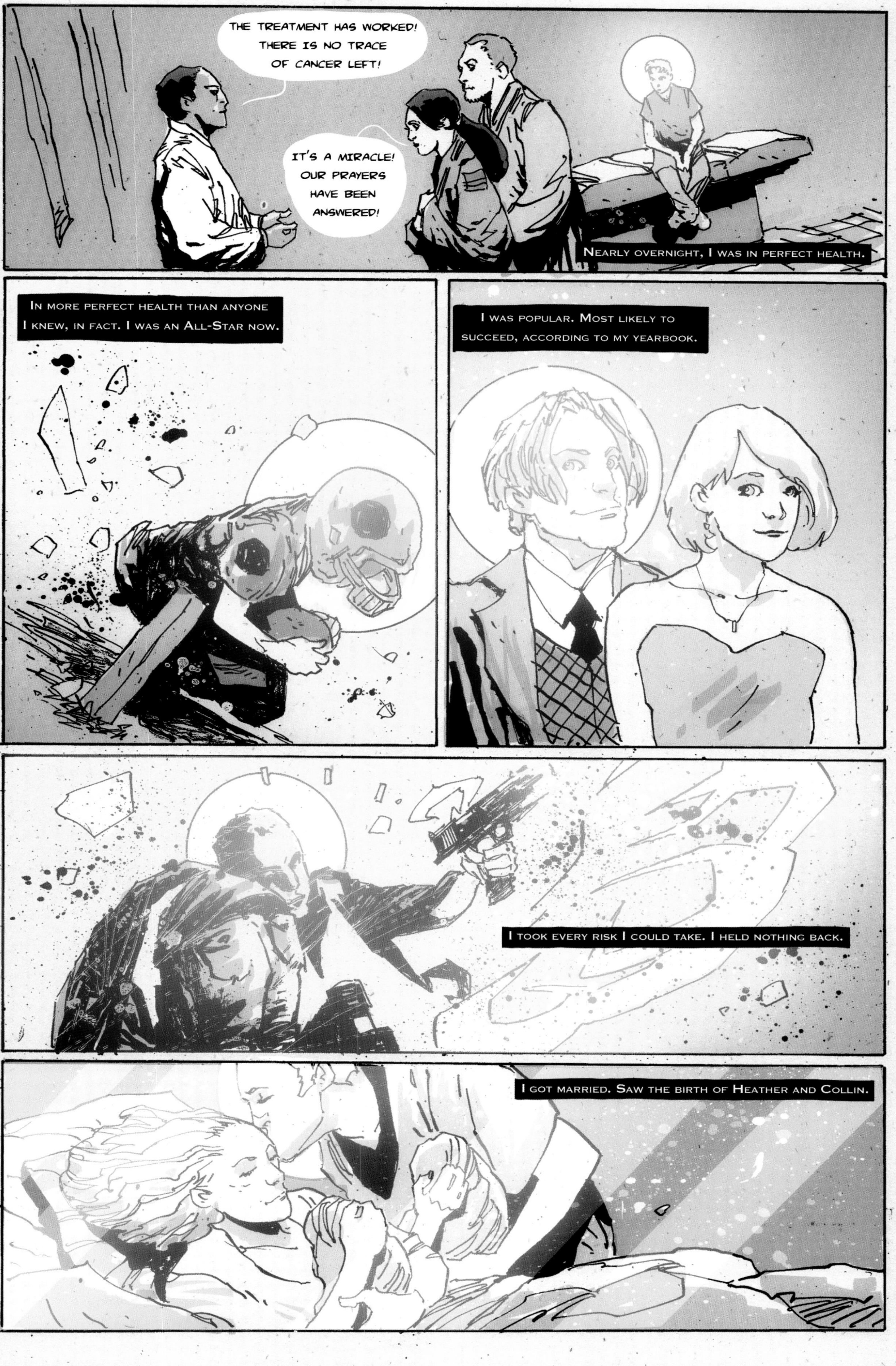
THE TREATMENT HAS WORKED! THERE IS NO TRACE OF CANCER LEFT!
IT'S A MIRACLE! OUR PRAYERS HAVE BEEN ANSWERED!
NEARLY OVERNIGHT, I WAS IN PERFECT HEALTH.
IN MORE PERFECT HEALTH THAN ANYONE I KNEW, IN FACT. I WAS AN ALL-STAR NOW.
I WAS POPULAR. MOST LIKELY TO SUCCEED, ACCORDING TO MY YEARBOOK.
I TOOK EVERY RISK I COULD TAKE. I HELD NOTHING BACK.
I GOT MARRIED. SAW THE BIRTH OF HEATHER AND COLLIN.

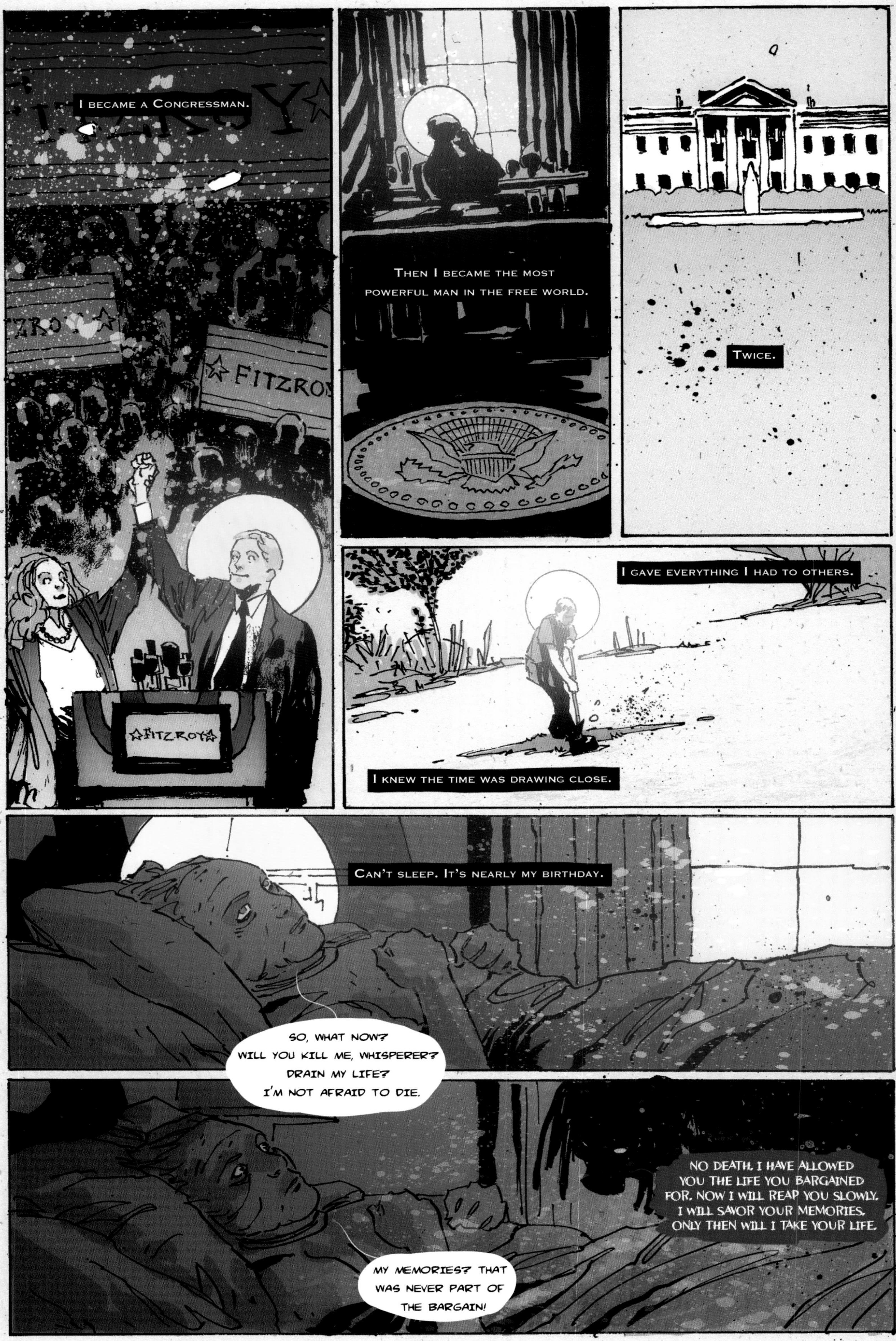
I became a Congressman.
FITZROY
FITZROY
FITZROY
Then I became the most powerful man in the free world.
Twice.
I gave everything I had to others.
I knew the time was drawing close.
Can't sleep. It's nearly my birthday.
SO, WHAT NOW? WILL YOU KILL ME, WHISPERER? DRAIN MY LIFE? I'M NOT AFRAID TO DIE.
NO DEATH. I HAVE ALLOWED YOU THE LIFE YOU BARGAINED FOR. NOW I WILL REAP YOU SLOWLY. I WILL SAVOR YOUR MEMORIES. ONLY THEN WILL I TAKE YOUR LIFE.
MY MEMORIES? THAT WAS NEVER PART OF THE BARGAIN!

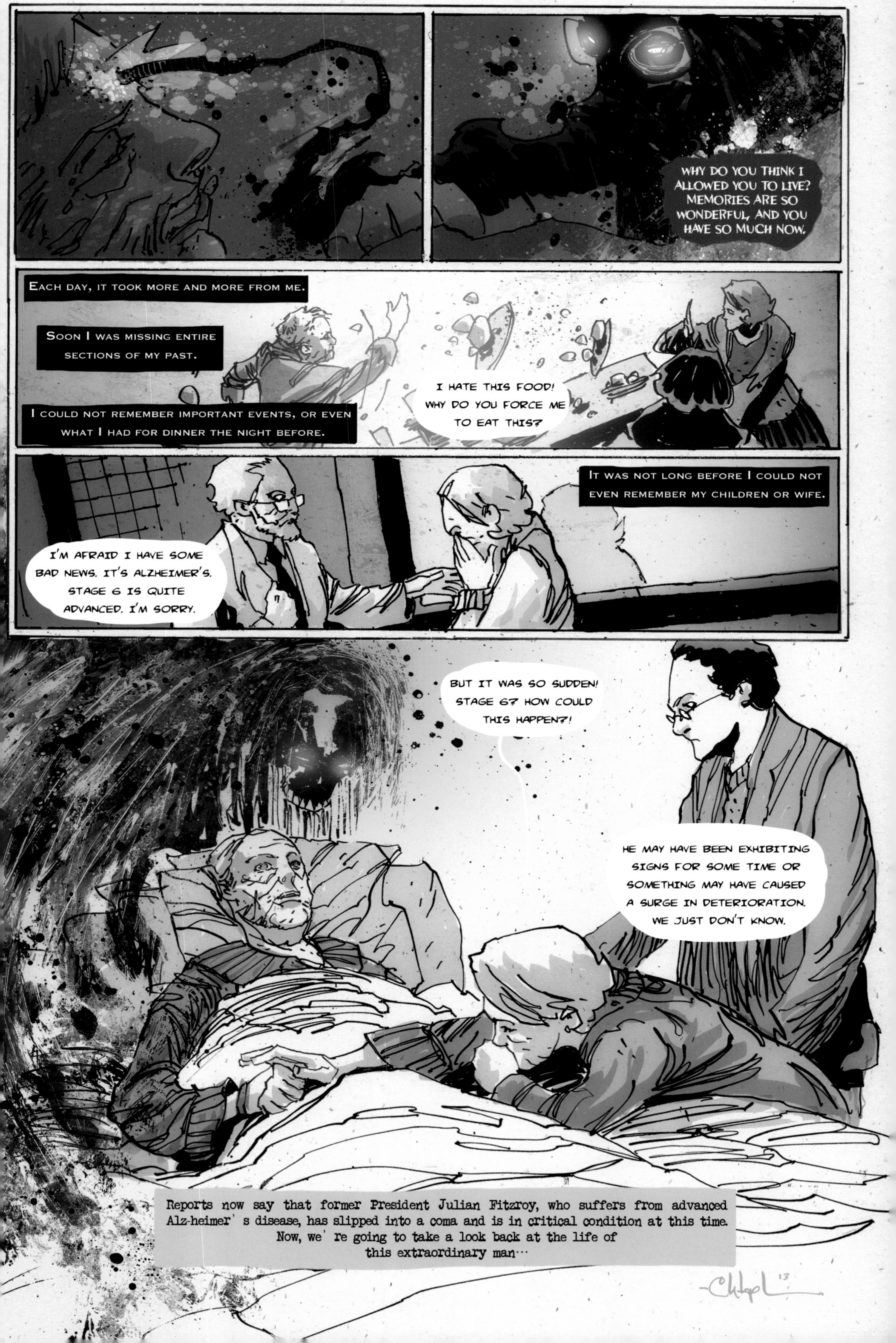
WHY DO YOU THINK I ALLOWED YOU TO LIVE? MEMORIES ARE SO WONDERFUL, AND YOU HAVE SO MUCH NOW.
EACH DAY, IT TOOK MORE AND MORE FROM ME.
SOON I WAS MISSING ENTIRE SECTIONS OF MY PAST.
I COULD NOT REMEMBER IMPORTANT EVENTS, OR EVEN WHAT I HAD FOR DINNER THE NIGHT BEFORE.
I HATE THIS FOOD! WHY DO YOU FORCE ME TO EAT THIS?
IT WAS NOT LONG BEFORE I COULD NOT EVEN REMEMBER MY CHILDREN OR WIFE.
I'M AFRAID I HAVE SOME BAD NEWS. IT'S ALZHEIMER'S. STAGE 6 IS QUITE ADVANCED. I'M SORRY.
BUT IT WAS SO SUDDEN! STAGE 6? HOW COULD THIS HAPPEN?!
HE MAY HAVE BEEN EXHIBITING SIGNS FOR SOME TIME OR SOMETHING MAY HAVE CAUSED A SURGE IN DETERIORATION. WE JUST DON'T KNOW.
Reports now say that former President Julian Fitzroy, who suffers from advanced Alz-heimer' s disease, has slipped into a coma and is in critical condition at this time. Now, we' re going to take a look back at the life of this extraordinary man···

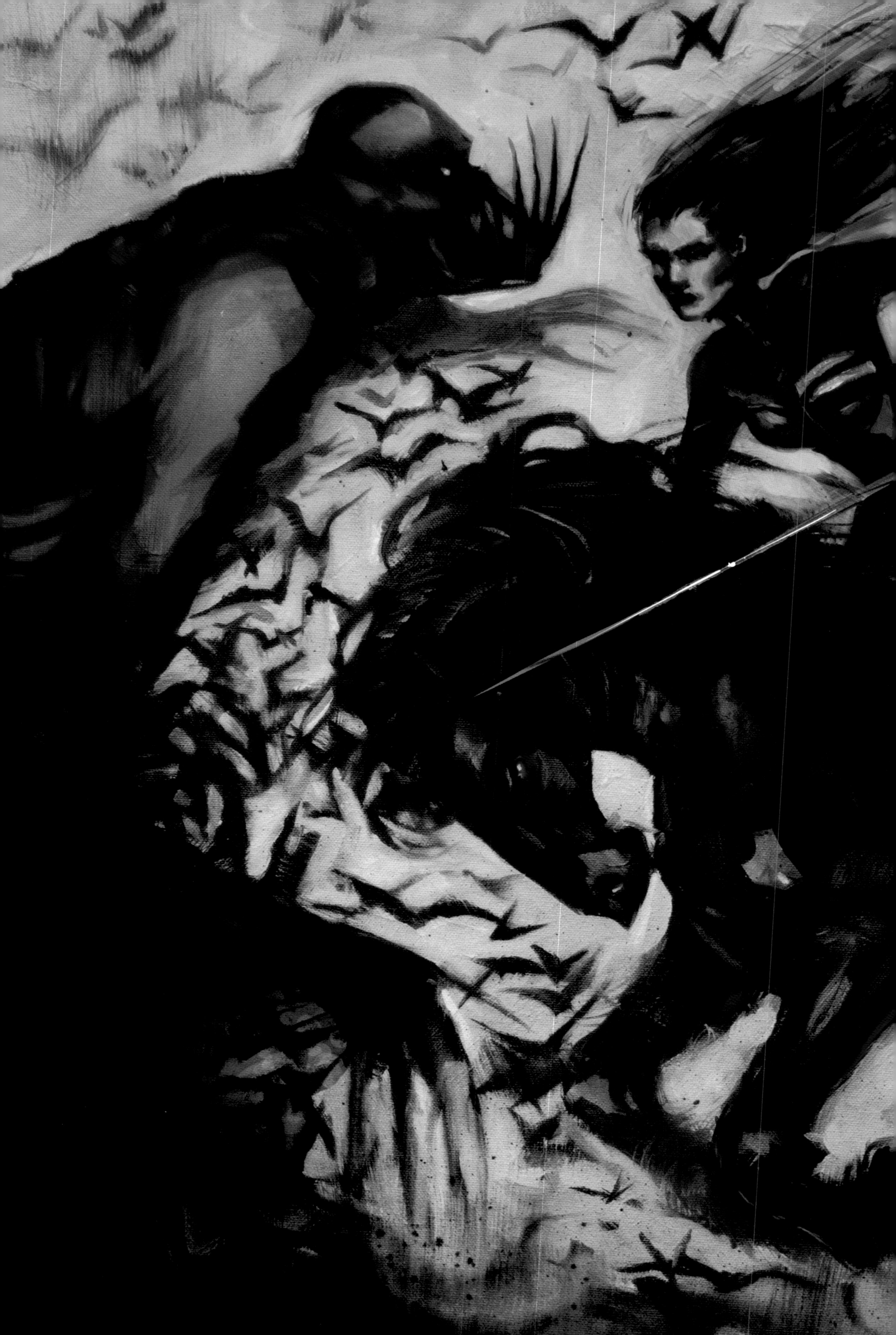

PINUP BY DANIELLE OTRAKJI

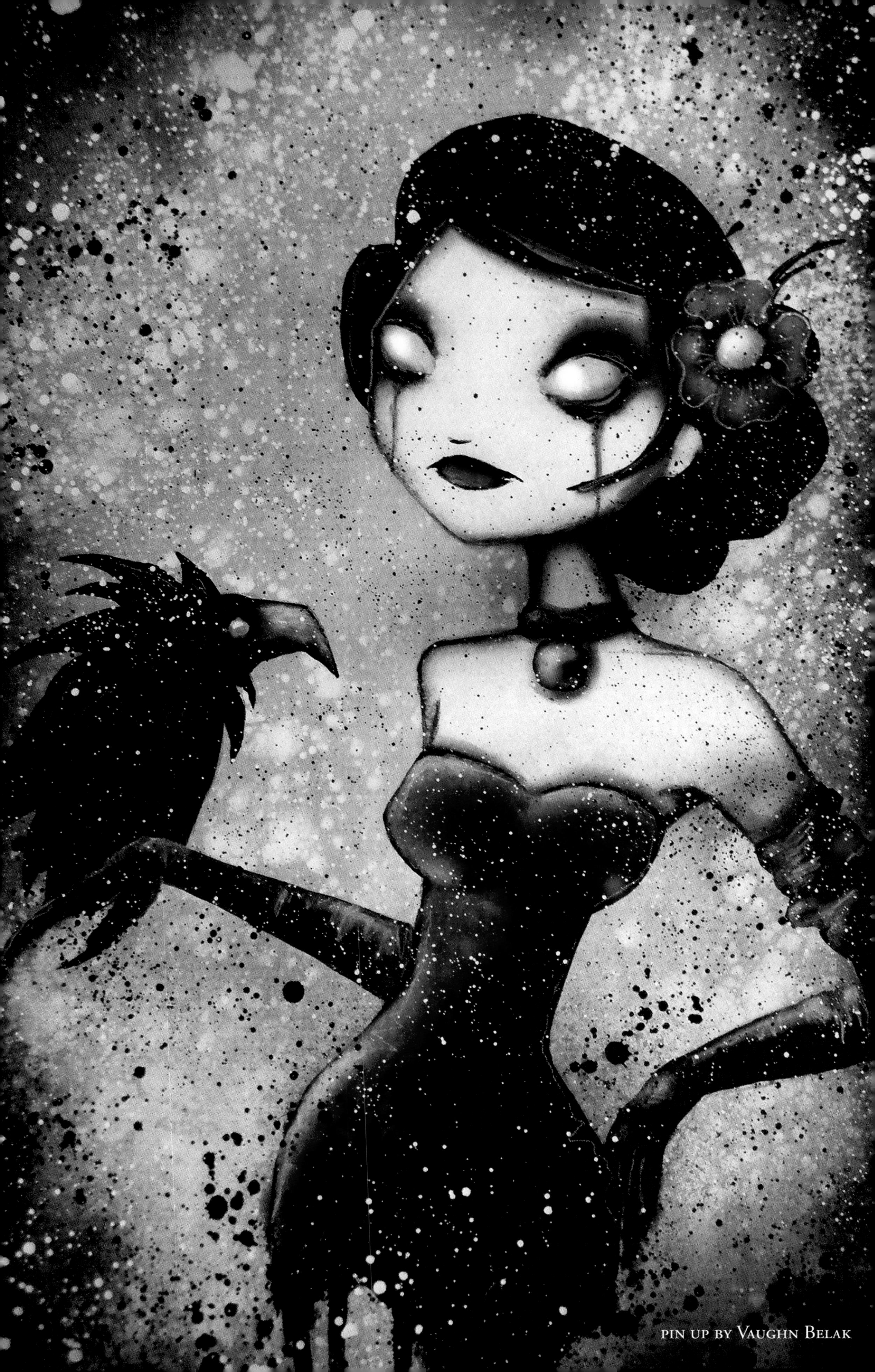

pin up by Vaughn Belak

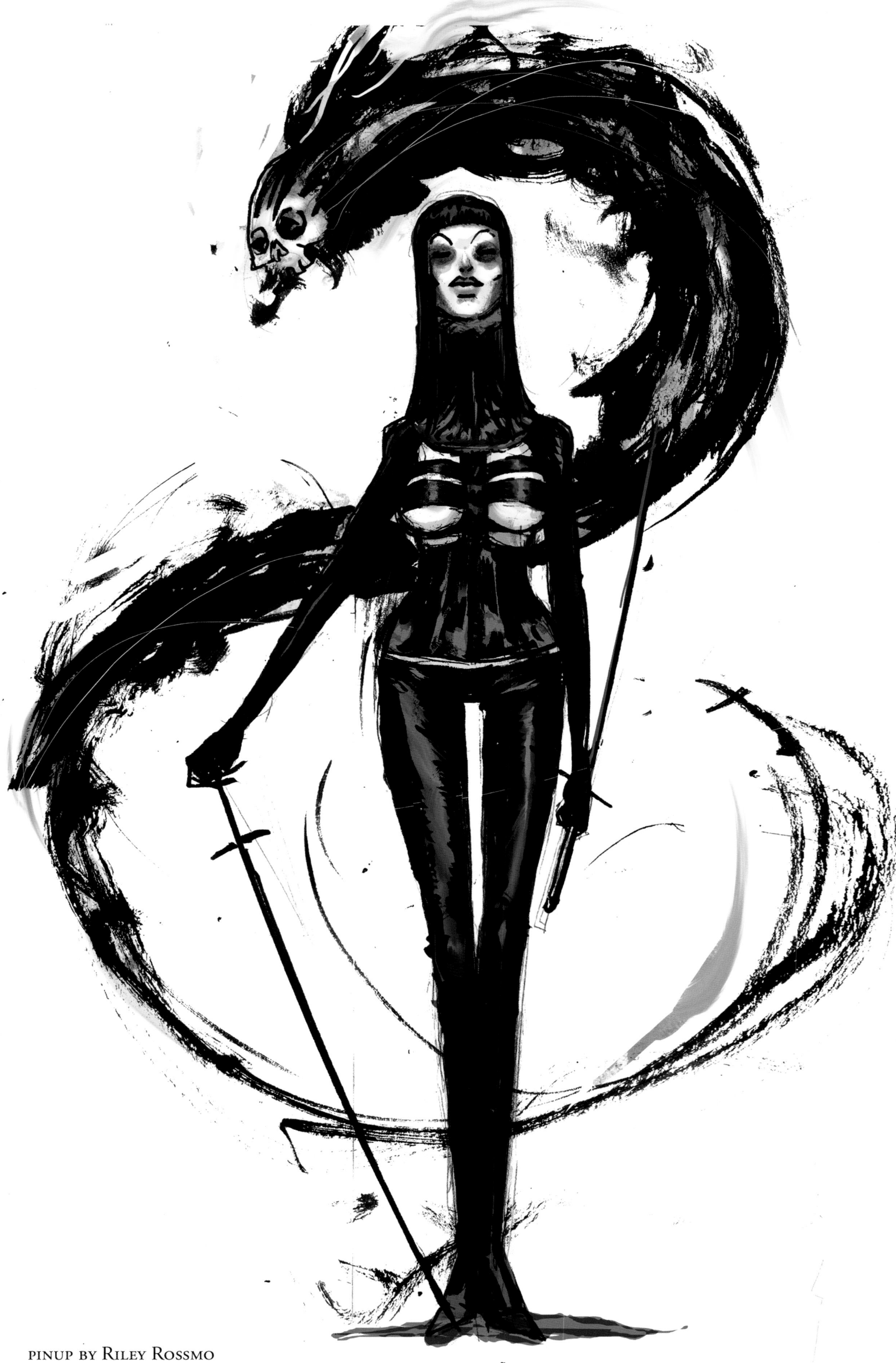

PINUP BY RILEY ROSSMO

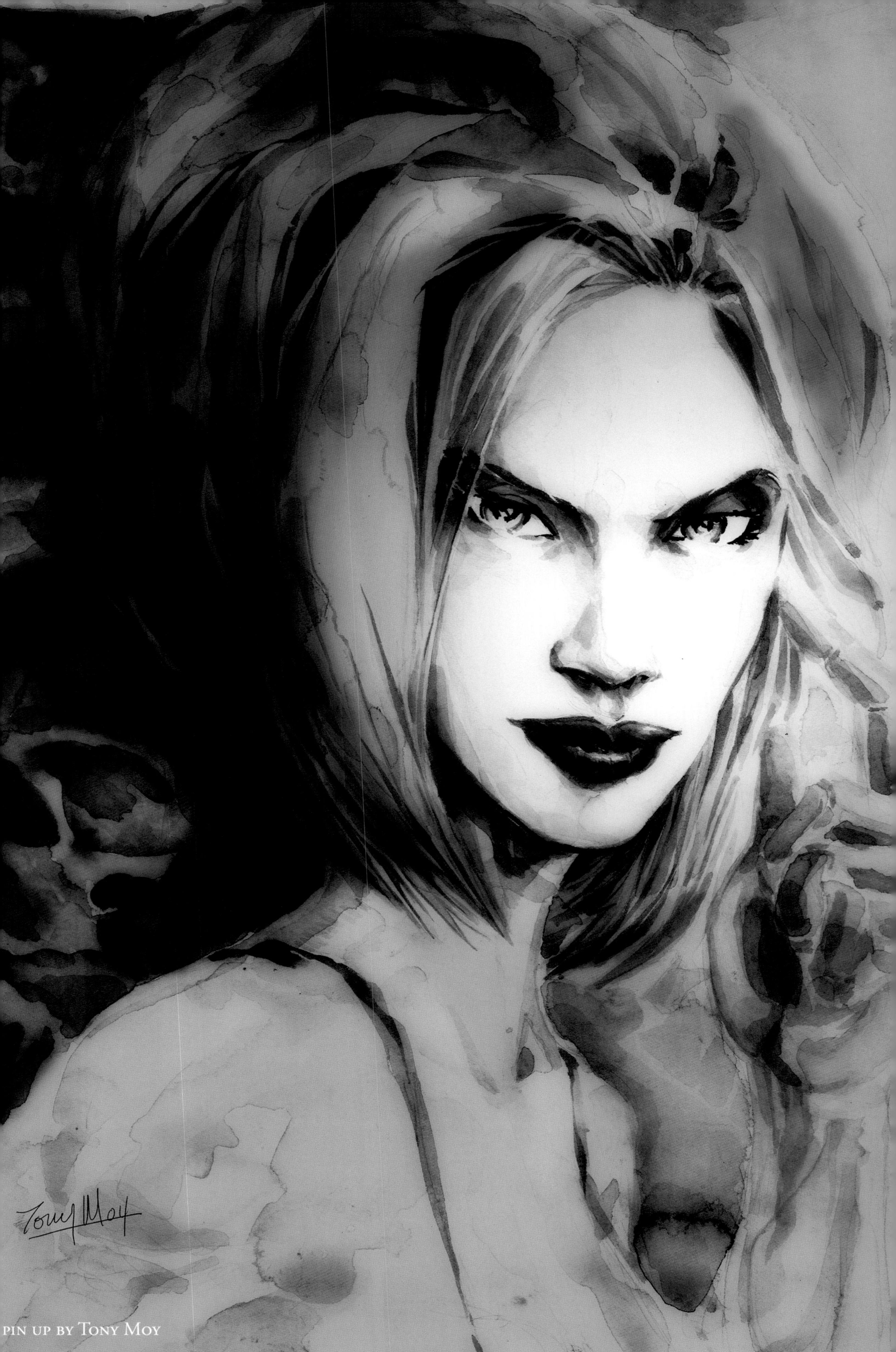
Tony Moy

PIN UP BY TONY MOY

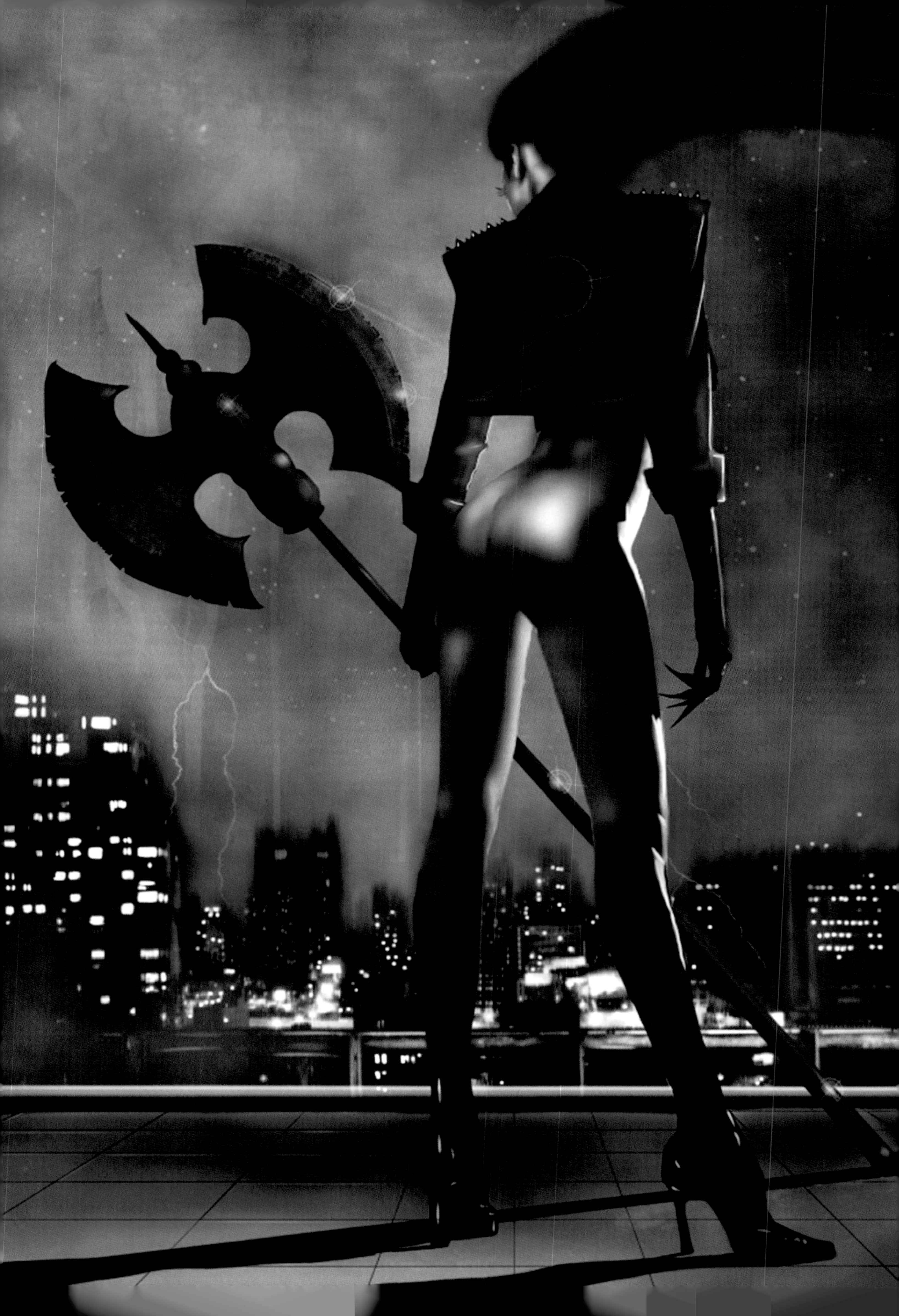

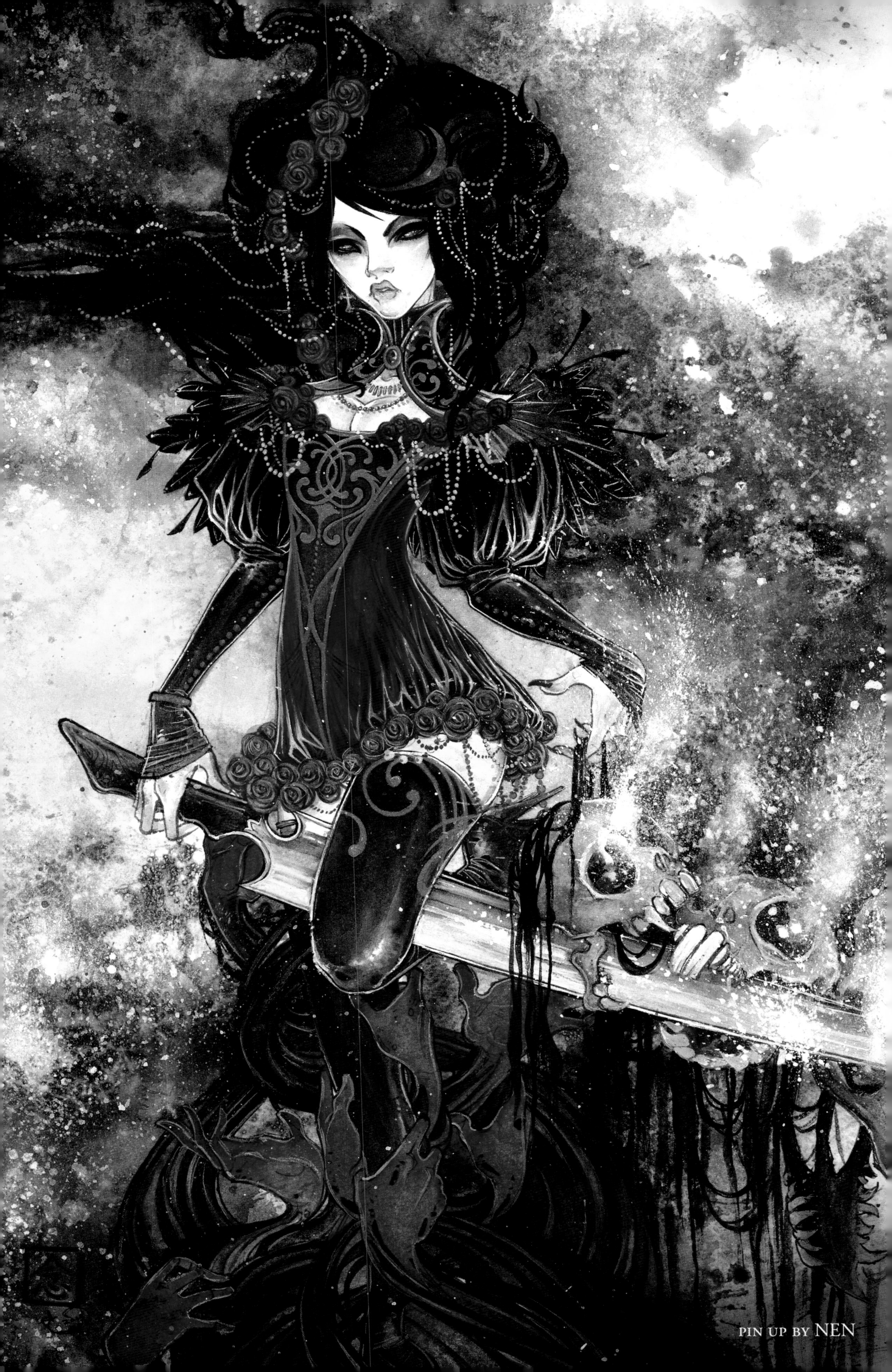

PIN UP BY NEN

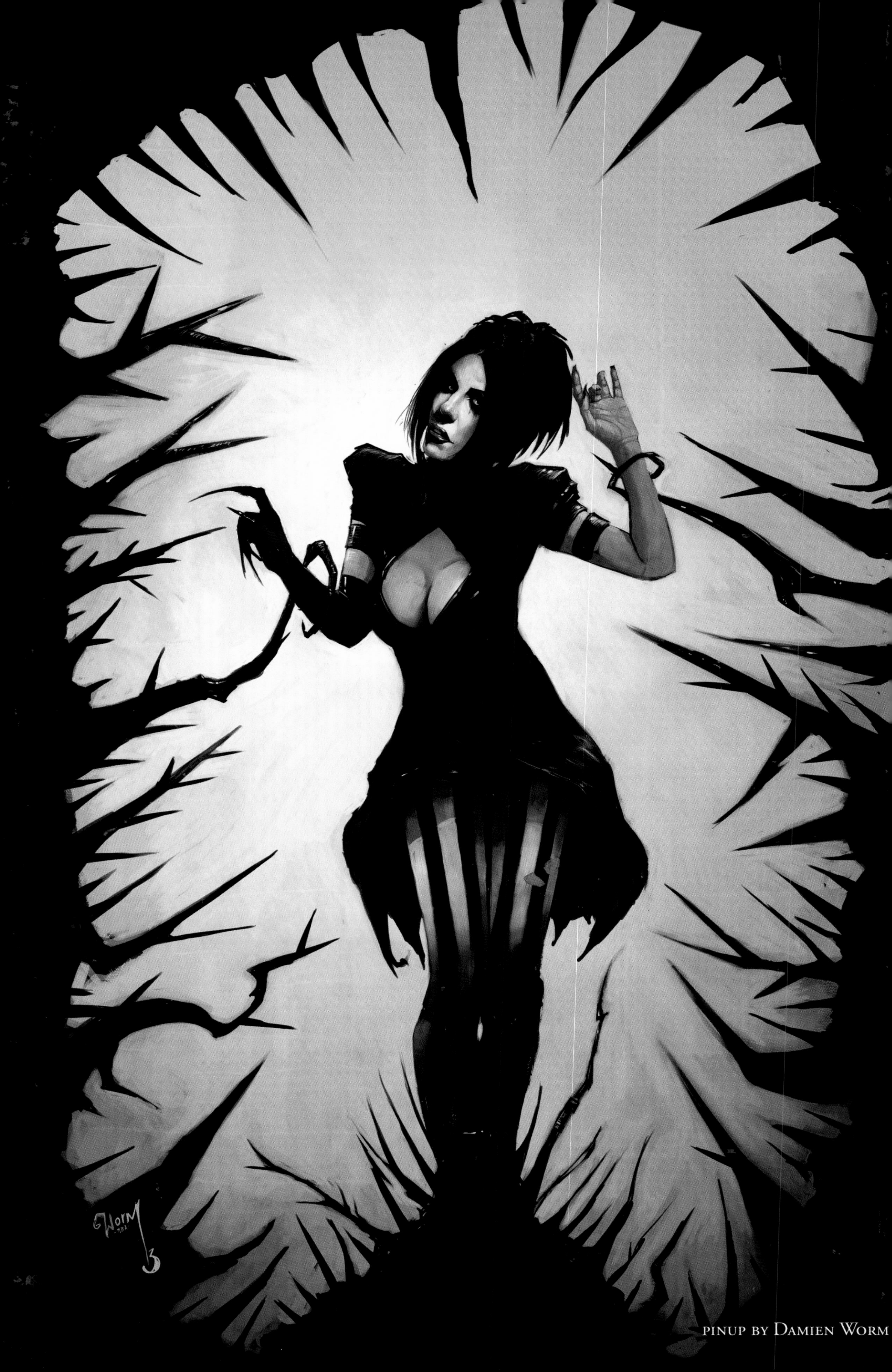
Worm
MBA
3

PINUP BY DAMIEN WORM

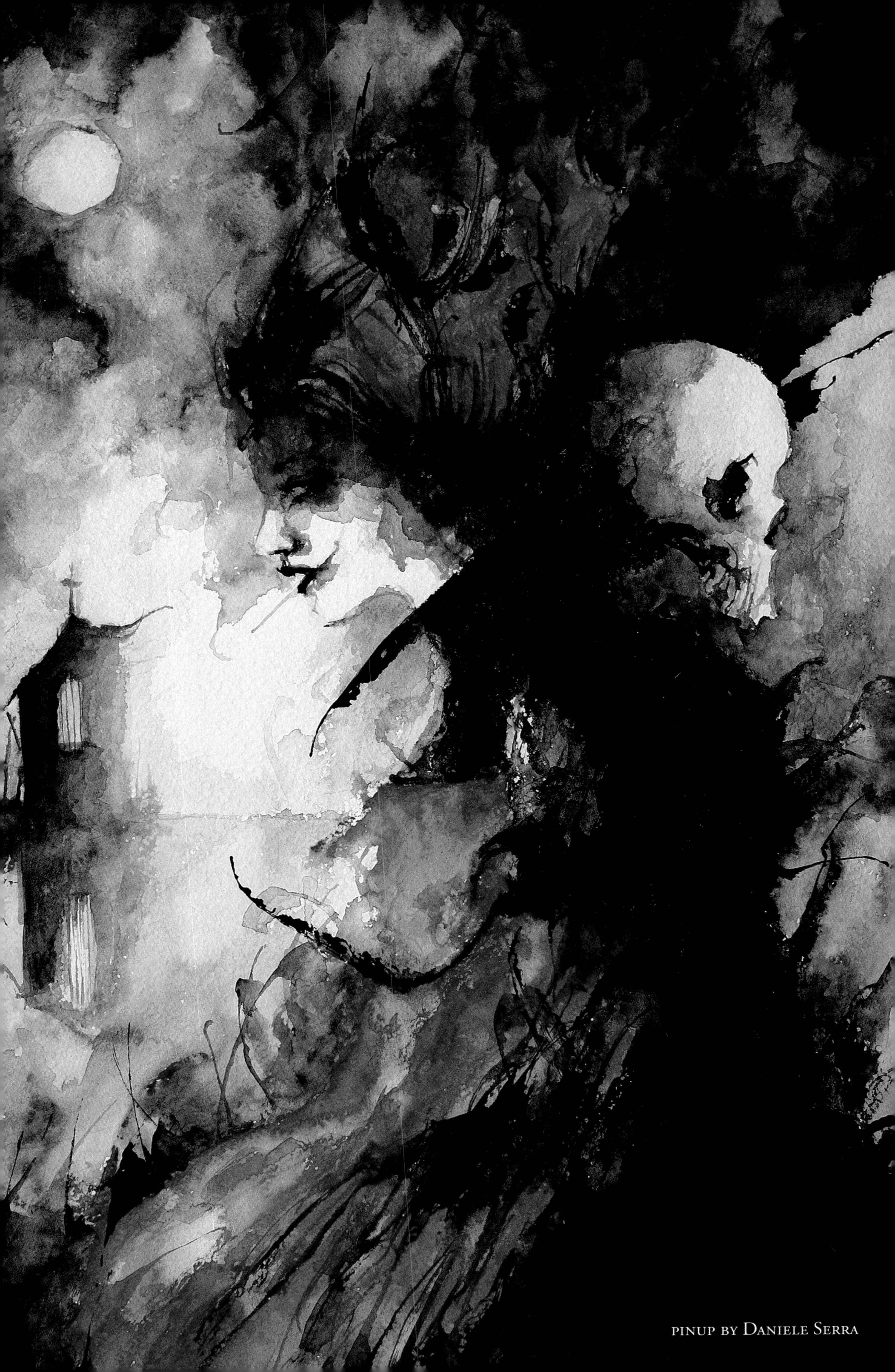

PINUP BY DANIELE SERRA

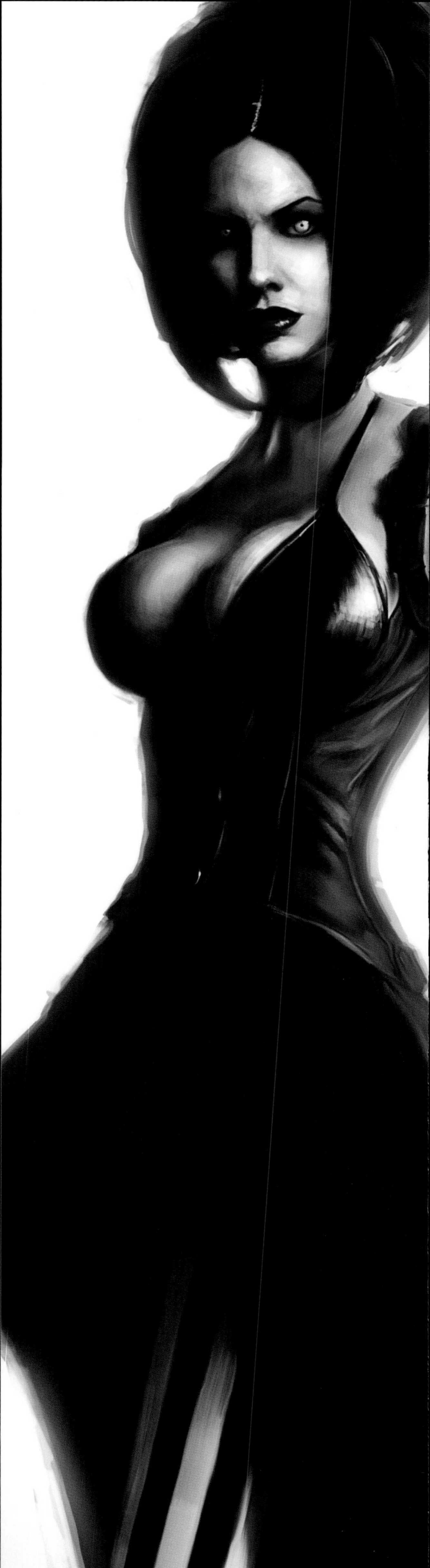

er 1A issue 1
by menton3

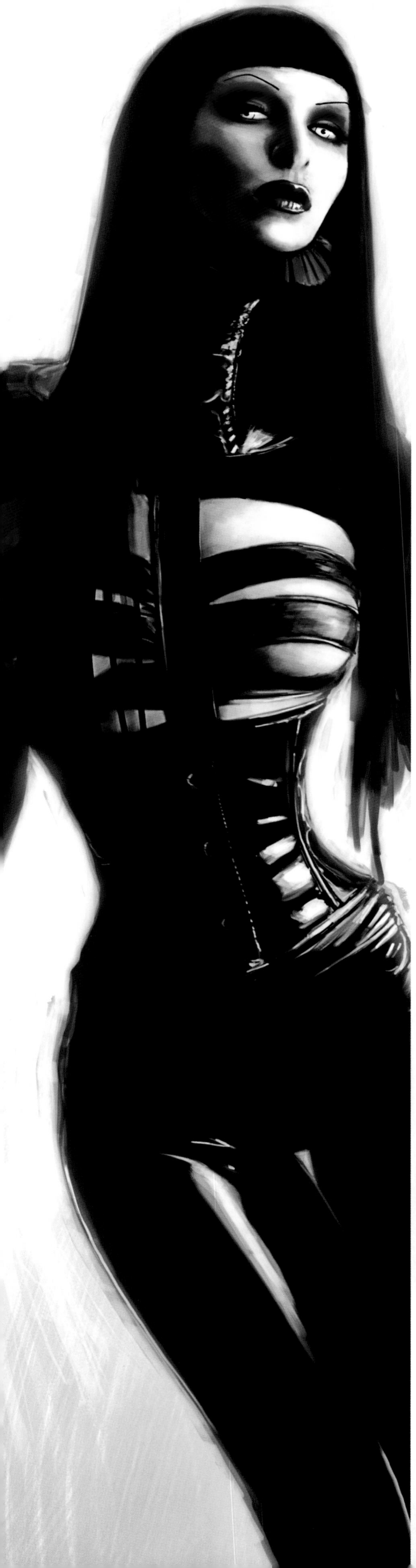
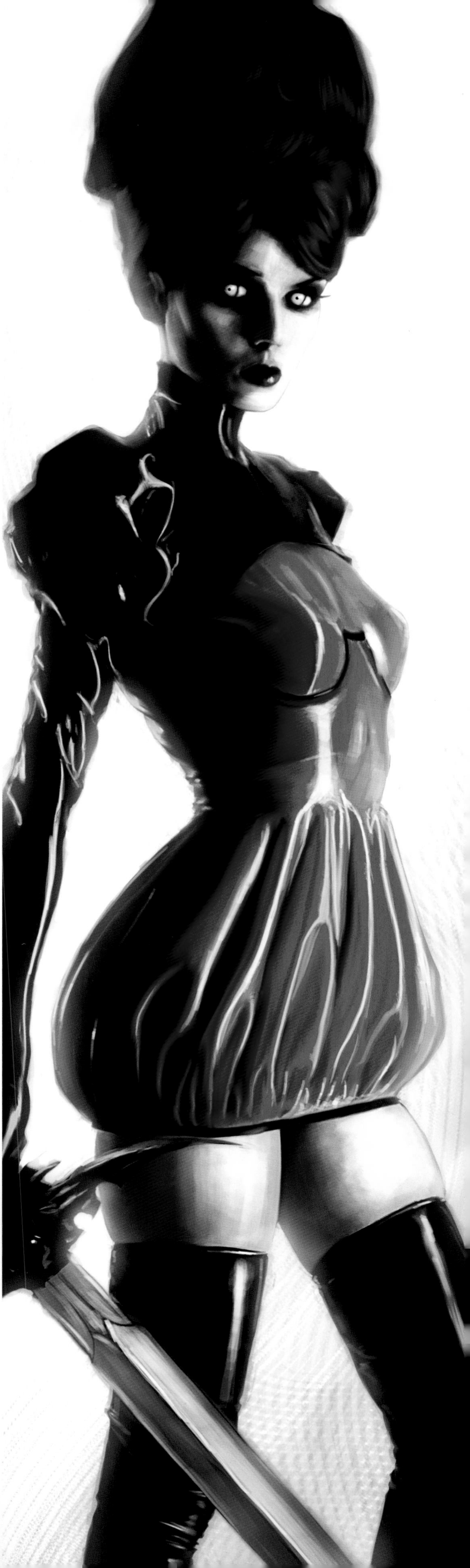

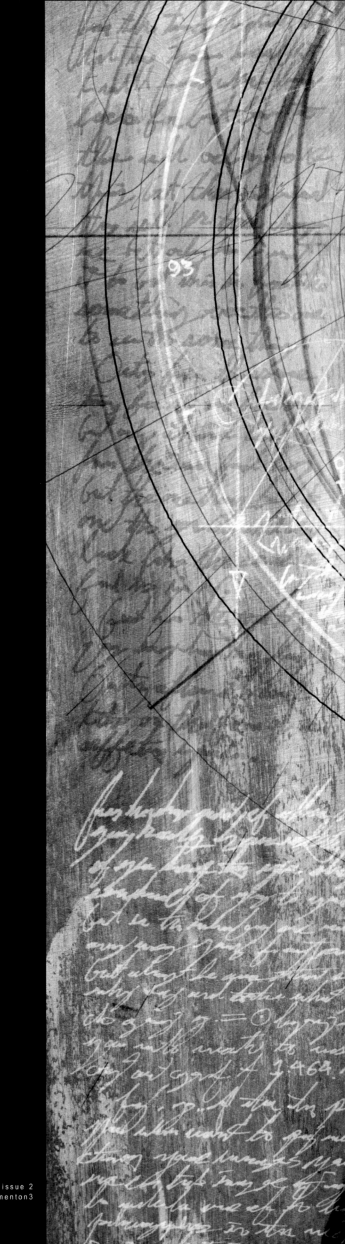

Cover 1A issue 2
by menton3

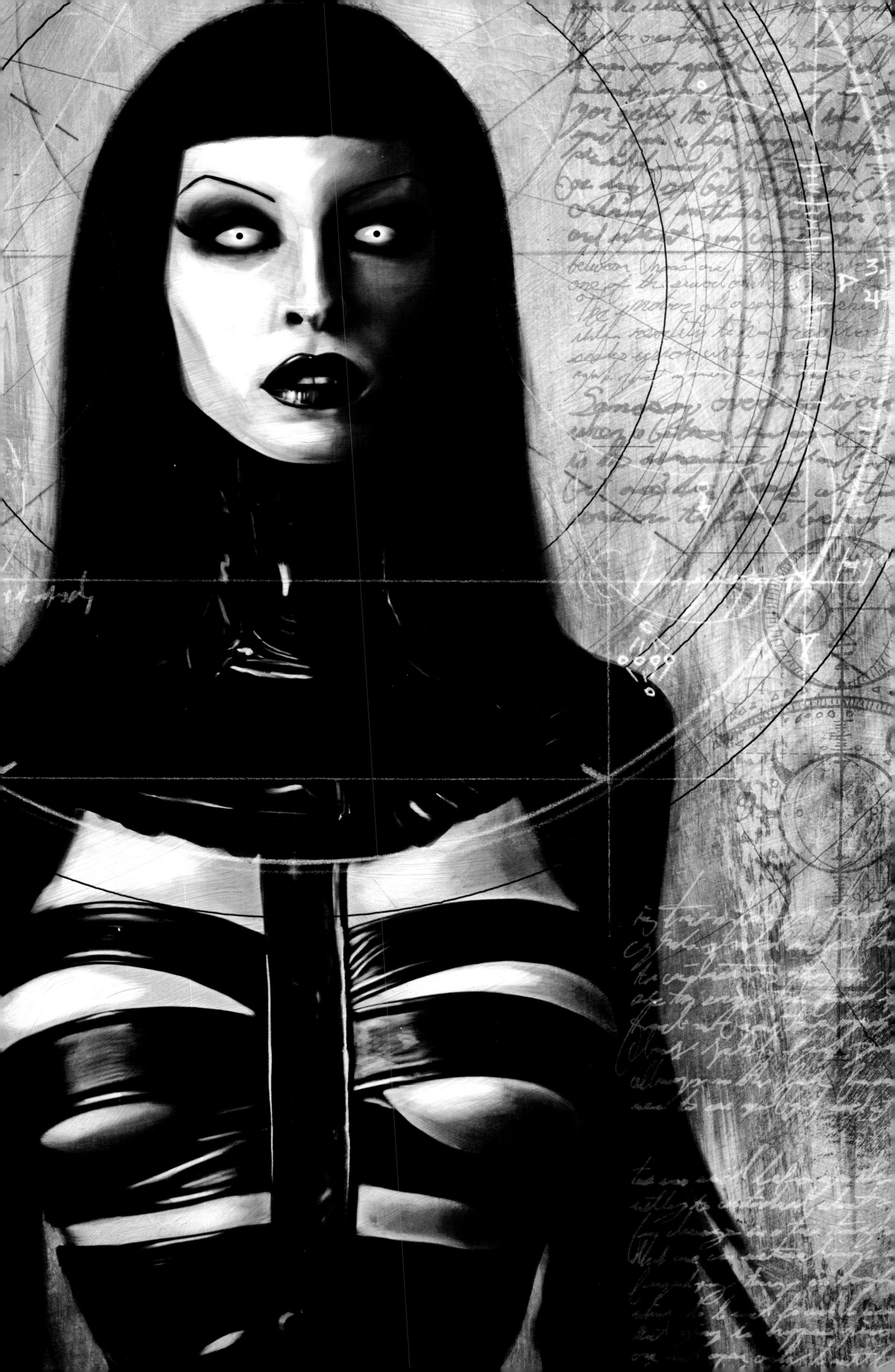

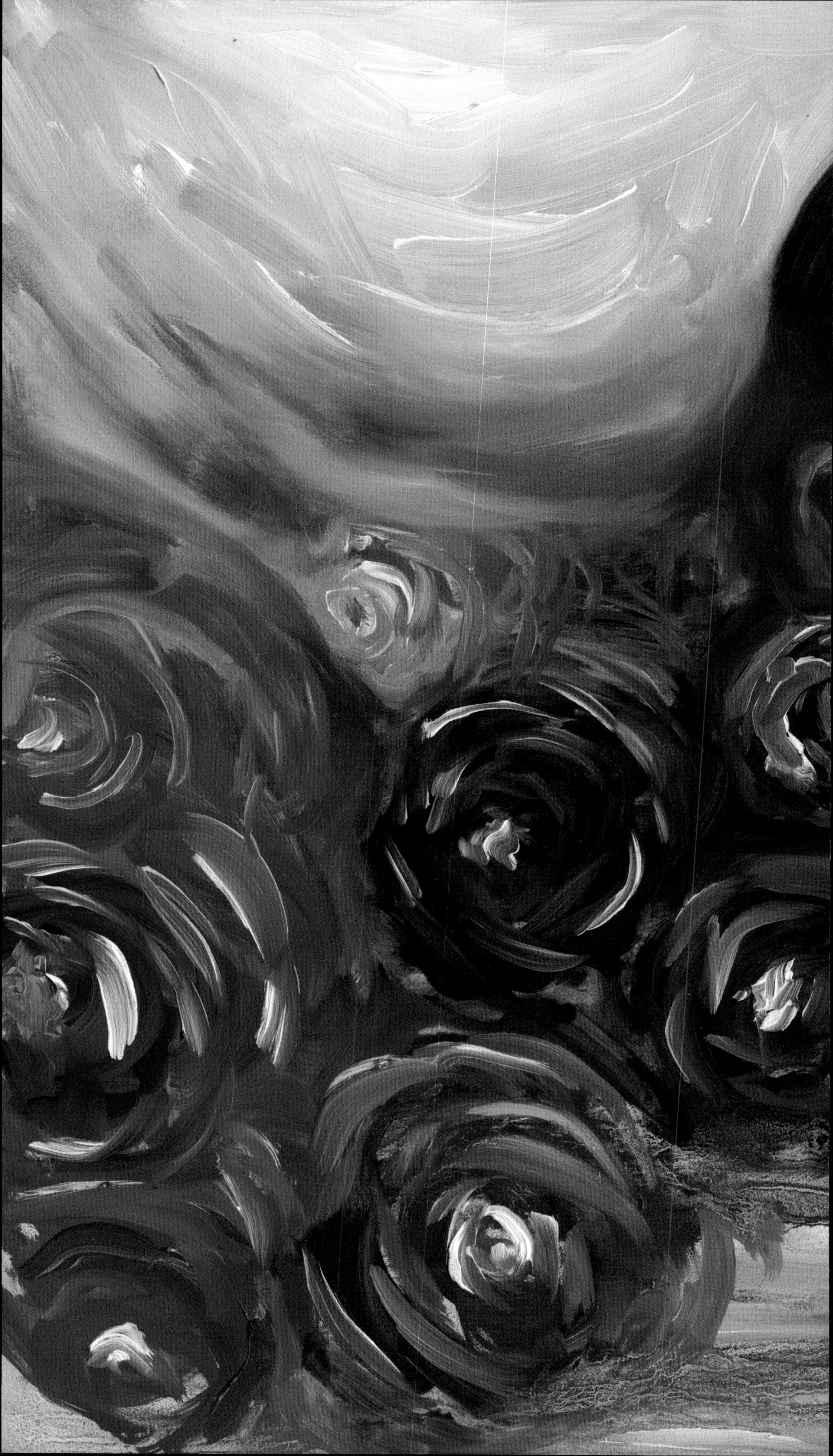

ty clare 2 " by menton3
Oil on Panel 11x14

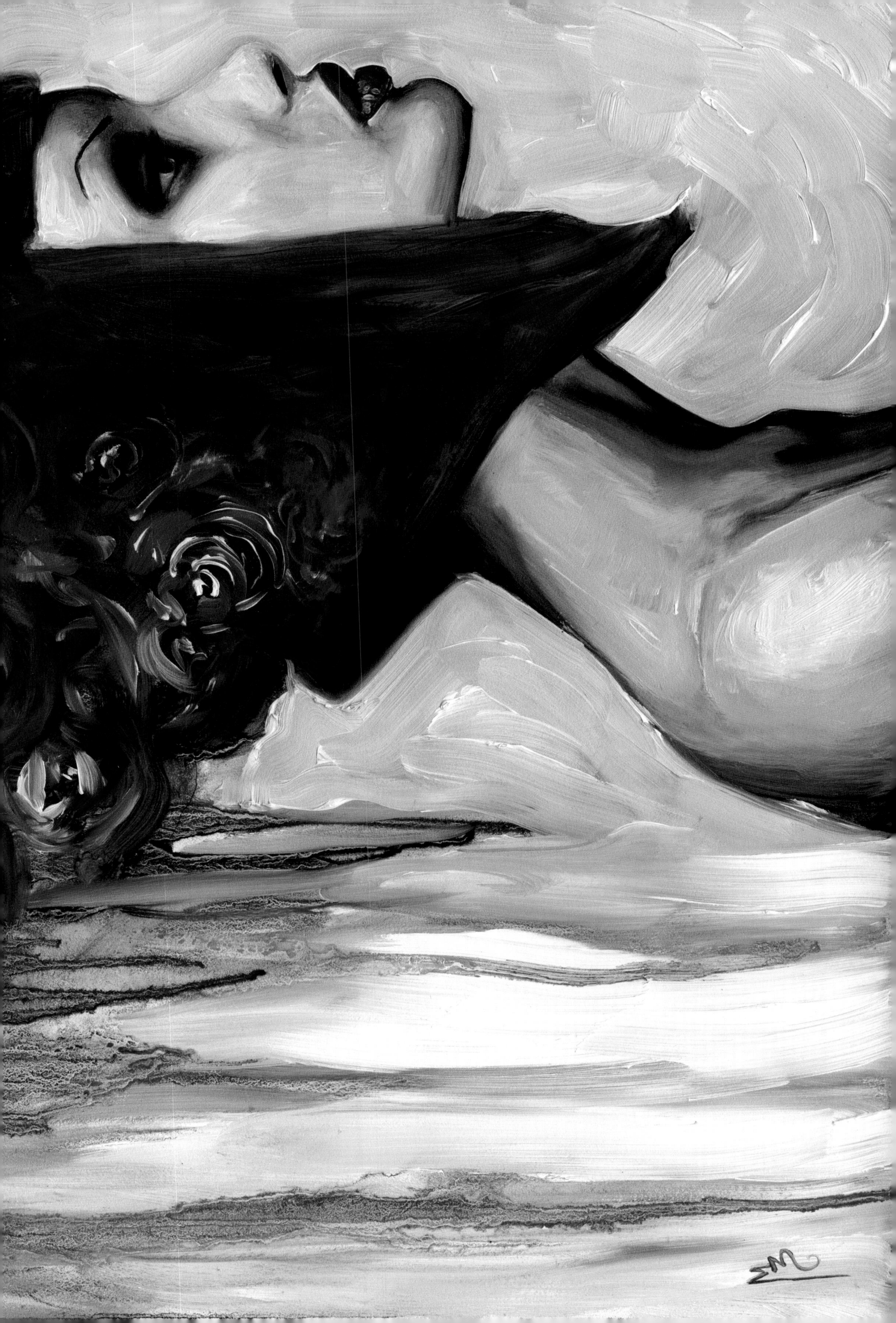

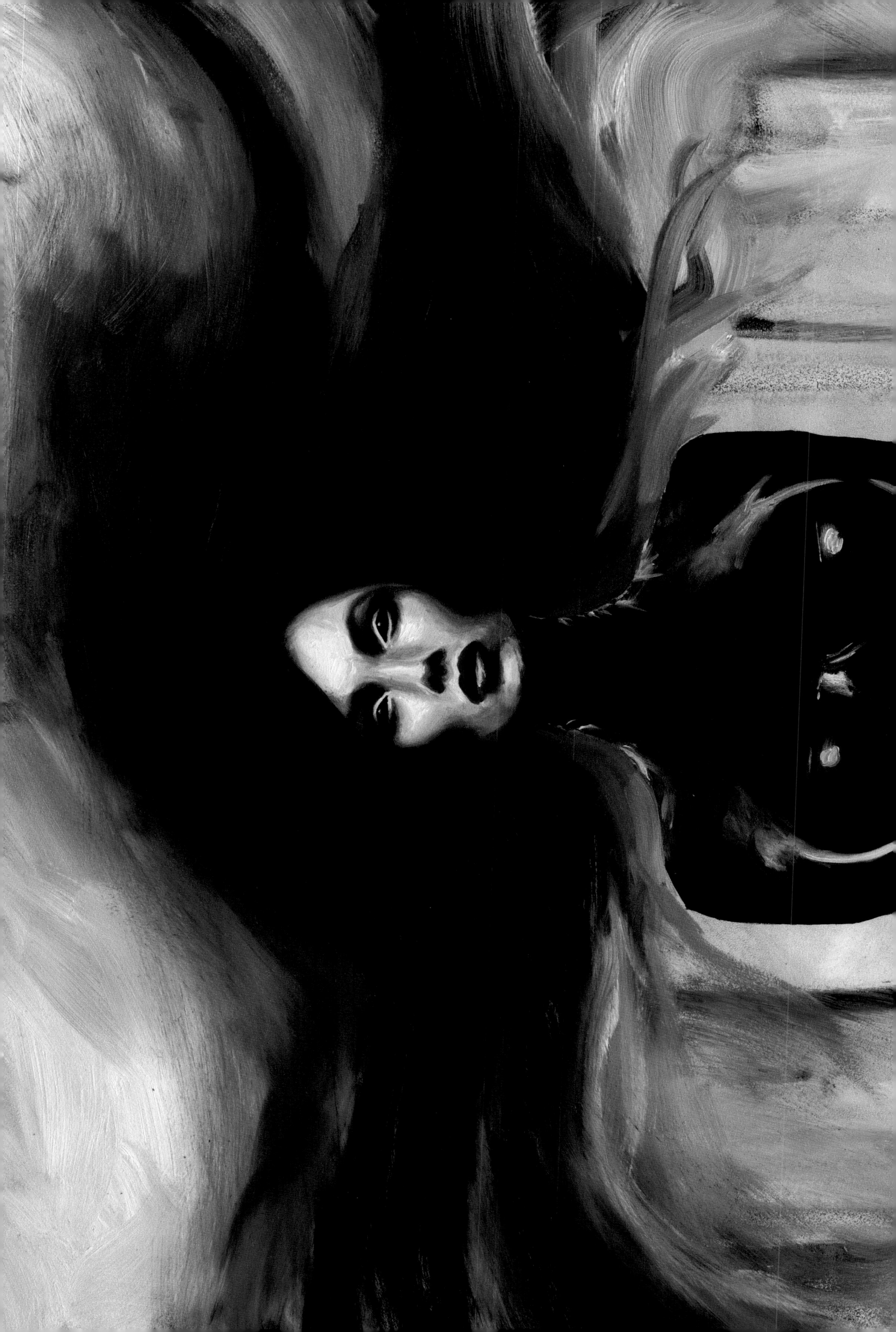

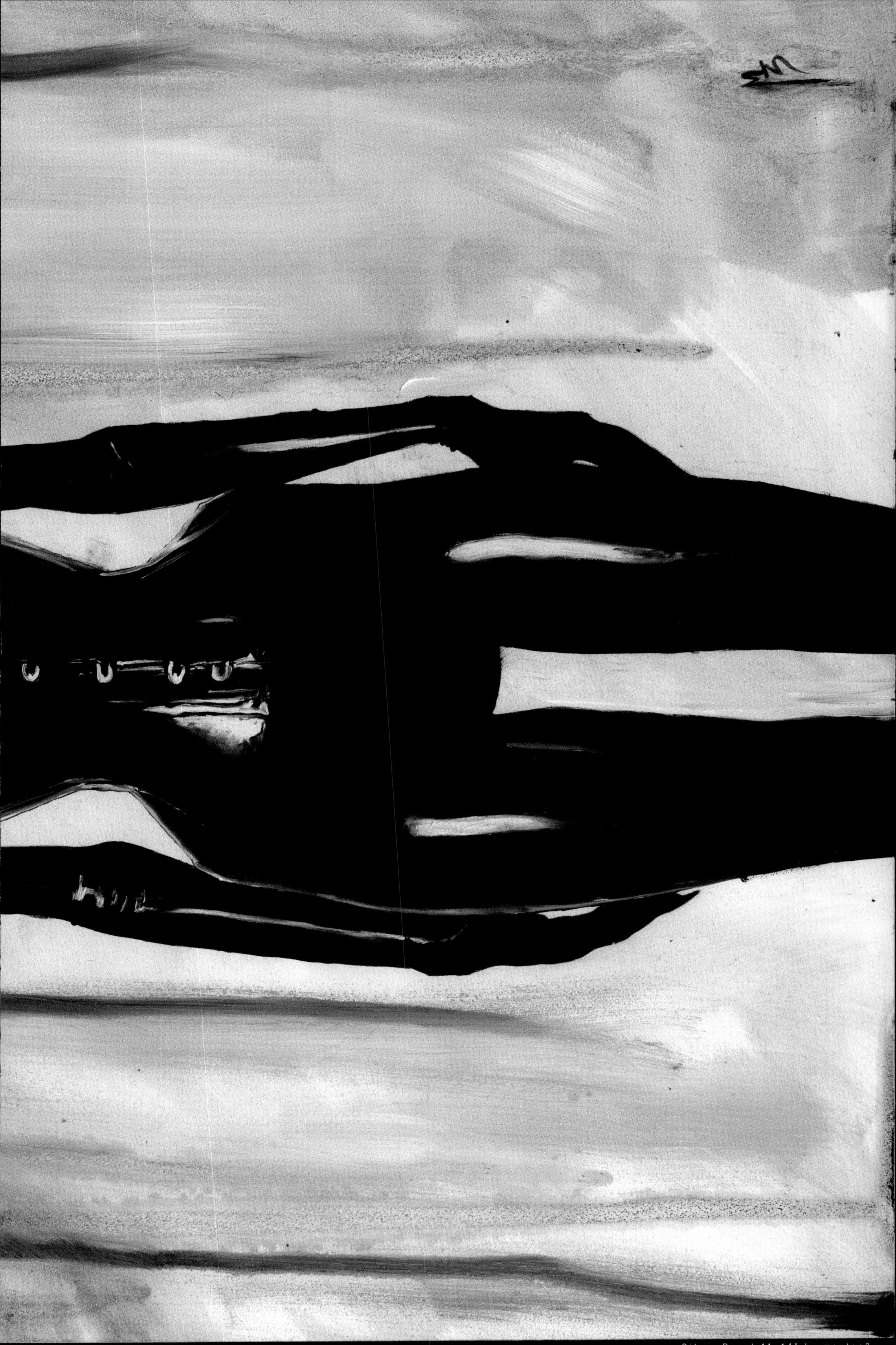

Oil on Panel 11x14" by menton3

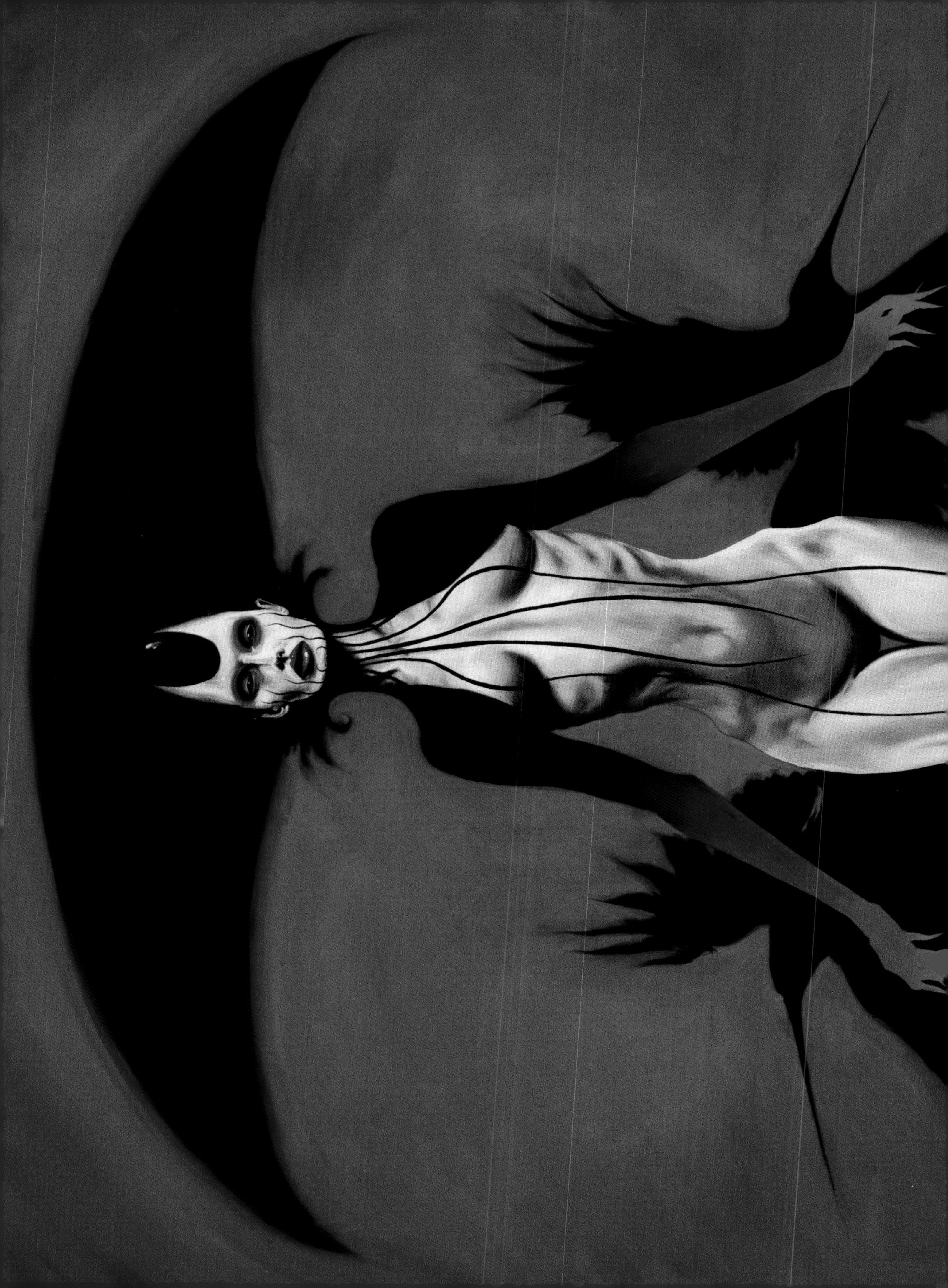

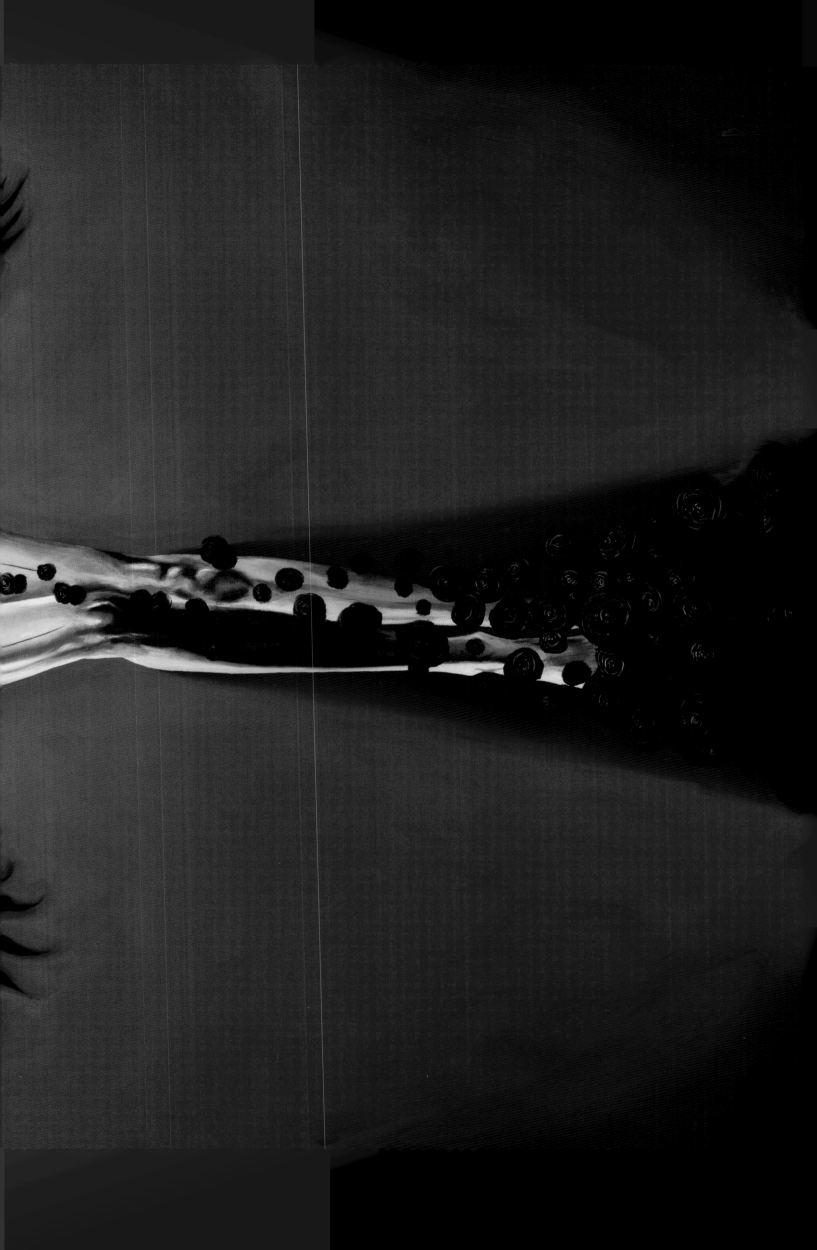

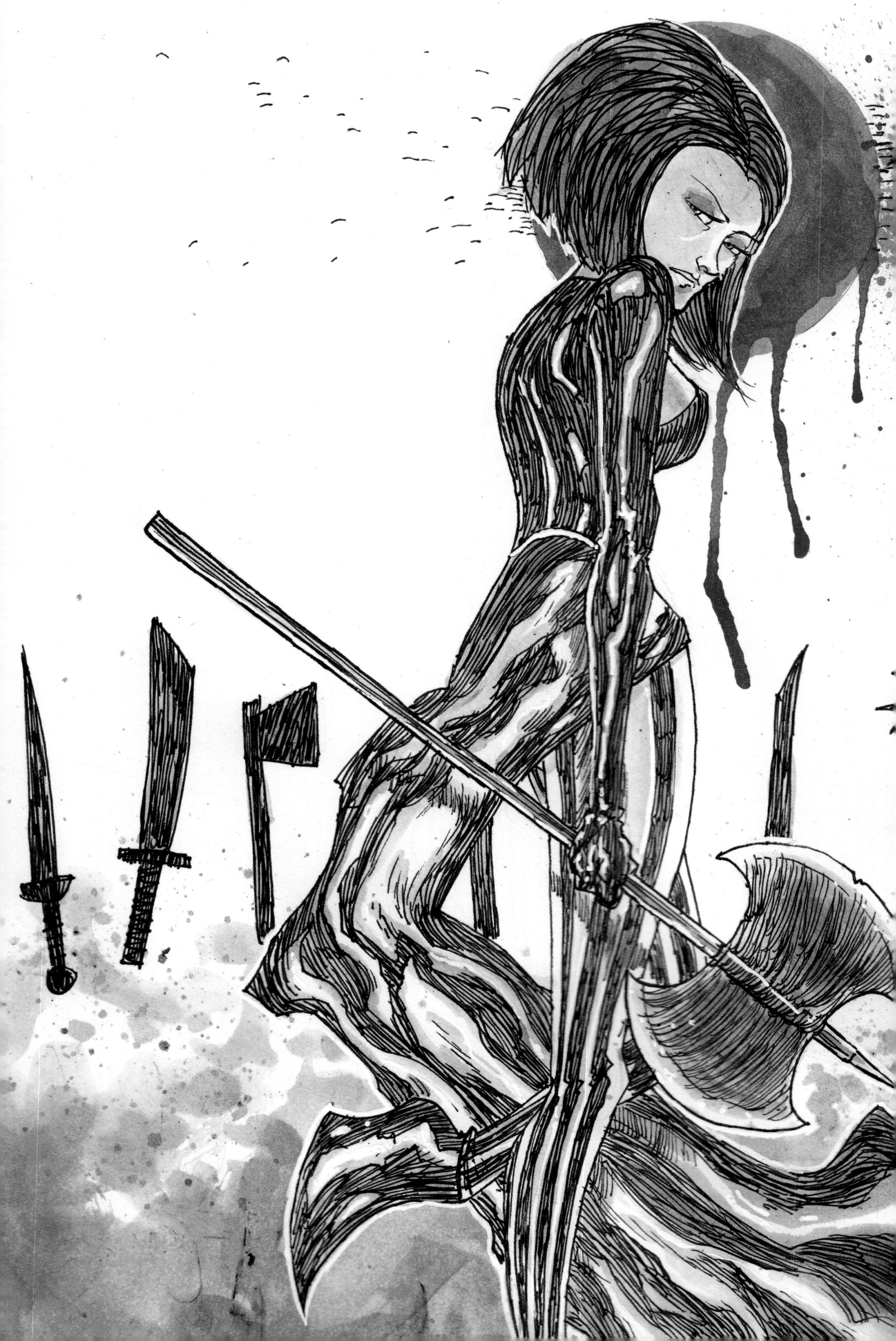

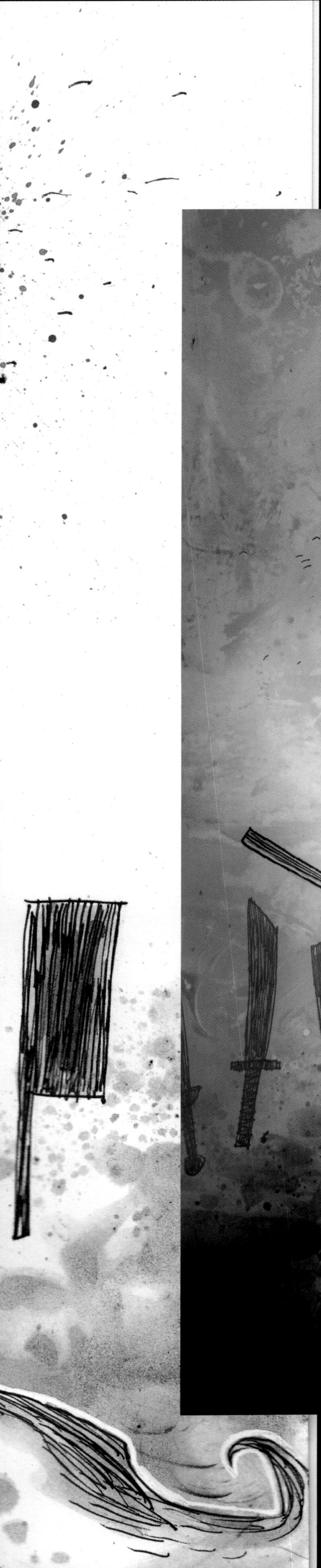

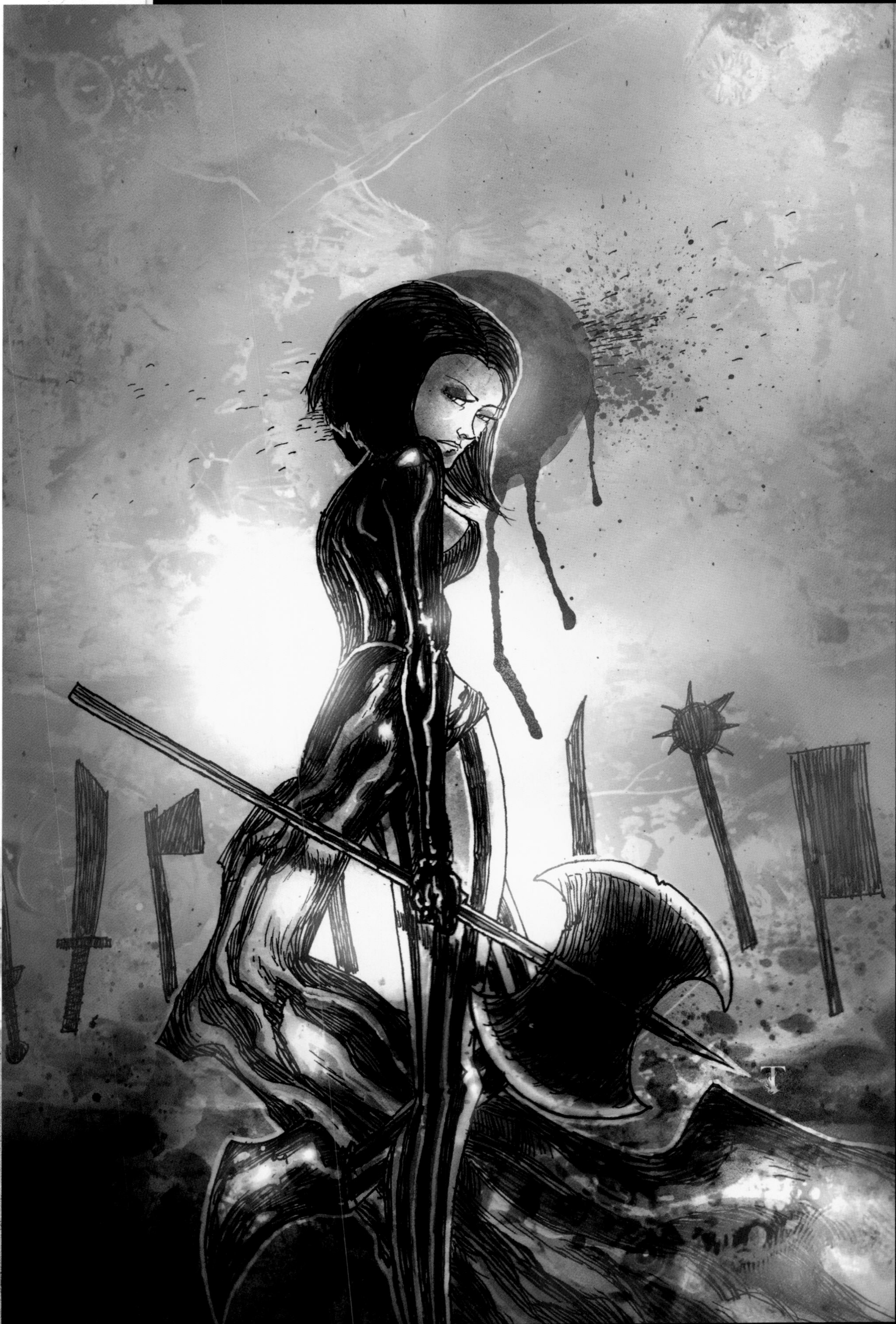

cover B issue #2 by Ben Templesmith

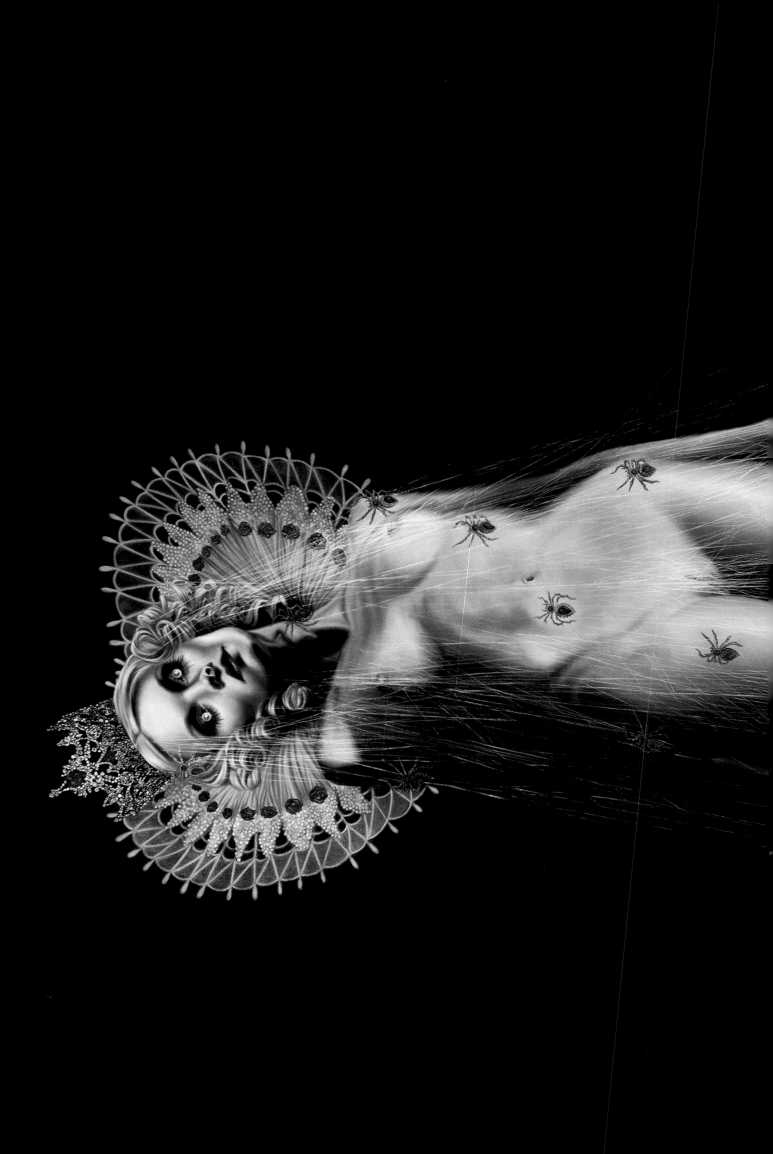

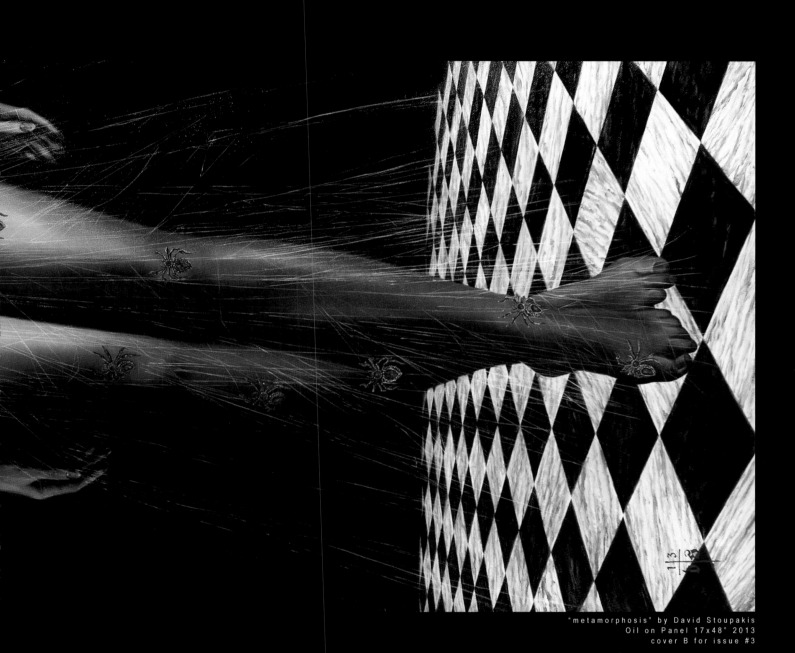

"metamorphosis" by David Stoupakis
Oil on Panel 17x48" 2013
cover B for issue #3

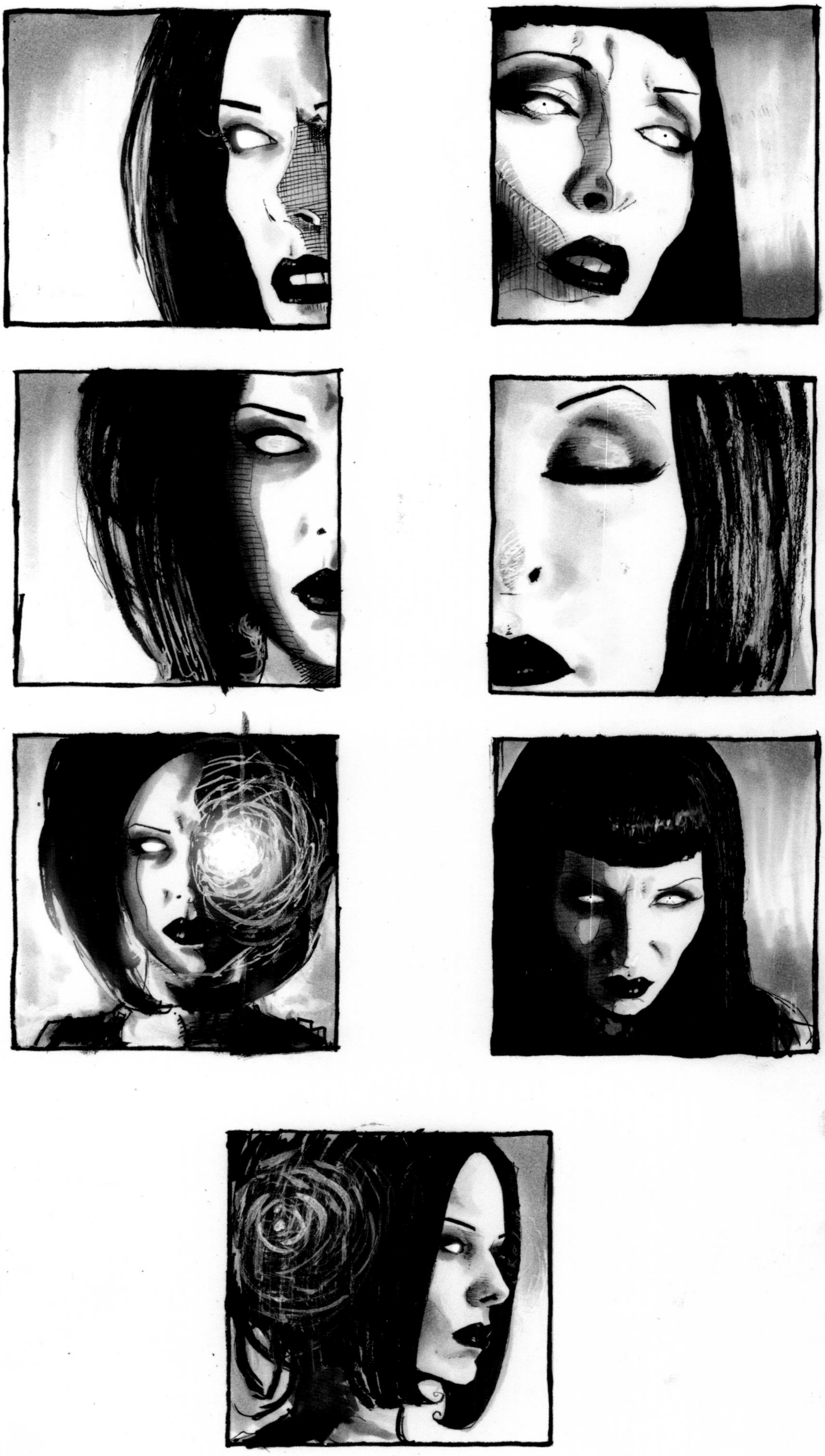

Dec 10th 2013

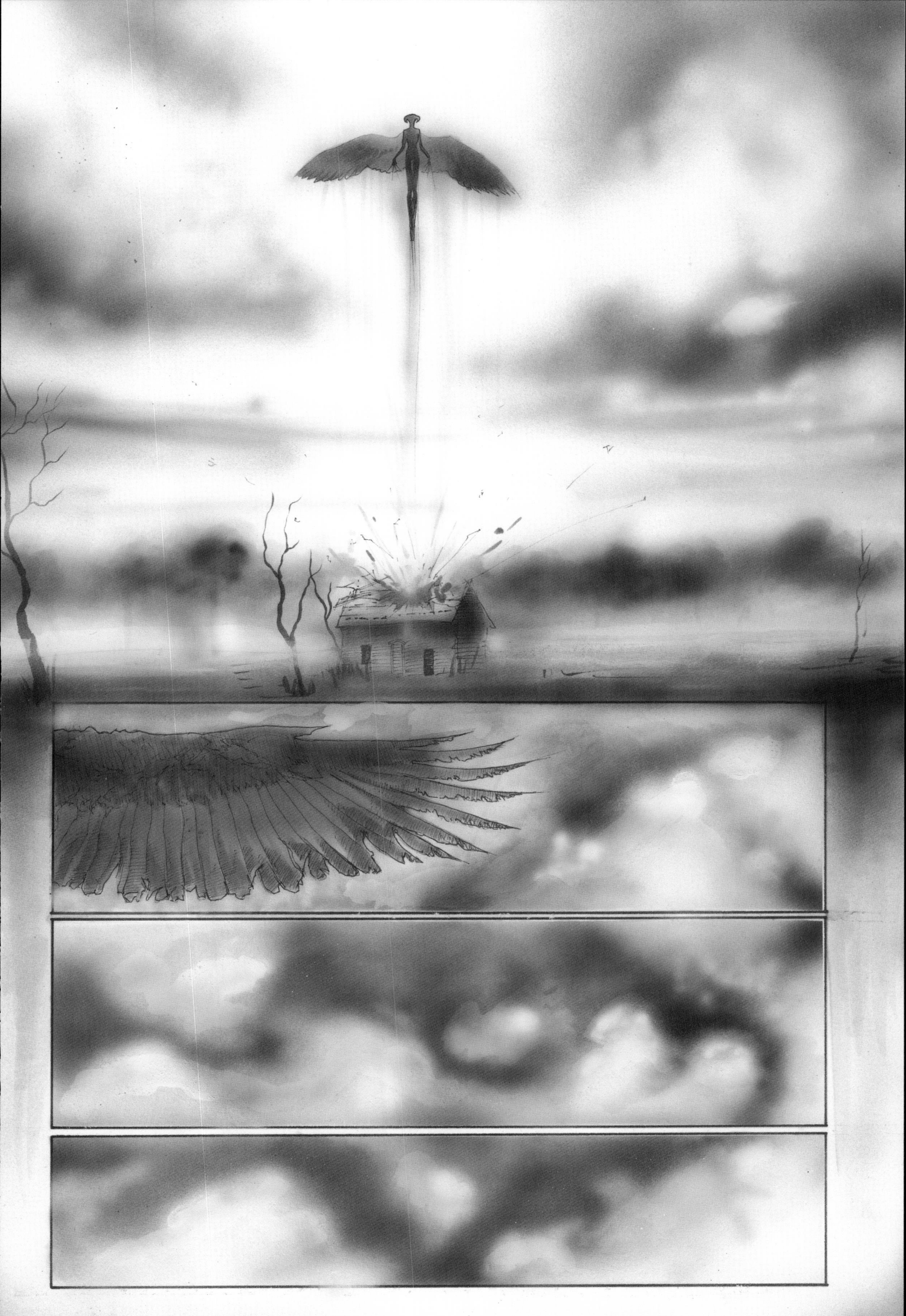

original art scans for book 3
by menton3

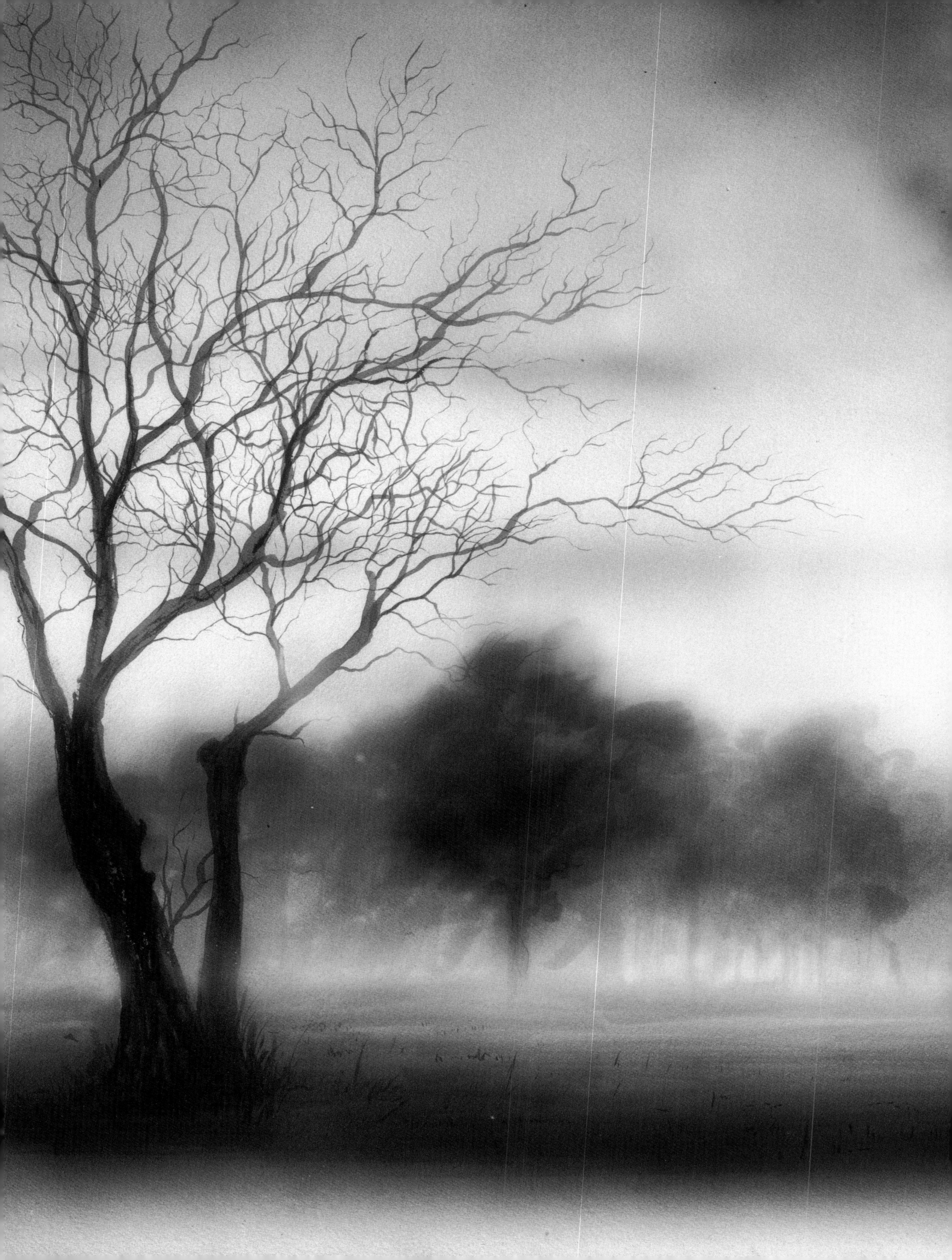

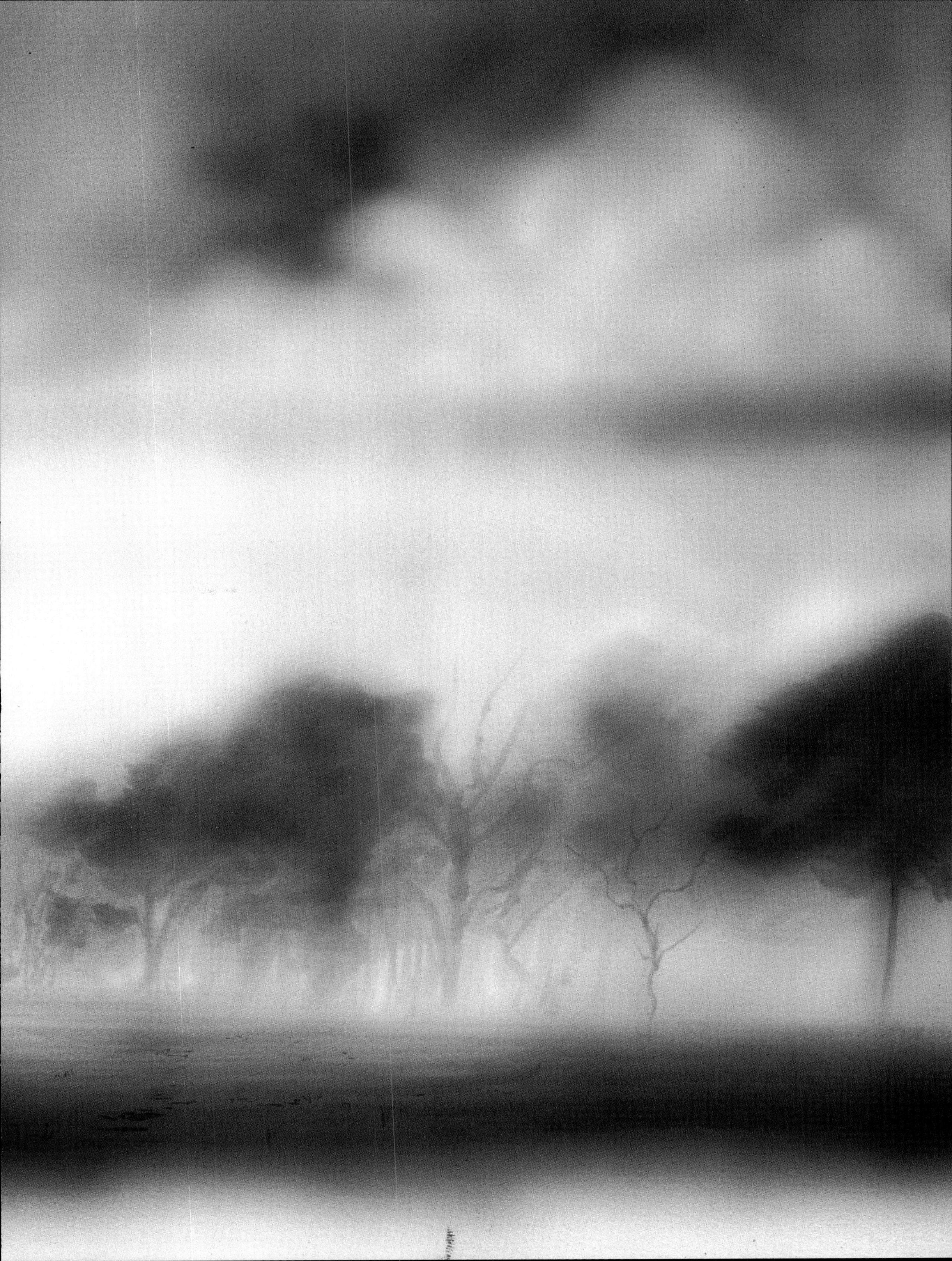

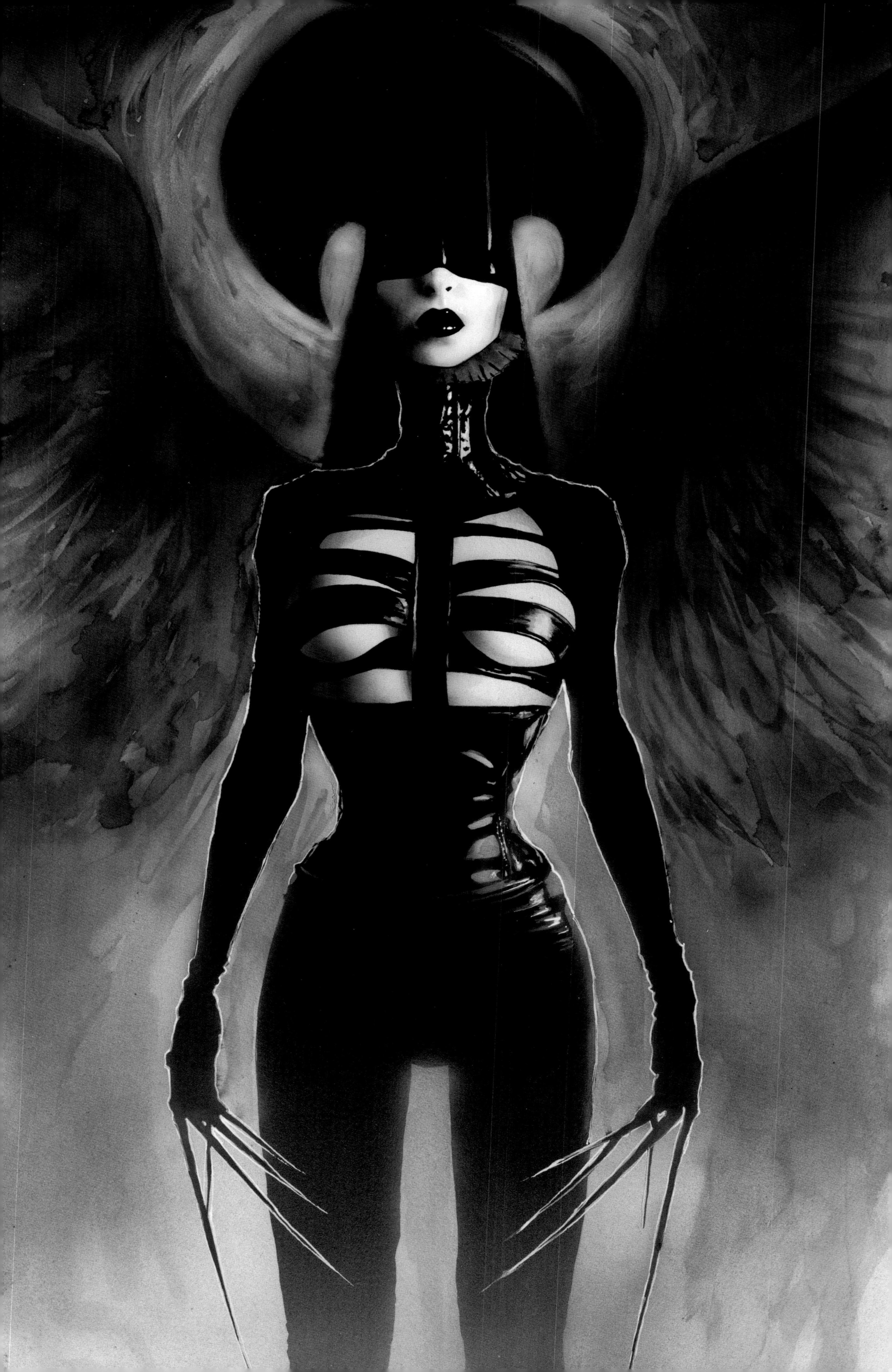

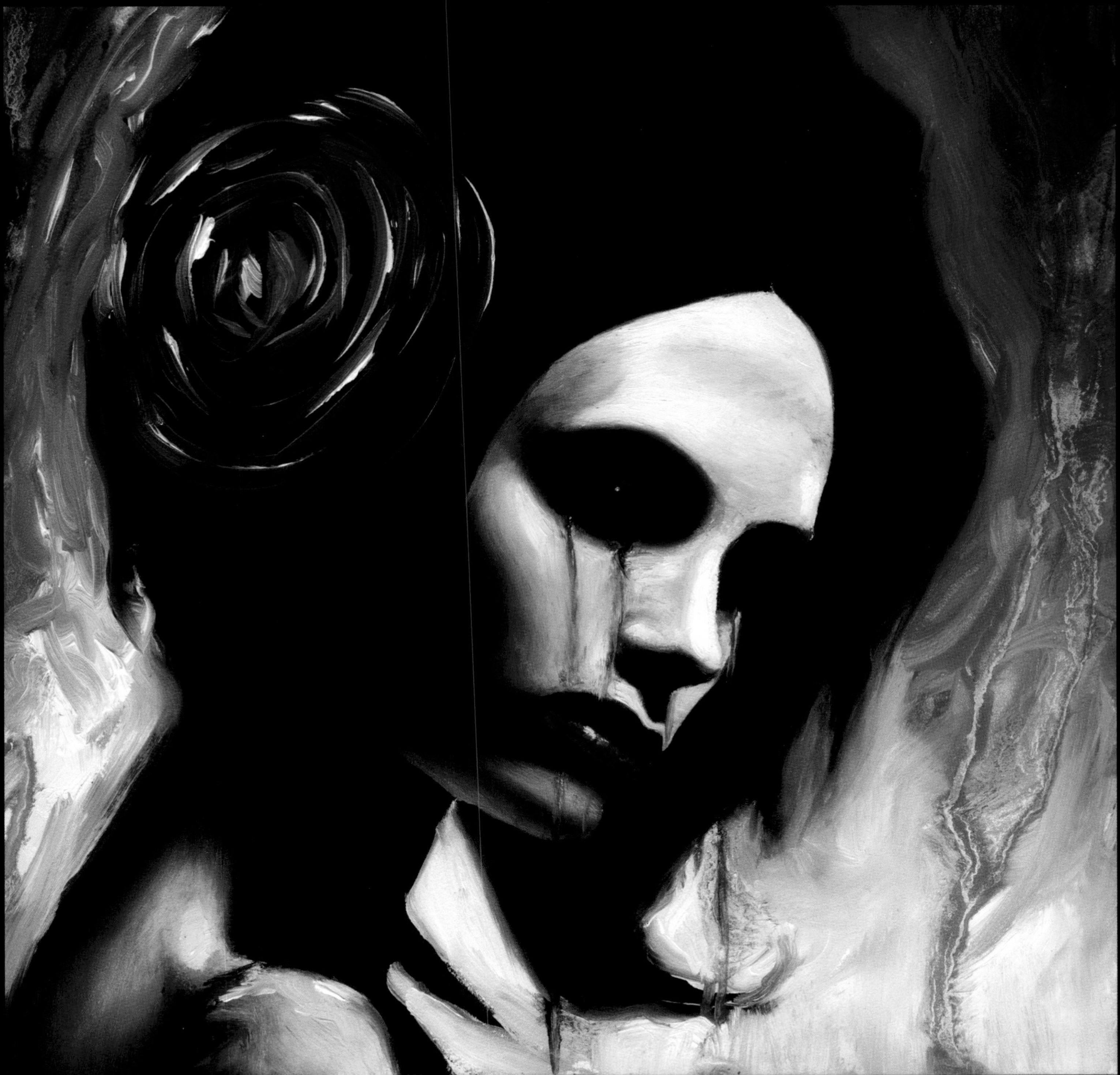

original art scans for book 3
by menton3

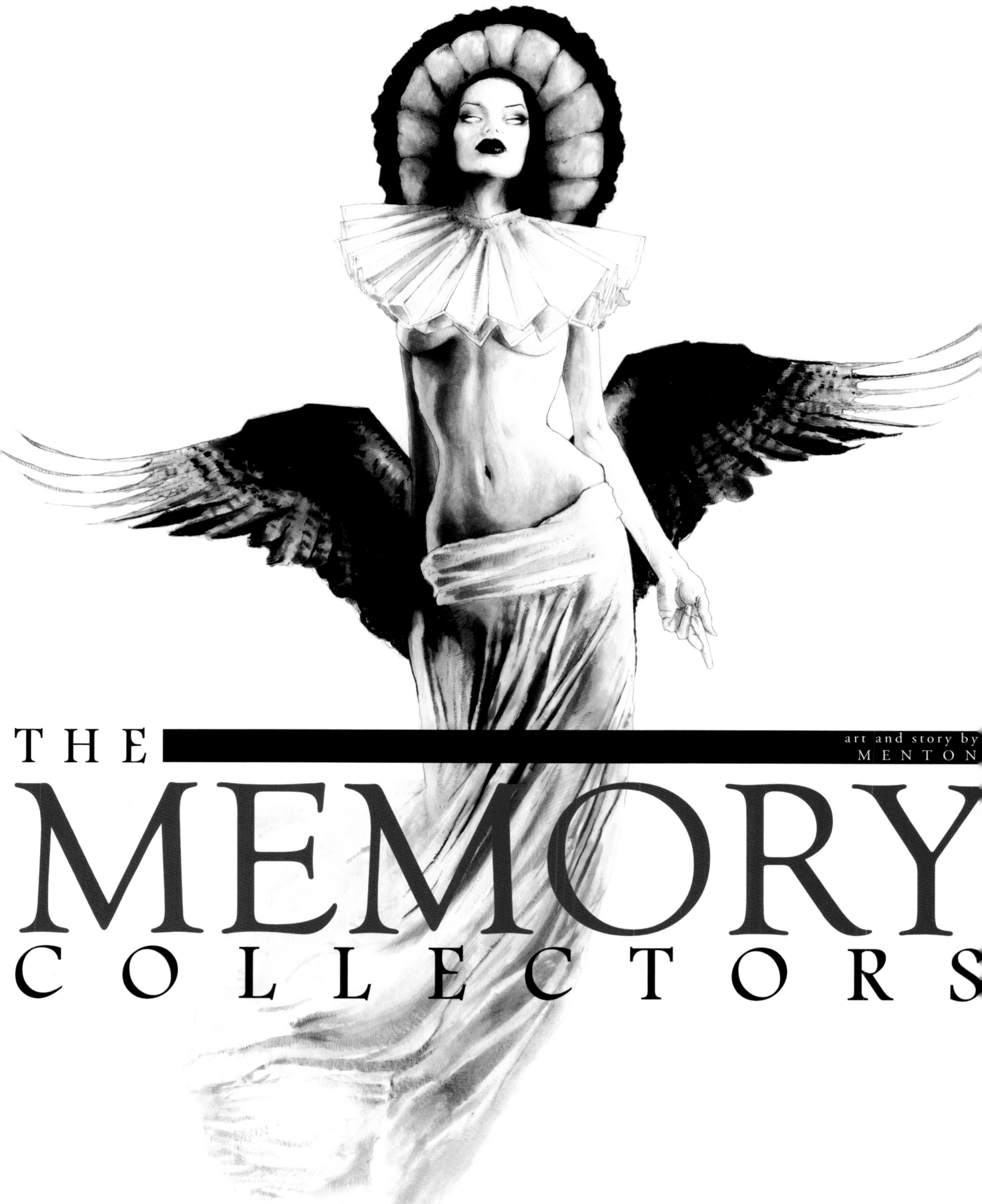

THE MEMORY COLLECTORS

art and story by
MENTON